Bonhoeffer's Religionless Christianity in Its Christological Context

Bonhoeffer's Religionless Christianity in Its Christological Context

Peter Hooton

LEXINGTON BOOKS/FORTRESS ACADEMIC
Lanham • Boulder • New York • London

Published by Lexington Books/Fortress Academic
Lexington Books is an imprint of The Rowman & Littlefield Publishing Group, Inc.
4501 Forbes Boulevard, Suite 200, Lanham, Maryland 20706
www.rowman.com

6 Tinworth Street, London SE11 5AL, United Kingdom

Copyright © 2020 The Rowman & Littlefield Publishing Group, Inc.

All rights reserved. No part of this book may be reproduced in any form or by any electronic or mechanical means, including information storage and retrieval systems, without written permission from the publisher, except by a reviewer who may quote passages in a review.

British Library Cataloguing in Publication Information Available

Library of Congress Cataloging-in-Publication Data Available

Library of Congress Control Number: 2020930447

ISBN 978-1-9787-0933-1 (cloth)
ISBN 978-1-9787-0935-5 (pbk)
ISBN 978-1-9787-0934-8 (electronic)

For Reni
without whom this book would not have been written.

Contents

Acknowledgments		ix
Introduction		1
1	"We Are Approaching a Completely Religionless Age"	9
2	Bonhoeffer's Critique of Religion	35
3	Religionless Christianity in Its Christological Context	69
4	Nonreligious Interpretation	115
5	Mystery, Faith, and Wholeness	141
6	Christ without Religion	163
Bibliography		199
Index		205
About the Author		211

Acknowledgments

It has been a privilege and a delight to spend several years reading Bonhoeffer and reflecting on his writings, and to have had the benefit of the work of scholars such as Eberhard Bethge, Ernst Feil, Ralf Wüstenberg, John de Gruchy, Clifford Green, Wayne Floyd, and Michael DeJonge, who have contributed so much to our understanding of him.

The book was written for the most part at St Mark's National Theological Centre in Canberra and owes much to the wise and generous counsel and encouragement of people there, especially the Rev'd Dr. Jane Foulcher, the Rev'd Dr. Ockert Meyer, and Associate Professor David Neville. I am indebted, too, to the Rev'd Dr. Keith Clements, former general secretary of the Conference of European Churches, Professor Terry Lovat of the University of Newcastle in Australia, and Professor Robert Vosloo of Stellenbosch University in South Africa, for their enriching comments and suggestions.

I am also grateful for the support of Charles Sturt University's Research Centre for Public and Contextual Theology, of which I am a member, and the Australian Centre for Christianity and Culture, whose executive director, the Rt. Rev'd Professor Stephen Pickard, has warmly endorsed this project.

I thank Neil Elliott and Gayla Freeman for so graciously facilitating my publishing journey with Lexington Books/Fortress Academic.

Introduction

The German theologian Dietrich Bonhoeffer (1906–1945) believed Western civilization to be "approaching a completely religionless age"[1] to which Christians must respond and adapt. This book explores Bonhoeffer's own response to this challenge—his concept of a religionless Christianity—and its place in his broader theology. It does this, first, by situating the concept in a present-day Western sociohistorical context, which includes an assessment of the current state of the secularization debate. It then considers Bonhoeffer's understanding and critique of religion, before examining the religionless Christianity of his final months in the light of his earlier Christ-centered theology. The work of nonreligious interpretation and the place of mystery, paradox, and wholeness in Bonhoeffer's thinking are also given careful attention—and nonreligious interpretation is taken seriously as an ongoing task. The book aspires to present religionless Christianity as a lucid and persuasive contemporary theology; and does this always in the presence of the question which inspired Bonhoeffer's theological journey from its academic beginnings to its very deliberately lived end—the question "Who is Jesus Christ?"

The parallels between Bonhoeffer's concept of religionless Christianity and his earlier theology allow me to argue that religionless Christianity is a natural, though by no means inevitable, outcome of his ongoing theological endeavor. I make no claim, though, to a comprehensive exposition of the whole of Bonhoeffer's theology. Rather, I draw selectively on elements in the earlier writings which seem to me not only to enable the emergence of the concept of religionless Christianity but also to serve as necessary aids to understanding what Bonhoeffer intended by it. I believe the religionless Christianity which characterizes Bonhoeffer's prison theology thus to depend on certain critical continuities in his thinking, as well as on developments both in his theological outlook (principally, the progressive disclosure of a more inclusive Christology) and in the world of his experience.

The study prioritizes Christology over other categories of theology because, for Bonhoeffer, all theology has its origin in the mystery of God's becoming human, and because the question "who is Christ actually for us today?"[2] is the one with which religionless Christianity is principally concerned. Christology does not always have the stage to itself, but its foremost associates in this book—ecclesiology and Christian ethics—remain largely under a christological umbrella.

Bonhoeffer's religionless Christianity is heavily contextualized. It is, therefore, necessary not only to examine his understanding of religion as a historically conditioned and "transitory form of human expression"[3] but also to take account of the personal-historical circumstances which helped shape the idea of a religionless Christianity.

The book is divided into six chapters.

The first investigates the historical premise which grounds Bonhoeffer's sense of the need for a new form of Christianity. If he was wrong about the approach of a "completely religionless age," then it would seem he may also have been wrong about the need for Christianity to redefine itself against religion. And a world of more than two billion Christians (to say nothing of the other major faith traditions) is clearly not a religionless one. There is nevertheless strong evidence of a sustained decline in the overall significance of religion as a cultural property of the West today. Modernity does not necessarily lead to secularization, but it does foster plurality, and encourage the exercise of choice among alternatives, including religious alternatives, and alternatives to religion. While a majority of Westerners continue to acknowledge at least a vestigial Christian identity (with much smaller numbers either embracing religion wholeheartedly, or denying it outright), religion generally plays at best a small role in their lives. In many social contexts, the governing presumption is now one of unbelief. This is not the future Bonhoeffer predicted, but it is sufficiently like it to support a broadly positive assessment of his historical presupposition. Most people do not depend on God to make everyday sense of their lives, and Christians have little choice but to accept the largely secular reality in which they find themselves.

The second chapter probes Bonhoeffer's understanding and critique of religion. Bonhoeffer's views on religion owe much to Karl Barth, who convinced him of the vanity of all human efforts to establish communion with God. There is no human way to God but only God's way to us. All religion, for Bonhoeffer, is essentially hubris—a vain reaching out to God from below. Bonhoeffer finds in Matthew 8:17 ("He took our infirmities and bore our diseases"[4]) "the crucial distinction" between Christianity and religion.[5] This distinction, between the powerful, but ultimately illusory, God of religion, and the compassionate, vulnerable God of the gospel, lies at the heart of both Bonhoeffer's critique of religion and his concept of a religionless Christianity. Other elements of the critique of religion—its otherworldly preoccupation with personal salvation, its tendency to see God as the solution only to problems we cannot yet solve, its confinement to a particular sphere of life, and its unjustified assumptions of privilege and authority—all are honed by this distinction. What remains, when religion is set aside, is simply the gift of God's Word[6] to human beings. Religion is not to be confused with faith, and the collapse of religion, properly understood, need have no adverse implications for confidence in God's self-revelation. Quite the opposite is true in fact. Through *faith* in Jesus Christ, we are called not to *religion* but to *new life* with God.

Chapter 3 explores Bonhoeffer's concept of religionless Christianity in its broader theological, and predominantly christological, context. Bonhoeffer raises the prospect of a religionless Christianity in just a handful of letters smuggled out of his Berlin prison cell in the spring and summer of 1944. All were addressed to his dear friend, Eberhard Bethge, who found in them persuasive evidence of a decisive new theological beginning. Bonhoeffer begins with a restatement of the question that has consistently informed his theology. What, he asks, is Christianity, "or who is Christ actually for us today?"[7] Life, history, and theology have together conspired to convince him that God expects us to manage our lives "without God."[8] The powerful God of religion is gone. God has consented "to be pushed out of the world and onto the cross," and helps us now only by virtue of being "weak and powerless" in the world.[9] We are called "to share in God's suffering at the hands of a godless world."[10] God *is* the encounter with the crucified and risen Christ, and we are restored to new life with God by the act of faithful participation in the being of Jesus, "the human being for others."[11]

The key elements of Bonhoeffer's prison theology are not themselves new. As Bethge observes, "[t]he building blocks are there and are being used."[12] But they now stand in a somewhat different arrangement. The new look is important, but to ignore its provenance is to risk a serious misunderstanding of what Bonhoeffer means by religionless Christianity. Chapter 3 highlights elements of Bonhoeffer's thinking which seem to me to enable the emergence of his prison theology. Prominent among them are Bonhoeffer's intensely relational concept of person, his understanding of transcendence, his idea of freedom, the notion of vicarious representative action, the emphasis on conformity to Christ, the concept of Christ *pro me* and *for others*, and his overarching vision of one reality in Christ.

There is also in this chapter an emphasis on the considerably more inclusive view of Christ's place in the world that emerges, particularly, in the *Ethics*. "Religionless" Christians, no less than "religious" ones, are firmly associated, in Bonhoeffer's mind, with a community of believers. But whereas the young Bonhoeffer is convinced that Christ is present *only* in the church, he is compelled, by the logic of his Christology, progressively to moderate this understanding. Because Jesus bears the whole of human nature,[13] because, in him, the form of humanity is created anew,[14] and because, through him, all human beings, without exception, are reconciled with God,[15] it necessarily follows that Jesus Christ is present in every human being. The church is obliged to reflect this understanding. While it is indeed remarkable that "only a part of humanity recognizes the form of its savior,"[16] Jesus Christ can only be proclaimed "as the one in whom God has bodily taken on [all] humanity."[17]

Chapter 4 explores, and expands on, Bonhoeffer's approach to nonreligious interpretation. Bonhoeffer knew that, if Christianity was to transition successfully to a religionless age, it would have to change not only its ways of thinking but also its ways of speaking. He hoped to shape practical expressions of a new, religionless form of Christianity, and understood this work to demand a proper hermeneutical foundation, including language suitable for people who knew little of Christian scripture and tradition. Nonreligious interpretation would have a crucial supporting role to play in establishing religionless Christianity. By finding new ways of explaining existing theological and biblical concepts, nonreligious language must convey what Bonhoeffer believed religious language to be no longer capable of conveying convincingly. It must tell people "what it means to live in Christ and follow Christ."[18] It must address the question of Christ's contemporary identity and bear exemplary witness to the relevance of Jesus Christ today.

Bonhoeffer did not underestimate the difficulty of this task and made very little progress with it. He may have left us only one example, in the letter of July 16, 1944, where he equates "repentance" with "ultimate honesty."[19] I believe nonetheless that Bonhoeffer would have persevered with the work of interpretation if he had had the chance to do so, and that this work must go on if we are to treat Bonhoeffer's concept of religionless Christianity as it should be treated—as fully functional theology, rather than as fragment, or historical artifact. My own initial response to this challenge is set out in this chapter.

Chapter 5 looks at the place of mystery and paradox in Bonhoeffer's thinking, and at his determination to preserve a sense of life's wholeness in the face of growing fragmentation. Religionless Christianity is thus brought into relation, on the one hand, with theology's irreducible mandate to preserve and protect the mystery of God's becoming human in Jesus Christ, and, on the other, with Bonhoeffer's own need to make sense of a life that has taken him from a place of privilege, security, and relative certainty to one of moral ambivalence and extreme peril. Bonhoeffer warns that we must not, under any circumstances, allow ourselves to be "torn apart" by past regrets and future aspirations,[20] but have instead to learn the lesson that the mature human being is always "wholly present," a "complete self," wherever that person happens to be.[21]

Bonhoeffer is under no illusion, though, that we can absorb this lesson and reach this state unaided. Just as real peace is to be found only in wholeness, so is true wholeness to be found only in God, which means, for Bonhoeffer, in the encounter with Jesus Christ. This is an experience of faith rather than a truth of religion. And it is in faith that we begin our lives new each day; in that self-contained, solar whole which is "long enough to find or to lose God, to keep faith or to fall into sin and disgrace."[22]

The final chapter brings the critique of religion and Bonhoeffer's Christ-shaped theology together in an account of religionless Christianity which further underscores its consistency with key elements of his earlier work. Religionless Christianity is intended to facilitate a Christian response to life in a world where God is no longer commonly regarded as an essential element of human self-understanding. It distinguishes between the powerful, but chimerical, God of religion, and the agapeic, vulnerable God of the gospel. Knowledge of God comes only through God's self-revelation in Jesus Christ, and this event—the event of God's becoming human—is decisive for ontology, and for ethics.

In the encounter with Jesus Christ, we reach the boundary, or limit, of our existence. We come face-to-face with the archetypal Other,[23] and it is this encounter which gives us confidence that we are not alone in a world of our own imagining. But Jesus Christ is not only "the boundary of the being that has been given to [us]."[24] He is also the one who stands where we should stand but cannot, before God, *pro nobis*.[25] Indeed, as the one "through whom are all things and through whom we exist" (1 Cor. 8:6), he is the mediator of all our relationships. To think otherwise is to fall prey to the illusion of immediacy, for there is in truth "no way from us to others than the path through Christ, his word, and our following him."[26] In Jesus Christ, we recognize our true humanity as something shared and never solitary. There is no such thing as the truly isolated, autonomous individual. There are separation and plurality, but the sense of self, of I-ness, is grounded exclusively in relationship, with God, and with other people. Life is innately social and necessarily involves accepting responsibility for other people. Human freedom, too, is comprehensible only as a relation, grounded in God's own free decision "to be bound to historical human beings."[27] Just as God has chosen to be free for human beings rather than from them, so is their freedom now a freedom only for others.

Religionless Christianity does not recognize the traditional division of reality into sacred and profane realms. It concedes just "*the one realm of the Christ-reality [Christuswirklichkeit], in which the reality of God and the reality of the world are united.*"[28] Bonhoeffer's concept of the Christ-reality signals Christ's inclusiveness. In Jesus Christ, all humanity is reconciled with God. There are no exceptions. No-one is excluded from Christ's work of redemption. The Christ-reality is also representative of human wholeness. "As reality is *one* in Christ, so the person who belongs to this Christ-reality is also a whole."[29] One does not have to choose between Christ and the world. "Belonging completely to Christ, one stands at the same time completely in the world."[30] Life in the Christ-reality is a fully responsible, compassionate, exceptionless sharing in the pains—as well as the delights—of finite creaturely existence.

Bonhoeffer seeks to spare Christians the choice between what he sees as two unsatisfactory alternatives: a choice between heaven and earth; the choice between a self-enclosed, entirely secular humanism, and a finally unconvincing, otherworldly transcendentalism. In Bonhoeffer's religionless Christianity, a genuine existentialism (a thoroughly worldly life of constant decision, risk, responsibility, and uncertainty) is held in dialectical tension with a genuine Other (a real outside), while the power of Christ's freeing and redeeming love unlocks a larger life of constant and profound fellowship with Jesus Christ. His death and resurrection do not point to new life in some other place but rather to a new way of living—of "being for others"—in this, now post-religious, one.

Christians might thus reasonably be expected to place their trust in the God "who is weak and powerless in the world" simply because they know God, so understood, to be loving and faithful. They will be content to "live as those who manage their lives without God" because they know that the God whose absence is so keenly felt by once religious people is not, and never was, the God "before whom [they] stand continually."[31] They depend on the power of love that comes to them by virtue of Christ's passion. They know that "only the suffering God can help,"[32] because only in the presence of the crucified and risen Christ, only in the presence of the one who is both fully human and wholly God, does the human encounter with God take place.

The real encounter with God will always be an incontrovertible, because faithful, experience of O/otherness. Jesus Christ, says Bonhoeffer, confronts us "in every step we take, in every person we meet." It is "God himself [who] speaks to us from every human being."[33] It is Jesus Christ himself who presses the claim of the other on us. Christians must learn to recognize, and to acknowledge, Christ in every human being because, in the God-reconciled world of the incarnation, every human being bears the image of God. And this must serve to inform and guide Christian conduct in pluralistic societies, where Jesus Christ is but one of many expressions of belief in the transcendent.

Bonhoeffer's religionless Christianity, read in the context of his broader theology, draws ideas of otherness and interdependence, which are not easily held together, into complementary relationship. Together they provide a strong foundation for a radical theological anthropology. In Jesus Christ, God assumes "the whole of human nature."[34] Our sense of I-ness rests on our awareness of the active presence of God (the divine You) in *other* people.[35] We have our being only in relation to a You, and thus *ex*-ist "always and only in ethical responsibility,"[36] by accepting, or rejecting, an external claim. In Bonhoeffer's theology, it is not the *idea* of "being for others" that is new. Notions of selflessness have frequently been advanced as a Christian ideal. These, however, are generally presented as the antithesis of a more natural human inclination to prioritize an independent sense of self—an ethical autonomy—which does not depend on the claims made on us by others. Bonhoeffer, though, believes that to assume human beings are somehow wired to live this way—"atomistic[ally],"[37] in ethical isolation—is to misunderstand, fundamentally, the nature of life. The idea of "being for others" is not a new way of being human. It is, rather, the only way of being truly human and is as such characteristic of Christ's inclusiveness; of life lived, theologically speaking, in the *Christuswirklichkeit* shared by God and human beings, whence springs the sense of human wholeness, and confidence in God's unfailing goodness and compassion. We may, of course, repudiate this, and cling instead to that illusory notion of the isolated individual which religion, as Bonhoeffer conceives it, shares with some expressions of secularity, but, for Bonhoeffer, the reality is that our "being for others" is synonymous with the life with God which is our life, and thus with our humanity.

NOTES

1. Dietrich Bonhoeffer, *Letters and Papers from Prison*, ed. John de Gruchy (Minneapolis: Fortress Press, 2010), DBWE 8: 362.
2. *Letters and Papers*, DBWE 8: 362.
3. *Letters and Papers*, DBWE 8: 363.
4. The NRSV is generally used for citing the Bible. The only exceptions are to be found in citations included in extracts from Bonhoeffer's own writings.
5. *Letters and Papers*, DBWE 8: 479.
6. Other than in some direct quotes, (the) "Word" is capitalized whenever it is understood to refer to God's becoming human in Jesus Christ.
7. *Letters and Papers*, DBWE 8: 362.
8. *Letters and Papers*, DBWE 8: 478.
9. *Letters and Papers*, DBWE 8: 479–80.
10. *Letters and Papers*, DBWE 8: 480.
11. *Letters and Papers*, DBWE 8: 501.
12. Eberhard Bethge, *Dietrich Bonhoeffer: A Biography*, ed. Victoria J. Barnett (Minneapolis: Fortress Press, 2000), 860.

13. Dietrich Bonhoeffer, *Discipleship*, ed. Geffrey B. Kelly and John D. Godsey (Minneapolis: Fortress Press, 2003), DBWE 4: 217.
14. Dietrich Bonhoeffer, *Ethics*, ed. Clifford J. Green (Minneapolis: Fortress Press, 2005), DBWE 6: 96.
15. *Ethics*, DBWE 6: 66–67.
16. *Ethics*, DBWE 6: 96.
17. *Ethics*, DBWE 6: 403.
18. *Letters and Papers*, DBWE 8: 389.
19. *Letters and Papers*, DBWE 8: 478.
20. *Letters and Papers*, DBWE 8: 278.
21. *Letters and Papers*, DBWE 8: 324.
22. Dietrich Bonhoeffer, "Biblical Reflection: Morning," in *Theological Education at Finkenwalde: 1935–1937*, ed. H. Gaylon Barker and Mark S. Brocker (Minneapolis: Fortress Press, 2013), DBWE 14: 864.
23. In this book the capitalized "Other" denotes God.
24. Dietrich Bonhoeffer, "Lectures on Christology (Student Notes)," in *Berlin: 1932–1933*, ed. Larry L. Rasmussen (Minneapolis: Fortress Press, 2009), DBWE 12: 305.
25. "Lectures on Christology," DBWE 12: 324, 327. The Latin term *pro nobis* means "for us."
26. *Discipleship*, DBWE 4: 95.
27. Dietrich Bonhoeffer, *Act and Being*, ed. Wayne Whitson Floyd Jr. (Minneapolis: Fortress Press, 2009), DBWE 2: 90.
28. *Ethics*, DBWE 6: 58. The emphasis, in quoted passages, belongs always to the author of the work cited.
29. *Ethics*, DBWE 6: 62.
30. *Ethics*, DBWE 6: 62.
31. *Letters and Papers*, DBWE 8: 479.
32. *Letters and Papers*, DBWE 8: 478–79.
33. Dietrich Bonhoeffer, "Sermon on Matthew 28:20, Barcelona, April 15, 1928," in *Barcelona, Berlin, New York: 1928–1931*, ed. Clifford J. Green (Minneapolis: Fortress Press, 2008), DBWE 10: 494.
34. *Discipleship*, DBWE 4: 217.
35. Dietrich Bonhoeffer, *Sanctorum Communio,* ed. Clifford J. Green (Minneapolis: Fortress Press, 2009), DBWE 1: 54–55.
36. *Sanctorum Communio*, DBWE 1: 48.
37. *Sanctorum Communio*, DBWE 1: 33.

Chapter 1

"We Are Approaching a Completely Religionless Age"

In the first of the theological letters written to his friend and future biographer Eberhard Bethge from Tegel military prison, Dietrich Bonhoeffer confidently declares, "We are approaching a completely religionless age; people as they are now simply cannot be religious anymore."[1] Even those who still clearly liked to think of themselves as religious seemed now to have something quite different in mind. The implications of this transformation were, to Bonhoeffer's way of thinking, momentous. Nineteen hundred years of Christian preaching and theology rested on the assumption of a "religious a priori" in human beings; what Bonhoeffer's doctoral supervisor at the University of Berlin, Reinhold Seeberg, had described as "a purely formal, primeval endowment of the created spirit or ego that renders it capable of, and in need of, the direct awareness of the absolute Spirit."[2] Seeberg believed that even nonreligious people were *potentially* religious. They, too, possessed the religious a priori.

If though, says Bonhoeffer, it were to become evident that the religious a priori was in fact just "a historically conditioned and transitory form of human expression," then it would be reasonable to assume that people could become "radically religionless."[3] And if we should be forced to conclude, as Bonhoeffer believed we were, that Christianity in its Western form[4] was but a stage on the way to a "complete absence of religion," then what would it mean to speak of Christ, the church, and Christian life in a religionless world?[5]

While this is clearly an important question if its presuppositions are correct, it quickly becomes much less interesting if they are not. There is a prior question to be answered, and it naturally has to do with the credibility of the religionless premise that grounds Bonhoeffer's sense of the need for a new form of Christianity. Does it still merit serious consideration? Did it ever do so? We clearly do not live in anything resembling a "completely religionless age," and have no currently compelling reason to think that we are likely to do so, any time soon. Assuming this to be the case then, what might be the implications, for Bonhoeffer's religionless Christianity, of abandoning its most basic assumption; or is there, perhaps, some other way of construing Bonhoeffer's claim that better fits the world we know, and that keeps the notions of "religionlessness" and "religionless Christianity" effectively in play?

WHAT DID BONHOEFFER MEAN BY RELIGION, AND ITS ABSENCE?

Bonhoeffer's own sense of religion was shaped progressively by a critique which had its roots in the early theology of Karl Barth. Bonhoeffer's critique of religion served, in due course, to ground the counter-concept of a religionless Christianity and is, as such, the subject of the next chapter. What follows in this section is no more than a preview of this larger topic. It draws exclusively on Bonhoeffer's prison correspondence and is sufficient only to secure his participation in the discussion of what it means for religion to be present, or absent, in human beings.

By April 1944, Bonhoeffer had come to believe that Christians were no longer able to speak persuasively, in language fit for the time, about Christ and Christianity. The "age of inwardness [*Innerlichkeit*] and of conscience," too, had passed and, with it, "the age of religion altogether."[6] He wonders how we might now aspire to speak of God "without religion, that is, without the temporally conditioned presuppositions of metaphysics,[7] the inner life, and so on?"[8] Here we have the two characteristics that came essentially to define the religious outlook for the Bonhoeffer of the prison letters: metaphysics and inwardness, with their shared emphasis on the supernatural and personal salvation. When metaphysics and inwardness lose the power to convince, or otherwise to satisfy, the inquiring mind, then the whole precarious edifice of religion is at risk of collapse. And metaphysics and inwardness may indeed be said largely to have lost that power in the modern world—in a "world that has come of age."[9]

Bonhoeffer offers a historical explanation of his position in the letters of June 8 and July 16, 1944. In the first, he describes a centuries-long "movement toward human autonomy"[10] as having attained "a certain completeness" in his time. Human beings now have the capacity to address all of life's important issues "without recourse to 'Working hypothesis: God.'"[11] In the second, he briefly rehearses a series of largely seventeenth-century developments in theology, philosophy, politics, and law, which, by encouraging belief in the independent operations of human reason and natural law (*etsi deus non daretur*[12]) collectively conspired to make "the autonomy of human beings and the world . . . the goal of thought."[13]

Religion's problems with the natural sciences began even earlier, in the fourteenth and fifteenth centuries, with Nicholas of Cusa and Giordano Bruno "and their—'heretical'—doctrine of the infinity of the universe."[14] An infinite universe is, by definition, "self-subsisting" and, while modern physics and cosmology may have restored some sense of boundaries—by positing a beginning to the universe and speculating about its end—earlier finite cosmologies have been permanently displaced, and God with them.[15]

The argument advanced by Bonhoeffer in this brief exposition of modern European intellectual history, inspired by his prison reading of Wilhelm Dilthey and Carl Friedrich von Weizsäcker, is a familiar and still broadly respectable one. It can be presented as an example of secularization theory; of the idea that historical developments over the past several hundred years have engendered a progressive, and likely continuing, decline in the significance of religion as a Western cultural expression.[16] Already, some years previously, in the *Ethics* fragment "Heritage and Decay," where he gives a more extensive historical account of Europe as a "reality whose only foundation is Christ," Bonhoeffer had written, "The corpus christianum, the Western-Christian order, which was ruled and held together by emperor and pope as commissioned by Jesus Christ, was shattered in the Reformation."[17] This, he said, heralded the beginning of "the great process of secularization . . . at the end of which we stand today."[18]

Bonhoeffer could see that God was "being increasingly pushed out of a world come of age," out of the world of human experience. But he had no time for those who sought either to discredit the natural sciences (by "tak[ing] up arms—in vain—against Darwinism and so on"), or to confine God to the functions of a *deus ex machina*, as the answer to life's "so-called ultimate questions . . . needs and conflicts."[19]

Indeed, Bonhoeffer saw no point, and no merit, in "trying to persuade this world that has come of age that it cannot live without 'God' as its guardian."[20] This was like trying to turn an adult back into a child, by making people "dependent on a lot of things on which they in fact no longer depend."[21] It was symptomatic of the misguided attempt by Christian apologists and "the secularized offshoots of Christian theology"—psychiatrists and existential philosophers!—"to prove to secure, contented, and happy human beings that they are in reality miserable and desperate."[22] Meanwhile, by condemning the rise of human autonomy as "the great falling-away from God," Christians were simply inviting an increasingly self-confident world to think of itself as anti-Christian.[23]

As is generally the case with Bonhoeffer, in whom life and thought were always closely intertwined, the conviction that religion was no more than a "transitory form of human expression," and that people could, and indeed already had, become essentially religionless, owed much to Bonhoeffer's own *Sitz im Leben*. He lived in turbulent times. Much of his relatively short life was spent in a country that was either at war or preparing for it, and otherwise largely defined by a variable mix of imperial ambition, vexed *amour propre*, political turmoil, economic malaise, social unrest, and the rise of Nazism. As a sensitive and intelligent man, with a strong sense of the custodial cultural responsibilities that belonged to the educated German middle class, Bonhoeffer was not one to be unmoved by history and clearly believed that he had a role to play in its unfolding.

In the 1930s, he had done his best to promote peace through the international ecumenical movement, and to uphold the primacy of Christ as Lord in the German Protestant church struggle (*Kirchenkampf*) between opponents and supporters of the Nazi regime. The world was now at war for the second time in a generation, and he was in prison, facing possible execution for treason. The church, abroad and at home, had managed to defend neither Christ nor peace, and he was left to depend, for life and the chance to participate in the rebuilding of Christian faith after the war, on the success of an assassination plot—of which he had explicit foreknowledge.[24] All the old certainties had vanished.

> [W]hat we have built up is destroyed overnight. Our lives, unlike our parents' lives, have become formless or even fragmentary. . . . It will be the task of our generation, not to "seek great things," but to save and preserve our souls out of the chaos, and to realize that this is the only thing we can carry as "booty" out of the burning house.[25]

In such a situation, it should not surprise us to find a creative mind drawing its own "radically religionless" conclusions.

NEITHER A PROFANE WORLD . . .

Here we come to a fork in the road. Both ways promise to reveal whether Bonhoeffer was right to predict the end of religion in the West. In one direction, the road is broad and well-lit. Its end is in sight. The other has more twists and turns but is ultimately more rewarding.

The broad path encourages bold statements of the obvious. Clearly, a world of more than two billion Christians (to say nothing of the other major faith traditions) is not a religionless one. Importantly, the numerical center of gravity of Christianity has shifted over the past hundred years, from Europe and North America, to Africa, Latin America, and Asia; but, even so, Christianity in its Western form is in no immediate danger of disappearing. There are still more Christians in Europe (though only just) than on any other continent, and more Christians in the United States than in any other country.[26]

Meanwhile, events such as "September 11," March 2004 (Madrid), July 2005 (London), November 2015 (Paris), March 2016 (Brussels), July 2016 (Nice), May 2017 (Manchester), June 2017 (London), August 2017 (Barcelona), and March 2019 (Christchurch) have transformed religion, for religious and secular Westerners alike, into a geopolitical issue. If, says Tom Greggs, we may describe the Cold War as definitive for the generation after Bonhoeffer, then it is religion and issues surrounding religion that can be said to define the political landscape for the current generation. Religion "is back on the agenda in a way it has not been for a long time."[27] Once we understand this, we are free to approach Bonhoeffer's concept of "religionlessness" essentially as historical artifact.

... NOR A DEVOUT ONE

But there is still the second road to explore, and this will take longer. I begin with the sociologist and theologian Peter Berger's assertion that, in a world "characterised by an explosion of passionate religious movements," Europe is the obvious exception.[28] Berger thinks it reasonable to affirm that no other part of the world, possibly excepting Australia, is as secular as contemporary Western and Central Europe.[29] This claim, however, is obviously not intended to embrace the West as a whole. The United States in particular is widely seen as presenting a very different picture. Berger observes that "[i]t has become something of a cliché to state that the United States is a religious society, Europe a secular one." The reality is naturally more complicated, but the cliché remains perfectly serviceable.[30]

Thus, we cannot simply substitute the word "secular" for the word "religionless" and assume Bonhoeffer to have been right about the future direction of Western civilization. The American experience poses a potentially insuperable obstacle to any generalizations about religion and the West, and is likewise subversive of secularization theory, at least to the extent that secularization theory assumes a direct causal link between modernity and secularity.[31]

Berger believes it is time to discard the notion that modernity is necessarily bad for religion, which most sociologists of religion now believe to be demonstrably false.[32] A theory which binds secularity and modernity inescapably together is incapable of explaining the differences in religious outlook between the United States and Europe. We are unlikely to persuade other than the most parochial human beings that Belgium, for example, is more modern than the United States, and America is simply too big an exception to prove the rule. Berger is thus led to dismiss secularization theory as a finally invalid "extrapolation of the European situation to the rest of the world."[33]

He goes on to suggest though that, while modernity does not always lead to secularization, it does lead, "in all likelihood necessarily," to pluralism. Human society has, until relatively recently, generally been characterized by high degrees of cultural homogeneity. Modernity and associated phenomena—such as migration, urbanization, public education, and mass communication—now reinforced also by globalization, have undermined this homogeneity. In its place, a steadily expanding pluralism has created, even in religion, a "market in which individuals can, indeed must, make choices." Religion is no longer a given and has become instead "the object of reflection and decision."[34]

It may be argued that human beings have always had at least some ability to make choices in matters of religion, but the point that is being made here, in relation specifically to modernity, is that the opportunity to make them has very probably never previously been so widely available; nor has the exercise of this freedom ever previously been so broadly encouraged. And now, too, wherever human beings are truly free to choose their religion, they are likewise free to choose none. They can choose to be secular. Indeed, they may well choose to think of themselves—in Bonhoeffer's phrase—as "completely religionless." Berger suggests that

> Europeans make more secular choices, Americans more religious ones. But even an individual who declares adherence to a very conservative version of this or that religious tradition has chosen to do so, must remember that fact, and will be at least subliminally aware of the possibility of reversing that decision at some future time.[35]

The decision not to believe in God, freely taken and exercised by a substantial and growing number of people throughout the Western world, represents a distinctively modern[36] choice, the significance of which was not lost on Bonhoeffer in 1944. He writes to Bethge on June 8 that it has become increasingly clear, over the past hundred years or so, that "everything gets along without 'God' and does so just as well as before. . . . The world . . . is sure of itself in a way that it is becoming uncanny for us." And it seems that nothing—not even a second world war—can seriously impair confidence in autonomous humanity's inexorable progress.[37]

UNDERSTANDING SECULARITY

Berger denies any necessary connection between modernity and secularity. Modernity does, however, bring plurality, and encourages the exercise of choice among alternatives, including religious alternatives, and alternatives to religion. The drivers of choice, though, are historically and culturally embedded, and may lead to very different outcomes in different parts of the world. Secular choices are not simply a function of changes ushered in by modernity.

But what do we mean by secularity? Two views are considered here: the first, a critique by the philosopher Charles Taylor, has features in common with Berger's rejection of mainstream secularization theory; the second, based on the work of sociologists Steve Bruce and David Voas, offers a robust defense of the secularization paradigm. Both provide assessments of religion's evolutionary pathway and trajectory in the West which tend, in their own quite distinctive ways, to support a broadly sympathetic contemporary reading of Bonhoeffer's religionless premise.

Taylor offers a tripartite characterization of secularity in the Western world, describing it first in terms of public spaces which "have been allegedly emptied of God, or of any reference to ultimate reality";[38] then in relation to a general decline in popular religious belief and practice; and finally as a function of a change of situation, or worldview, where belief in God is no longer axiomatic but is instead understood to be just one option among others, "and frequently not the easiest to embrace."[39]

Taylor prefers to think of belief and unbelief not as competing convictions but rather as varieties of "lived experience."[40] The moral/spiritual life is lived in different ways. It has for us a more or less satisfactory form or shape, and includes a place, whether an activity or a condition, where "life is fuller, richer, deeper, more worthwhile, more admirable, more what it should be."[41] There is naturally another side to this, a "negative slope," a place of exile. In this condition, at its worst, all sense of the place of fullness is lost, although "the misery of absence" is nonetheless keenly felt.[42] And then there is also that moderately stable middle ground, which is neither a place of exile nor of fullness but a place of order and routine which gives meaning to our lives, keeps the threat of exile at bay, and, most importantly, provides "some sense of continuing contact with the place of fullness; and of slow movement towards it over the years."[43]

It will be obvious that, for believers, the notion of fullness will include some idea of God, of transcendence, and that this will not be the case for unbelievers, who may generally be expected to regard fullness as an exclusively human potentiality. But we are still speaking here essentially of contrasting beliefs and have yet to establish what is meant by "a sense of the difference of lived experience."[44] Taylor suggests the best way of doing this is to distinguish between a gift received and a self-sufficiency grounded in the wholly human power of reason.[45] Believers expect to *receive* power or fullness "in a relation," and to be transformed by it. They have a sense of the "without."[46] While, for unbelievers, the way to fullness lies entirely "within."

Theirs is the power of autonomous reason which, at its cool and critical best, sees the world as it is, and engages with it in ways that promote the best interests of human beings.[47]

There are also modes of unbelief which, as Taylor points out, attribute fullness to sources of power other than autonomous reason. But these alternative sources of power are likewise immanent rather than transcendent. "They are to be found in Nature, or in our own depths, or in both," and have the capacity "to heal the division within us that disengaged reason has created, setting thinking in opposition to feeling or instinct or intuition." These views have features in common with the religious critique of Enlightenment, "in that they stress reception over against self-sufficiency," but, in their determinedly self-conscious immanence, are frequently at least as stridently antireligious as the disengaged ones. And then, of course, there are those who, in a thoroughly postmodern spirit, deny both "the claims of self-sufficient reason" and "Romantic notions of . . . recovered unity," emphasizing instead "the irremediable nature of division" and the essentially delusionary nature of fullness, "which is at best a necessary dream, something we may have to suppose to make minimum sense of our world."[48]

But whether we choose the condition of belief or unbelief, we are rarely truly certain of anything, utterly doubt-free, oblivious of any and all threats to our settled understanding of the world.[49] We are now also largely denied the experience of "immediate certainty" formerly available to Western Christians, and still familiar to people in many other parts of the world, an essentially religious condition which does not distinguish between "experience and its construal."[50] Almost no one in the West these days is comfortable with such a simple view of reality. We may well claim to hold such a view, but we know that it is still, ultimately, a construal—one interpretation among others—and that it will not go unchallenged. In light of this, says Taylor, we all learn to negotiate two points of view, one reflecting our version of reality (and largely closed to others); the other acknowledging the presence of alternatives "with which we have in various ways to coexist."[51] Taylor also draws attention to what he calls a change in the default option—from the presumption of belief to the presumption of unbelief—in an ever-larger number of social contexts, and nowhere more so than in the academy where the secular orientation has achieved virtual hegemony.[52]

Taylor's understanding of secularity assumes a particular relationship to religion in each of its three modes. In the first, religion is "that which is retreating in public space"; in the second, it is "a type of belief and practice which is or is not in regression"; while in the third, believers and unbelievers are caught up together in lives charged with ambiguity and deprived of old certainties. But what, without underestimating its celebrated conceptual flexibility, are we to make of religion itself in these circumstances?[53]

Taylor believes that, if we confine ourselves to a particular civilization (what is now "the modern West" and was previously Latin Christendom), our task becomes a little easier, because here we are no longer in a world which assumes "the place of fullness" to be always somewhere else, outside or beyond human life, but rather in one in which it is held by many to be found (albeit in different ways) exclusively within human life.[54] This new, contested understanding of the place of fullness is rooted in the modern world's acceptance of a natural order, governed by intelligible physical laws, which allows, but does not require, inference to a creator God. Those who choose to make such an inference are clearly religious, and this, Taylor suggests, facilitates a reasonably straightforward reading of religion in terms of belief in the transcendent.[55]

But does human fulfillment necessarily entail the recognition of a good that is both independent of, and greater than, ourselves?[56] For Christians, the answer to this question must obviously be yes. People may, however, just as easily choose to believe in nothing greater than themselves. They may embrace an utterly self-sufficient humanism which begins and ends with them. And while there may be exceptions to this thesis, which assumes such a thoroughgoing humanism to be exclusively a product of modernity,[57] Taylor is confident that a self-sufficiency of this kind has never previously been so comprehensively incorporated into the general, everyday life of society.[58]

Contemporary secularity is not to be equated, though, with an exclusive, self-sufficient humanism. It is rather the shared context within which believers and unbelievers alike seek the experience of fullness. Nor are we obliged simply to choose between exclusive humanism on the one hand and religion on the other. There are other options, including nonreligious antihumanisms of the postmodern variety ("deconstruction" and "post-structuralism"), as well as noninstrumentalist philosophies, such as deep ecology, which seek to recover a sense of the world as biosphere, and of human wholeness, without recourse to religion.[59] Taylor thinks it nonetheless true to say, however, that Westerners now live in a secular age which is unique in human experience because it can envisage, as a mass choice, "the eclipse of all goals beyond human flourishing."[60]

THE IMMANENT FRAME

But how might we best portray the spiritual character of the present age, where, for so many Westerners, belief in God is hard, if not impossible? Taylor describes a process of "disenchantment," in which the "porous self" is replaced by the "buffered self," for whom the mind assumes a place and agency distinct from the "outer" world. We now live mainly in our heads, exploring depths within that for most of human history have been thought to lie outside ourselves, in the "enchanted world." Given such a profound change of orientation, it is perhaps hardly surprising that the new buffered self has little time for the supernatural and the arcane.[61]

With the buffered self comes a previously unfamiliar insistence on privacy, and on "zones of intimacy." These are still social spaces, but they are spaces shared with relatively small numbers of people. We now have a much stronger sense of individuality, and of social orders which (far from having any claim to divine origin) exist, instrumentally, for the good of human beings, and to which we choose to belong for that reason.[62] These qualities—of interiority, instrumental individualism, and humanism—together constitute what Taylor calls "the immanent frame,"[63] a self-sufficient natural order which stands in stark and deliberate contrast to the beguiling, but essentially vain, otherworldliness of the old dispensation. This new self-understanding is underwritten by a new science, governed by impersonal, apparently universal laws, which may possibly reflect divine intent but do not depend on it.

The immanent frame could thus be said to encourage an exclusively materialist worldview, and it is common for people to insist that it can sensibly be interpreted only in this way. Taylor, though, consistent with his understanding of contemporary secularity, believes the immanent frame to provide the context for Western life as a whole. It includes believers as well as nonbelievers. As such, the most we can claim is that it permits, and may even be thought to encourage, the denial of transcendence but does not require it. We live in a society where virtually no view goes unrepresented. There will, of course, be places where some (otherwise familiar) voices are barely heard, but no voice is entirely lost, just as none has the field quite to itself. "An atheist in the Bible belt has trouble being understood," but is far from incomprehensible. People everywhere know that views they find perplexing, even reprehensible, are warmly embraced by others in the same society.[64]

All this, says Taylor, gives us a sense of what it means to stand in the windswept "Jamesian open space" at the heart of a cross-pressured culture, where those who feel they should, or must, abandon transcendence mourn nonetheless the "loss of a world of beauty, meaning, warmth," and the prospect of "a self-transformation beyond the everyday"; while those who are drawn most strongly to God still fear the universe could turn out to be meaningless after all, thereby rendering their desire for God nothing more than "the self-induced illusion that materialists claim it to be."[65] Taylor clearly does not believe that we are approaching a religionless age, but he would have us understand that we live in an essentially secular one, where the governing presumption is frequently one of unbelief, and which embodies, for perhaps the first time in human history, the extensive embrace of an exclusive, self-sufficient humanism which leaves no room for God.

DEFENDING THE SECULARIZATION PARADIGM

Neither Berger, who argues from modernity to plurality (rather than from modernity to secularity), nor Taylor, who treats secularity as the contemporary context within which both belief and unbelief come to expression, deny the secular worldview a prominent place at the table, but they do contest its hegemony. Bruce and Voas, on the other hand, who set out to defend the secularization paradigm from a growing band of critics, do not seriously doubt its eventual final triumph.

Bruce, like Taylor, assumes religion to involve belief in the transcendent but includes in his definition of religion a sharper sense of the divine's relation to the world. Thus, Bruce thinks of religion "substantively, as beliefs, actions, and institutions based on the existence of supernatural entities with powers of agency . . . or impersonal processes possessed of moral purpose . . . that set the conditions of, or intervene in, human affairs."[66] In this context, the secularization paradigm seeks to explain religion's progressive marginalization in the West.

Bruce argues for a causal relationship between "the social power of religion, the number of people who take it seriously, and how seriously anyone takes it."[67] As the social power of religion declines, so, for each new generation, does its credibility. With religion now essentially a matter of choice rather than of socialization, options multiply, boundaries become porous, and this "encourages first relativism—all roads lead to God—and then indifference as it becomes harder to persuade people that there is special merit in any particular road."[68]

Bruce defends the use of church attendance figures as a statistical measure of Christianity's decline in Western Europe on the ground that they allow researchers to measure, and to make comparisons over time with respect to, a particular type of religious behavior; and because going to church "requires some effort and thus shows some degree of commitment" on the part of the respondent.[69] According to Bruce, researchers have been able to correlate church attendance with other elements of religiosity in meaningful ways. One seldom finds, for example, a large number of respondents who call themselves Christian, or say they believe in a "personal creator God," or who otherwise claim a place of importance for religion in their lives, and who are not also regular churchgoers.[70]

Bruce is thus ready to treat church attendance "as a reliable index of underlying belief and commitment."[71] According to the Mannheim Eurobarometer, church attendance in Western Europe declined sharply over the thirty years from 1970 to 1999. In France, for example, the percentage of the population attending church at least weekly fell from 23 to 5 percent, in Belgium from 52 to 10 percent, in Holland from 41 to 14 percent, in Germany from 29 to 15 percent, in Italy from 56 to 39 percent, and in Ireland from 91 to 65 percent.[72] In Britain, census data shows that, on Sunday March 30, 1851, between 40 and 60 percent of the population attended public worship.[73] One hundred and fifty years later, the comparable figure was around 9 percent.[74] Outside Europe, there have been similarly steep declines in weekly church attendance in Canada (from 67 percent in 1946 to 19 percent in 2003) and in Australia (from 30 percent in 1960 to 7.5 percent in 2001).[75]

Bruce, though, is especially drawn to Voas's study of changes in European Christianity, which is based on an analysis of the first wave (2002–2003) of the European Social Survey (ESS).[76] The survey questions on religion seek to elicit both affirmations of identity and evidence, if any, of religious practice. They cover affiliation (current or past identification with a religion), practice (frequency of attendance at religious services, frequency of private prayer), and belief (self-rated religiosity, importance of religion in the respondent's life). Voas treats all six variables as indicators of "a single underlying quality of religiosity" and combines them into a scale measure of that quality.[77] He divides respondents, by nationality, into five-year cohorts (beginning 1915–1920, through 1980–1984) for the purposes of analysis, and seeks to answer two questions which have long divided observers and interpreters of religious change in Europe: is there change in more than one direction; and how should we regard "the large subpopulation that is neither religious nor unreligious"?[78]

Voas believes the answer to the first question to be no. He finds a similar pattern of decline in all of the countries surveyed,[79] together with some convergence on the mean. "The more religious countries (particularly in the Catholic group) have declined most; the more secular countries (especially in Scandinavia) have declined least."[80] Voas finds no evidence to support the conjecture that Europeans become more religious as they get older. Rather, he contends, the evidence points unambiguously to the generational nature of religious decline.[81]

Voas notes, with respect to the second question, that people cannot simply be divided into two groups: the religious and the nonreligious. There are still significant levels of residual involvement in Christian practice, and outbreaks of occasional Christianity such as we are accustomed to see, for example, at Christmas and Easter, which suggest either a reluctance, or the absence of any felt need, to commit to one end of the scale or the other. These occasional Christians "are neither regular churchgoers (now only a small minority of the population in most European countries) nor self-consciously non-religious."

Voas calls this generally ill-defined attachment to a vestigial Christian identity "fuzzy fidelity," and applies this label to all three aspects of religious involvement—belief, practice, and affiliation.[82]

One can no longer assume, for example, from the simple fact that many people continue to profess belief in God, that they are "basically Christian." They may prefer to think of themselves as "spiritual" and to acknowledge a higher power of some kind without embracing anything resembling traditional Christian doctrine. Voas refers in this context to the 2001 Scottish Social Attitudes Survey, where those who said they believed in God "divided fairly equally between 'a personal creator God,' 'a higher power or life-force,' and 'there is something there.'"[83]

Some commentators see in the distinction between religion and spirituality the promise of a "new spiritual awakening" of faith in God.[84] This distinction is not, however, especially helpful to us here. Spiritual people may generally be thought to fall into the "fuzzy fidelity" category, and to be included in Bonhoeffer's critique of religious "inwardness." There is also a problem of direction: spiritual people, like religious ones, are inclined to believe that there is a human way to God "from below"—they *decide*, in a sense, who God is *for them*. This, as we will see in the following chapter, is the starting point for Bonhoeffer's comprehensive critique of religion.

Other observers, such as Graham Ward, assert—contra the "ideological secularism" of the sociologists—a publicly visible resurgence of religion. Ward, however, concedes that this is not a "return of religion" as such but a new "hybrid, fluid and commercialized" form of "religiousness," which is taking place in the West against a background of declining traditional Christian observance.[85]

Most Europeans, says Voas, still have a largely familial or cultural sense of a specific religious background, but whether this contributes anything of substance to a functioning sense of self is highly uncertain.[86] The prevailing attitude to religion is one of indifference, rather than of outright rejection or hostility.

> Many of those in the large middle group who are neither religious nor unreligious are willing to identify with a religion, are open to the existence of God or a higher power, may use the church for rites of passage, and might pray at least occasionally. What seems apparent, though, is that religion plays a very minor role (if any) in their lives.[87]

In all of the countries included in the ESS, the religious component of the population has shrunk from generation to generation, while the wholly secular component has grown. But the impact of these changes on the "fuzzy" intermediate group has varied from country to country. In the most religious (in Greece and Italy, for example), this group has increased in size, while in the least religious (Sweden and the Czech Republic), it has reduced slightly. Other countries have witnessed either no or, at most, modest growth in the "fuzzy" intermediate component of their populations. While these results could be said to favor those critics of secularization theory who argue that there is no single pattern of religious change in Europe, Voas thinks otherwise.

The question is whether this large intermediate group is to be taken as "a sign of secularisation, or conversely as a religious market waiting for the right product to come along." Or again, might we not, perhaps, reasonably see members of this group as self-consciously unaffiliated, believing individuals; people who have chosen quite deliberately to believe without belonging?[88]

Voas believes the data to point unambiguously to a Europe-wide secularizing trend, revealing as it does—despite some variations in pace—"a common trajectory of religious decline." He thinks it fair to assume that "people stop being religious more quickly than they start being wholly secular," and that change is slow because it occurs largely from generation to generation. "Fuzzy fidelity" may therefore be expected to characterize a substantial part of the population for a long time, but it is still a passing phenomenon. Voas warns against the tendency to regard "fuzzy fidelity" as some "new kind of religion, or a proxy for as yet unfocused spiritual seeking." It is what it is, "a staging post on the road from religious to secular hegemony."[89]

It is, of course, still possible to argue that the progressive drop in levels of support for institutional Christianity across Europe provides evidence of religious change, rather than of decline. The large number of people in the intermediate group may include many who "continue, and will continue, to value the services provided by the churches they no longer attend." But if this were so, says Voas, then we should expect to see, at the very least, high levels of stability in the neither-religious-nor-secular population. This conclusion is not, however, supported by extrapolation from existing trends, which points instead to a long-term decline in the proportion of "fuzzy" Christians as an effect of the eclipse of the wholly religious subpopulation by its steadily expanding, wholly secular counterpart.[90] The effect is already visible in the most secular countries (France, Norway, Sweden, Hungary, and the Czech Republic), and others will soon reach this point unless there is a sudden marked change in direction.[91]

Bruce argues that American "exceptionalism"—the fact that Americans "are more likely than Europeans to claim a religious identity, to go to church, and to pray"—is no reason to abandon the secularization paradigm, although the fact that the United States is more religious than other postindustrial societies cannot simply be overlooked. Indeed, if the mandatory link between modernization and secularization, on which the paradigm depends, is to be sustained, it must be possible to demonstrate either that religion in the United

States is in decline or that "American exceptionalism can be explained by principles consistent with the secularisation paradigm, or both."[92]

Bruce thinks it possible to do both. He points, for example, to the emergence among American social scientists of a new consensus around a figure of 20 percent (it was previously 40) for weekly church attendance nationwide, after research undertaken in the 1990s alerted them to a possibly substantial gulf between attendance claims and actual churchgoing. Thus, while it is certainly still true to say that churchgoing is a more common practice in America than it is in much of Europe, there has been a nonetheless significant drop in church attendance in the United States since the 1950s.[93]

Bruce believes, with Oxford sociologist of religion Bryan Wilson, that "while Europeans secularised by abandoning the churches, Americans secularised their churches."[94] Religion in the United States today is mainly about "personal growth." The very content of American Christianity has been secularized. Bruce here quotes the American sociologist of religion Wade Clark Roof, who describes "the religious stance" in the United States today as "more internal than external, more individual than institutional, more experiential than cerebral, more private than public."[95]

Whether the United States is simply moving more slowly than Europe down the same secularizing path, as Bruce believes, or is on a different path, consistent with its own very different experience of nation-building, as Berger, Davie, and Fokas affirm, is not an issue that needs to be resolved here. It is sufficient for our purposes to bear in mind that for many, if not most, Europeans and Americans, belief in God is no longer axiomatic. It requires a decision to be made and kept. It also requires at least some understanding of the reality that every belief and opinion, no matter how deeply held, is contestable, and likewise some recognition of the fact that the assumptions and patterns of behavior which govern the conduct of life in the West today have, for the most part, little if anything obviously to do with God.

CONCLUSION

Bonhoeffer believed the West to be on the verge of a religionless age. Autonomous human beings had no further need of God as a means either of understanding the world or of coping with it. Christian life and witness must adapt to the new situation if Christianity itself was not to become an anachronism.

We may assume that, had he survived the Second World War, Bonhoeffer, always a strongly contextual theologian, would have evolved a theology appropriate to the new world of his experience. In doing so, he would have been obliged to revise some of his assumptions, including the assumption that we "simply cannot be religious anymore."[96] This is obviously not true in any absolute sense—but it is not simply wrong either. There is strong evidence of a sustained decline in the overall significance of religion as a cultural property of the West today; and this is so whether we argue from modernity to plurality (Berger), or see secularity as the shared context within which believers and nonbelievers alike seek "the place of fullness" (Taylor), or choose simply to reaffirm the secularization paradigm (Bruce and Voas).

Modernity has not always led directly to secularity, but it has multiplied choice, and encouraged its exercise—to the extent that, in many Western social contexts, the governing presumption is now one of unbelief. We do not live in a religionless age and may never do so. But we do live in a largely secular one, an age of "disenchantment," whose distinguishing features—interiority, instrumental individualism, and humanism—together conspire to make it increasingly hard for people, simply and confidently, to believe in God. This is not the future Bonhoeffer predicted. It is, however, sufficiently like it to support a broadly positive assessment of his historical presuppositions.

Gerhard Ebeling was already firmly convinced, some sixty years ago, that Bonhoeffer had been right to assume a profound shift in religion's place and role in Western society. Religion now finds itself in a historically unique situation. Ebeling describes its nemesis, secularism, as "a novelty without parallel," a novelty "independent of statistics and prognosis." The actual numbers involved in any division of society into religious and nonreligious people are "a matter of indifference for the point [Bonhoeffer] is concerned to make." Our understanding of the very nature and scope of religious belief has changed. People are now at most partly religious. They are religious only "in the religious province of their being, whereas for the rest over broad stretches of their life their existence is in fact as non-religious as any."[97]

This view finds strong support in the work of Taylor, and of the sociologists of religion considered in this chapter. Old certainties have been lost and, with them, the normative sense of a beyond. The new plurality rests on a largely impersonal natural order, which may or may not have higher significance, including, possibly, but by no means necessarily, a divine sponsor. While a majority of Westerners continue to acknowledge at least a vestigial Christian identity (with much smaller numbers either embracing religion wholeheartedly, or denying it outright), religion generally plays at best a small role in their lives.

Bonhoeffer does not fear the approach of a religionless age. He sees the end of religion as fully consistent with God's purpose in Christ, which now includes securing Christ's presence in a world that is, quite properly, turning away from the historically conditioned and increasingly improbable—indeed, unbiblical—God of metaphysics and inwardness. But how, practically, in this situation, is Christ to become "Lord of the religionless as well?"[98]—especially when, for many people, this brief affirmation of Christ's sovereignty already says too much. Christianity now makes its way in a domain whose inhabitants (including many of those who still choose to call themselves religious) do not *depend* on God in any significant sense of the word. And Christians have effectively no choice but to accept the largely secular reality in which they find themselves. They, too, are included in Taylor's "immanent frame" and have nothing to gain by trying to deny a "world come of age" the essentially nonnegotiable, highly individualized, instrumental autonomy Westerners now take largely for granted.

Bonhoeffer provides us with at least the outline of a possible Christian response to this challenge in his prison correspondence, and richly anticipates it in his earlier work. If, however, we are to understand him properly, and do justice to his insights, we must first take a closer look at what Bonhoeffer understood by religion and the religious frame of mind.

NOTES

1. *Letters and Papers*, DBWE 8: 362.
2. Reinhold Seeberg, *Christliche Dogmatik* (Erlangen: Deichert, 1924–25), 1:103. The quote appears in an editorial footnote to Bonhoeffer's letter to Bethge of April 30, 1944. *Letters and Papers*, DBWE 8: 362, ed. fn. 11, tr. Isabel Best. The concept of the "religious a priori" was introduced into theology by Ernst Troeltsch in "Zur Frage des religiösen Apriori" ("On the Question of the Religious a Priori"), *Gesammelte Schriften* (Tübingen: J.C.B. Mohr, 1913), 2: 754–68. Bonhoeffer first criticizes it in his habilitation thesis, *Act and Being*, where he declares that "[a]ll that pertains to personal appropriation of the fact of Christ is not a priori, but God's contingent action on human beings. This holds true also for what Seeberg calls feeling and intuition, for the purely formal understanding of the word needs no other forms of thought than are supplied by the pure a priori of thought itself." *Act and Being*, DBWE 2: 58.
3. *Letters and Papers*, DBWE 8: 363.
4. The word "Western" here simplifies what, in Bonhoeffer's mind, and from an early twentieth-century German perspective, was a complex phenomenon. It embraced then, as it does now, and not always comfortably, significant differences in political and cultural outlook, values, and practices among its component parts. Michael DeJonge points out that, in the *Ethics* fragment "Heritage and Decay," Bonhoeffer

> uses two different terms for European political or cultural collectives. He uses the term *westlich* (western), but only in adjectival forms and always to the exclusion of Germany. Thus Bonhoeffer uses the term *westliche Völker* to refer to Germany's western neighbours, such as Holland, England, and especially France. When envisioning a European political-cultural unity that embraces both western people and Germany, Bonhoeffer uses the term *Abendland*. This distinction is obscured in the English translation, which renders both *westlich* and *abendländisch* as "western" and *Abendland* as "the West."

Michael P. DeJonge, "Bonhoeffer's Concept of the West," in *Bonhoeffer, Religion and Politics*, ed. Christiane Tietz and Jens Zimmermann (Frankfurt: Peter Lang GmbH, 2012), 40. Bonhoeffer contests the Anglo-Saxon predisposition to see the West as an expression, exclusively, of the liberal-democratic tradition (with which Germany could not identify), and to recognize only one kind of freedom: a freedom *from* "interference and tyranny." Bonhoeffer argues for a more complex idea of freedom *for* some larger purpose, which includes notions of duty and submission. DeJonge goes on to describe Bonhoeffer's somewhat strained vision of the future for Germany and the West:

> While he shares [the British ecumenist William] Paton's vision for an international, ecumenical post-war Europe, he resists Paton's requirement that Germany conform to an Anglo-French-American definition of Europe. And while Bonhoeffer resonates with the German distinction between Germany and its western neighbours, he wants to see beyond it to a positive relationship. The centre of his vision is the Christologically-defined *Abendland*, which acknowledges the split between Germany and its western neighbours while pointing beyond it.

DeJonge, "Bonhoeffer's Concept of the West," in Tietz and Zimmermann, 46.

5. *Letters and Papers*, DBWE 8: 363–64.
6. *Letters and Papers*, DBWE 8: 362.
7. In Bonhoeffer's theology, the word "metaphysics" is associated *positively* with God's mystery and ineffability, and *negatively* with what Bonhoeffer believed to be misleading and unhelpful "religious" notions of personal salvation and divine power.
8. *Letters and Papers*, DBWE 8: 364.
9. *Letters and Papers*, DBWE 8: 426. We must not imagine that Bonhoeffer saw this development as evidence of humanity's ethical progress, but rather that he used the phrase "world come of age" ("*der mündig gewordenen Welt*"), and its variations, as metaphors for the equivalent of the transition from adolescence to adulthood. As Green says, "[t]hose who are mündig are no longer children, *dependent* upon their parents. They are *independent*, and responsible for themselves. They must think for themselves and make their own decisions. They are accountable for their own actions before the law. They have rights and freedoms which were not theirs as children." Clifford J. Green, *Bonhoeffer: A Theology of Sociality* (Revised Edition) (Grand Rapids: Eerdmans, 1999), 252.
10. Bonhoeffer, says Green, uses the words *Mündigkeit* (maturity; "of age-ness") and *Autonomie* interchangeably, as, for example, in the letters of July 8 and 16, 1944, where the phrases "*die Mündigkeit der Welt und des Menschen*" and "*die Autonomie des Menschen und der Welt*" (*Widerstand und Ergebung* [Gütersloh: Gütersloher Verlagshaus, 2011], 511, 532) are equivalents. Green, *Theology of Sociality*, 250.
11. *Letters and Papers*, DBWE 8: 425–26. The expression "Working hypothesis: God" has its origin in Carl Friedrich von Weizsäcker's *Zum Weltbild der Physik* (Leipzig: Hirzel, 1943), which Bonhoeffer included in his prison reading on his brother Karl-Friedrich's recommendation. See Weizsäcker, *The World View of Physics*, trans. Marjorie Grene (Chicago: University of Chicago Press, 1957), 157: "Still every scientist must certainly set himself the goal of making the hypothesis 'God' superfluous in his field."

12. This Latin phrase is rendered in English "as if there were no God" (*Letters and Papers*, DBWE 8: 476). Bonhoeffer's German (*auch wenn es keinen Gott gabe*) is, however, closer to the Latin original (*non daretur*: English trans. "not given").

13. *Letters and Papers*, DBWE 8: 477. Both letters are heavily influenced by Bonhoeffer's more or less contemporaneous reading of Wilhelm Dilthey's *Weltanschauung und Analyse des Menschen seit Renaissance und Reformation* (*Worldview and Analysis of Humanity since the Renaissance and Reformation*). Bonhoeffer drew on Dilthey's understanding of modern European history, and on his language (autonomy, coming of age), for a critique of religion that heralded the approach of a genuinely religionless age. Ralf K. Wüstenberg, *A Theology of Life: Dietrich Bonhoeffer's Religionless Christianity*, trans. Douglas W. Stott (Grand Rapids: Eerdmans, 1998), 83.

14. *Letters and Papers*, DBWE 8: 477.

15. *Letters and Papers*, DBWE 8: 477–78.

16. Peter Berger, Grace Davie, and Effie Fokas, *Religious America, Secular Europe? A Theme and Variations* (Farnham, Surrey: Ashgate Publishing Limited, 2008), 141.

17. *Ethics*, DBWE 6: 111.

18. *Ethics*, DBWE 6: 113.

19. *Letters and Papers*, DBWE 8: 450.

20. *Letters and Papers*, DBWE 8: 426–27.

21. *Letters and Papers*, DBWE 8: 427.

22. *Letters and Papers*, DBWE 8: 427.

23. *Letters and Papers*, DBWE 8: 426.

24. This hope was largely extinguished by the failure of the attempt on Hitler's life at the *Wolfsschanze* (Wolf's Lair) in East Prussia on July 20, 1944.

25. *Letters and Papers*, DBWE 8: 387.

26. In December 2012, the Washington-based Pew Research Center judged Europe to be home to 26 percent of a global total of some 2.2 billion Christians, with Latin America and Sub-Saharan Africa (each with 24 percent) close behind. Pew Research Center, "The Global Religious Landscape," December 18, 2012, accessed June 23, 2016, http://www.pewforum.org/2012/12/18/global-religious-landscape-chr istians. By 2050, disparities in population growth are likely to have changed this picture significantly, with some 38 percent of the world's Christians projected to be living in Sub-Saharan Africa. Europe's share of the global total is expected by then to have fallen to around 16 percent. Pew Research Center, "Christianity Poised to Continue Its Shift from Europe to Africa," April 7, 2015, accessed April 20, 2019, https://www.pewresearch.org/fact-tank/2015/04/07/christianity-is-poised-to-continue-its-so uthward-march.

27. Tom Greggs, "Religionless Christianity in a Complexly Religious and Secular World: Thinking Through and Beyond Bonhoeffer," in *Religion, Religionlessness and Contemporary Western Culture*, ed. Stephen Plant and Ralf K. Wüstenberg (Frankfurt: Peter Lang GmbH, 2008), 116.

28. Berger, Davie, and Fokas, *Religious America, Secular Europe?*, 10.

29. Berger, Davie, and Fokas, *Religious America, Secular Europe?*, 11.

30. Berger, Davie, and Fokas, *Religious America, Secular Europe?*, 9. The book gives an account of "the relative religiousness of America and secularity of Europe"

which seeks to do justice to the complex historical, philosophical, institutional, and sociological dimensions of this widely held presumption.

31. Berger, Davie, and Fokas briefly summarize the history of this association:

> the idea of an organic link between modernisation and secularisation has dominated sociological thinking for the past 150 years—effectively since the beginnings of the discipline. Since 1970, however, it has been increasingly questioned. In the last quarter of the twentieth century, the markedly different situation in the United States, the growth of Christianity in the southern hemisphere, the presence of Pentecostalism all over the developing world, the affirmation of Islam in global affairs, increasingly heated debates for and against proselytism, and so on have prompted scholars of many disciplines to rethink the secularisation paradigm as it was inspired by the European case and to question the assumptions on which it was built.

Berger, Davie, and Fokas, *Religious America, Secular Europe?*, 2.

32. Berger, Davie, and Fokas, *Religious America, Secular Europe?*, 10.
33. Berger, Davie, and Fokas, *Religious America, Secular Europe?*, 10.
34. Berger, Davie, and Fokas, *Religious America, Secular Europe?*, 12–13.
35. Berger, Davie, and Fokas, *Religious America, Secular Europe?*, 14.
36. The word "modern" can seem a little dated in our highly fragmented "postmodern" twenty-first-century context, but has the advantage here of encompassing several generations, including Bonhoeffer's, and those of his liberal Protestant predecessors.
37. *Letters and Papers*, DBWE 8: 426.
38. Charles Taylor, *A Secular Age* (Cambridge, MA: Harvard University Press, 2007), 2.
39. Taylor, *Secular Age*, 3. Warner, VanAntwerpen, and Calhoun suggest it is this emphasis on "the 'context of understanding' in which commitments are formed . . . that sets *A Secular Age* apart from the vast body of sociological literature on secularization that precedes it." Michael Warner, Jonathan VanAntwerpen, and Craig Calhoun (eds.), *Varieties of Secularism in a Secular Age* (Cambridge, MA: Harvard University Press, 2010), 5. They also think it significant that Taylor nowhere deploys the term "post-secular" in *A Secular Age*, despite the widespread contemporary use of this term in academic and popular contexts. They attribute this at least partly to the fact that Taylor's sense of the secular has never been confined to a simple paradigmatic link between modernity and religious decline, loss of confidence in which has prompted the emergence of the term "post-secular." For Taylor, what some sociologists now choose to see as a "resurgence of religion is not evidence of a new post-secular dispensation." Warner, VanAntwerpen, and Calhoun, *Varieties of Secularism in a Secular Age*, 22.
40. Taylor, *Secular Age*, 4–5.
41. Taylor, *Secular Age*, 5.
42. Taylor, *Secular Age*, 6.
43. Taylor, *Secular Age*, 6–7.
44. Taylor, *Secular Age*, 8.
45. Taylor, *Secular Age*, 8. Taylor makes no mention of Bonhoeffer in *A Secular Age* but is sometimes reminiscent of him, as, for example, here, where in the

"We Are Approaching a Completely Religionless Age" 29

discussion of "fullness," he distinguishes between a gift received from "without" and the godless, self-sufficient "within" of autonomous human reason.

46. Warner, VanAntwerpen, and Calhoun maintain that Taylor wants "to change the way we think about belief" by infusing the experience of "fullness" with a real sense of the transcendent. Here, the *subjective* experience of fullness "is understood to be objective—the way the world is, or at least can sometimes be. . . . Our subjective stances may afford us more or better access to fullness, but it is not merely an interior state." We don't readily understand this. "Indeed, it is a reflection of our individualistic, psychological orientation and also our rationalistic, epistemological criteria for knowledge that we try to grasp fullness entirely in terms of subjective states; we say we have moments of transcendent experience . . . rather than moments when we experience the transcendent character of reality." Warner, VanAntwerpen, and Calhoun, *Varieties of Secularism in a Secular Age*, 11.

47. Taylor, *Secular Age*, 8–9.
48. Taylor, *Secular Age*, 9–10.
49. Taylor, *Secular Age*, 10–11.
50. Belief in God, says Taylor, is not the same now as it was 500 years ago. "The frameworks of yesterday and today are related as 'naïve' and 'reflective,' because the latter has opened a question which had been foreclosed in the former by the unacknowledged shape of the background." He illustrates this by drawing attention to ways of distinguishing between different kinds of experience—"between the immanent and the transcendent, the natural and the supernatural"—which people take in their stride today, but which are in fact a relatively recent product of modernity. "This hiving off of an independent, free-standing level, that of 'nature,' which may or may not be in interaction with something further or beyond, is a crucial bit of modern theorizing, which in turn corresponds to a constitutive dimension of modern experience." Taylor, *Secular Age*, 13–14.
51. Taylor, *Secular Age*, 12.
52. Taylor, *Secular Age*, 12–13.
53. Taylor, *Secular Age*, 15.
54. Taylor, *Secular Age*, 15.
55. Taylor, *Secular Age*, 15.
56. Taylor, *Secular Age*, 16.
57. Ancient Epicureanism is one such example.
58. Taylor, *Secular Age*, 19.
59. Taylor, *Secular Age*, 19.
60. Taylor, *Secular Age*, 19.
61. Taylor, *Secular Age*, 539–40.
62. Taylor, *Secular Age*, 540.
63. Taylor, *Secular Age*, 542.
64. Taylor, *Secular Age*, 556.
65. Taylor, *Secular Age*, 592–93. In one of a series of lectures he gave on William James at the Institute for Human Sciences in Vienna in 2000, Taylor describes him as "our great philosopher of the cusp," the one who "tells us more than anyone else about what it's like to stand in that open space and feel the winds pulling you now here, now there." Charles Taylor, *Varieties of Religion Today: William James Revisited*

(Cambridge, MA: Harvard University Press, 2002), 59. James, says Taylor, "sees religion primarily as something that individuals experience." Taylor, *James Revisited*, 4. James allows that religion gives rise to many different thoughts and theories but believes the range of religious feeling and conduct to be much more limited. He thus treats religious ideas as secondary to feelings and behavior, which are "the more constant elements" and the means by which religion "carries on her principal business." William James, *The Varieties of Religious Experience* (Mineola, NY: Dover Publications, 2002), 504. James has little time for the church and for theology but feels the frustration and pain of those whose religious inclinations are "checked in their natural tendency to expand" by the pressure to conform to a strictly material view of the world. James, *Varieties*, 204. He clearly sees how two very different epistemological standpoints lead believers and unbelievers to very different understandings of the nature of reality and the ethics of belief. People are forced to choose between two mutually exclusive worldviews, but having done so, will still often have some residual sympathy for the alternative. James takes a side in the debate between belief and unbelief, "but he helps you imagine what it's like to be on either." Taylor, *James Revisited*, 57. The image of the "Jamesian open space" reflects Taylor's own vision of a "cross-pressured" life lived "between the open [to transcendence] and closed perspectives." Taylor, *Secular Age*, 555. I use it in chapter 6 to describe people for whom Bonhoeffer's religionless Christianity may have special appeal, but do not mean to imply by this an intellectual convergence of any specific or substantial kind between James and Bonhoeffer. Bonhoeffer, as we shall see, was familiar with James's work, and respected it, but shared neither his philosophical pragmatism nor his views on religion. The significance, for my argument, of the "Jamesian open space" is its willing embrace of an unresolved tension between belief and unbelief, and an attendant openness to "the sense you have that there is something more, bigger, outside you." Taylor, *James Revisited*, 59.

66. Steve Bruce, *Secularisation: In Defence of an Unfashionable Theory* (Oxford: OUP, 2011), 1, accessed October 30, 2016, Oxford Scholarship Online, DOI: 10.10 93/acprof:osobl/9780199654123.001.0001.

67. Bruce, *Secularisation*, 2.

68. Bruce, *Secularisation*, 3. Hugh McLeod offers a very similar description of this process in *The Religious Crisis of the 1960s*, where he writes of "the end of Christendom." McLeod defines Christendom as "a social order in which regardless of individual belief, Christian language, rites, moral teachings, and personnel were part of the taken-for-granted environment. As the indifferent and the hostile claimed the right to do things differently, one of the pillars of Christendom fell." A growing pluralism had to accommodate disparate religious and moral values, while the significance of "Christian socialisation" for young people declined. "As Christianity lost a large part of its privileged position, the options in matters of belief, life-path, or 'spirituality' were open to a degree that they had not been for centuries." Hugh McLeod, *The Religious Crisis of the 1960s* (Oxford: Oxford University Press, 2007), 265.

69. Bruce, *Secularisation*, 16.

70. Bruce, *Secularisation*, 16.

71. Bruce, *Secularisation*, 16.

72. Bruce, *Secularisation*, 10.

73. Bruce, *Secularisation*, 9. Bruce explains the elasticity of the 1851 census data thus: "The census enumerators collected data for attendances (and many people attended more than once), so we can be sure only of the upper and lower limits, but we know that between 40 and 60 percent of the population attended public worship that day."

74. Bruce, *Secularisation*, 9. The British Humanist Association (BHA) quotes more recent figures that point, overall, to a continuing decline in the number of regular church attenders in the UK. The exception is the 2014 British Social Attitudes Survey, where 13.1 percent of respondents reported going to a religious service at least once a week. (The BHA notes in this connection that "self-reported Church attendance is invariably higher than actual recorded attendance.") Christian Research's "Religious Trends," No. 7, on the other hand, puts the number of people attending church in the UK on a particular Sunday in 2005 at 3,166,200, or just 6.3 percent of the population, while the Church of England's own average Sunday attendance figures have also continued to fall, from 1,005,000 in 2002 to 785,000 in 2013. British Humanist Association 2016, "Religion and Belief: Some Surveys and Statistics," accessed November 14, 2016, https://humanism.org.uk/campaigns/religion-and-belief-some-surveys-and-statistics/.

75. Bruce, *Secularisation*, 14–15. An Australian Community Survey run by NCLS (National Church Life Survey) Research gives a higher weekly figure (11 percent) for a more recent year (2016). NCLS Research notes, however, that "attendance rates obtained from sample surveys tend to be inflated compared to head counts and estimates from church leaders and administrators." The NCLS churches' own Estimates of Attendance Database suggests that, five years earlier, in 2011, 1.43 million (or just 6 percent) of Australians were attending church weekly. NCLS Research, "Local Churches in Australia," accessed April 20, 2019, www.2016ncls.org.au/resources/downloads/Local%20Churches%20in%20Australia-Research%20Findings%20from%20NCLS%20Research(2017).pdf.

76. David Voas, "The Rise and Fall of Fuzzy Fidelity in Europe," *European Sociological Review*, vol. 25, no. 2 (2009): 155–68, accessed November 2, 2016, www.esr.oxfordjournals.org, DOI:10.1093/esr/jcn044.

77. Voas, "The Rise and Fall of Fuzzy Fidelity in Europe," 157.

78. Voas, "The Rise and Fall of Fuzzy Fidelity in Europe," 155. Bruce acknowledges the limitations of "a single-time snapshot to represent change over time," but observes that, in the frequent absence of longitudinal studies, data from a single survey is often used "to draw conclusions about the past by treating each age cohort as if it is representative of its era." Bruce, *Secularisation*, 17.

79. The list of countries included in the ESS is not exhaustive, but it is extensive. There are twenty-one of them: Austria, Belgium, Czech Republic, Denmark, Finland, France, Germany, Greece, Hungary, Ireland, Italy, Luxembourg, Netherlands, Norway, Poland, Portugal, Slovenia, Spain, Sweden, Switzerland, and the United Kingdom.

80. Voas, "The Rise and Fall of Fuzzy Fidelity in Europe," 159. Voas observes that,

in the most secular countries—the Czech Republic, Sweden, and France—the curve appears to flatten out in the last couple of decades. People born in the early 1980s are much the same in religious terms as those born in the early 1960s. It is tempting to suppose that secularisation has run its course, leaving a certain amount of religion to fight another day. There may be some truth in this finding: no one expects atheism to become universal.

Voas, "The Rise and Fall of Fuzzy Fidelity in Europe," 159–60.
81. Voas, "The Rise and Fall of Fuzzy Fidelity in Europe," 160.
82. Voas, "The Rise and Fall of Fuzzy Fidelity in Europe," 161.
83. Voas, "The Rise and Fall of Fuzzy Fidelity in Europe," 161–62.
84. See, for example, Diana Butler Bass, *Christianity After Religion* (New York: HarperCollins, 2012).
85. Graham Ward, *The Politics of Discipleship: Becoming Postmaterial Citizens* (Grand Rapids, MI: Baker Academic, 2009), 131. http://search.ebscohost.com.ez proxy.csu.edu.au.
86. Voas, "The Rise and Fall of Fuzzy Fidelity in Europe," 162. Voas's analysis suggests that "[o]nly in the most religious countries do more than a quarter think that religion is personally somewhat important rather than unimportant. Elsewhere, the very large majority of these respondents see religion as not very important, and for a quarter or more it is very unimportant (0, 1, or 2 on the 0–10 scale)."
87. Voas, "The Rise and Fall of Fuzzy Fidelity in Europe," 164. There is clearly a degree of tension between Voas's concept of "fuzzy fidelity" and the more pressing need to choose between competing worldviews prominent in the thought of Taylor and James. They have in common, though, the quintessentially modern ingredients of choice and residual uncertainty; although, in the first instance (Voas), a decision is postponed, or avoided; while in the second, a decision is taken, but the element of doubt remains.
88. Voas, "The Rise and Fall of Fuzzy Fidelity in Europe," 165.
89. Voas, "The Rise and Fall of Fuzzy Fidelity in Europe," 167.
90. Voas, "The Rise and Fall of Fuzzy Fidelity in Europe," 167.
91. Voas, "The Rise and Fall of Fuzzy Fidelity in Europe," 167.
92. Bruce, *Secularisation*, 157.
93. Bruce, *Secularisation*, 159. Gallup surveys point to a decline in weekly church attendance by U.S. Catholics from 45 to 39 percent over the decade to 2017—the comparable figure in 1955 was 75 percent—while attendance by U.S. Protestants remained steady at 45 percent—and was in fact a little lower, at 42 percent, in 1955. Whereas, however, "largely because of the growth of the U.S. Hispanic population," the percentage of Americans identifying as Catholic has changed little over the past seventy years (22 percent today compared with 24 percent in 1955), the percentage of Americans identifying as Protestant has fallen sharply, from 71 percent in 1955 to 47 percent in 2017. Gallup expects this trend to continue "as older Americans are replaced by a far less Protestant-identifying younger generation," and as more Americans profess "no religious identity" (20 percent today compared with just 1 percent in 1955). Gallup, "Catholics' Church Attendance Resumes Downward Slide," April 9, 2018, accessed April 20, 2019, https://news.gallup.com/poll/232226/church-attendance-among-catholics-resumes-downward-slide.aspx?g_source=link_newsv9&g_campaign=item_2.

94. Bruce, *Secularisation*, 160.
95. Bruce, *Secularisation*, 165–66. W.C. Roof, "God is in the Details: Reflections on Religion's Public Presence in the United States in the Mid-1990s," *Sociology of Religion*, 57 (1996), 153.
96. *Letters and Papers*, DBWE 8: 362.
97. Gerhard Ebeling, *Word and Faith*, trans. James W. Leitch (London: SCM Press, 1963), 131–32.
98. *Letters and Papers*, DBWE 8: 363.

Chapter 2

Bonhoeffer's Critique of Religion

Ralf Wüstenberg believes Bonhoeffer to have had no "fixed *concept* of religion."[1] Religion was, rather, the "negative foil" for other important theological ideas.[2] Christoph Schwöbel similarly argues against the presence, in Bonhoeffer's work, of any formal definition of religion. Instead, says Schwöbel, we are given a list of things which reveal "a certain Wittgensteinian family resemblance,"[3] and which together typify the largely inflexible and impractical response of the church and theology to the emerging historical reality of "a world come of age."

While, however, it is necessary to acknowledge the episodic growth and development of the religious understanding in Bonhoeffer, it is, I think, no less clear that, by the end of his life, we have at our disposal a bold, comprehensive, and coherent account of what religion meant for him—and of its place in his theology—largely in the form of negative critique.

BONHOEFFER AND BARTH

Bonhoeffer's critique of religion begins with Karl Barth, who he later credits, in the first of the theological letters from prison, with being the only theologian before him to have begun thinking about something like a religionless Christianity.[4] The problem with Barth, though—or so it seemed to Bonhoeffer in April 1944—was that he did not take the argument far enough, leaving us with an essentially conservative "positivism of revelation."[5]

Bonhoeffer makes the case for and against Barth's critique of religion on several occasions in the prison letters,[6] and does so with particular clarity in the letter of May 5, 1944, where he writes,

Barth was the first theologian . . . to begin the critique of religion, but he then put in its place a positivist doctrine of revelation that says, in effect, "like it or lump it." Whether it's the virgin birth, the Trinity, or anything else, all are equally significant and necessary parts of the whole, which must be swallowed whole or not at all. That's not biblical. There are degrees of cognition and degrees of significance. . . . The positivism of revelation is too easy-going, since in the end it sets up a law of faith and tears up what is—through Christ's becoming flesh!—a gift for us. Now the church stands in the place of religion—that in itself is biblical—but the world is left to its own devices. . . . That is the error.[7]

These reproaches warrant consideration and will be examined shortly, but we must be careful not to overwhelm Bonhoeffer's very genuine praise of Barth with criticism. Bonhoeffer's understanding of religion rests firmly on the foundation provided by Barth's early theology. It was Barth, after all, who, in the second edition (1922) of his Commentary on *The Epistle to the Romans*, "led the God of Jesus Christ forward to battle against religion, πνεῦμα [spirit] against σάρξ [flesh]."[8]

Barth's Critique of Religion

In *Romans*, Barth gives an account of religion "scarred with the dualism of 'There' and 'Here.'" Religion, he says, makes of God a thing among other things. It reduces God to just "one factor in a contrast," a positive rather than a negative pole, a Yes rather than a No.[9] People cling to religion in the hope of eternal life, but the frontier of religion is in fact "the line of death which separates flesh from spirit, time from eternity, human possibility from the possibility of God."[10]

Grace is not to be confused with religion. They stand on opposite sides of the abyss that separates human beings from God. Grace is no longer grace when it is thought to be simply an extension of the religious experience with which we are already familiar. Grace "lies on the other side and no bridge leads to it."[11]

Religion is "the final human possibility." This vain reaching out to the divine compels us at last to recognize that "God is not to be found in religion." There is no human way to God. "Religion brings us to the place where we must wait, in order that God may confront us—on the other side of the frontier of religion. The transformation of the 'No' of religion into the divine 'Yes' occurs in the dissolution of this last observable human thing."[12] Religion thus allows us to know God "to be unknowable and wholly Other."[13] In the process, it reveals the full extent of humanity's falling away from God. By distinguishing the creature from the Creator, it brings the world into conflict with God. Religion breaks people in two and leaves them at war with themselves: a war of the spirit ("which delights in the law of God") against the flesh ("a world swayed by a wholly different law"). And in this conflict, neither party enjoys more than a temporary advantage over the other.[14]

Religion and the law together die with Christ on the cross, where "the last and noblest human possibility, the possibility of human piety and belief and enthusiasm and prayer, is fulfilled by being evacuated." The crucified Christ gives honor only to God. "Looking outwards from the Cross, we observe religion . . . as a particular aspect of human behaviour, to have been—taken out of the way."[15]

The risen Christ is the "new man," beyond all religion, "beyond all human possibility." Jesus Christ is the new creation, "the man who has passed from death to life,"[16] and who in this way testifies to the unqualified, categorical freedom of God. In him, religion and grace "confront one another as death and life."[17]

The church, like religion, stands on this side of the abyss which separates us from God. As such, it shares the limitations of religion. By aspiring to draw eternity into time, and make it visible, the church transforms the "Beyond" into "a metaphysical 'something,'" which is simply an extension of the world. It seeks to turn the divine into something temporal and practical "for the benefit of those who cannot live with the Living God, and yet cannot live without God (the Grand Inquisitor!)."[18] But this, says Barth, is no reason for Christians either to separate themselves from the church, or to divide it. "[T]he divine possibility cannot be apprehended save in the catastrophe of that human possibility which is the Church."[19] Christians must take the church as they find it and be prepared to share "the guilt of its inevitable failure." The "God-sickness of men" is a mark of the human condition. It will always be there in one form or another. The "religious-ecclesiastical possibility is inevitable," regardless of the final impossibility of the ecclesiastical religious undertaking itself.[20]

A Positivism of Revelation

Bonhoeffer found the distinction between the grace of God (which is known and received in *faith*, as God's gift to human beings) and *religion* (the human quest for God) enormously helpful and was quick to adopt it. Eberhard Bethge describes this distinction as among Bonhoeffer's "fundamental experiences as a student."[21] Barth, says Bethge, transformed the religious experience, which had been a source of real difficulty for Bonhoeffer, into a trivial thing. "For Barth, the certainty being pursued here was anchored not in people but in the majesty of God."[22] Martin Rumscheidt likewise observes that Barth's radical critique of religion appealed strongly to the young Bonhoeffer not least because it allowed him to recognize, as false and self-serving, religion's claim to transcend the purely human.[23]

By the time we come to the prison letters, however, the situation has changed. Bonhoeffer readily acknowledges his debt to Barth, by repeatedly praising Barth's early critique of religion, but now accuses him of allowing this subsequently to slide into a conservative "positivism of revelation."[24]

Bonhoeffer seems likely to have first come across the term "positivism of revelation" as a student of theology at the University of Berlin. Among those who used it there—apparently to signify an unquestioning faith in the unassailable truth of God's Word[25]—were the church historian Erich Seeberg, in his 1929 book on Luther,[26] with which Bonhoeffer was familiar.[27]

Gerhard Ebeling believed Bonhoeffer to have understood by "revelational positivism"

> a defence and restoration of biblical and ecclesiastical tradition conditioned by the rejection of liberal theology, in which for want of interpretation the world is left to itself, the individual elements in the tradition are passed off without differentiation for equally significant and equally necessary parts of the whole, the question of faith is held to be answered by presenting the "Faith of the church" and in that way a law of faith is erected.[28]

If we take Bonhoeffer's accusation seriously, and Ebeling's definition (which leans heavily on Bonhoeffer's letter of May 5, 1944) as our starting point, then we must assume Barth's attitude to religion to have changed over time, allowing him a flexibility beyond the observation, in *The Epistle to the Romans*, that religion takes us as far as we can go by ourselves and remains, as such, an activity worthy of "the vigour of noble and devoted men."[29] Wüstenberg finds evidence of such a change in *Church Dogmatics I/2*, where Barth makes the case for "true religion."[30]

True Religion

Barth begins this section of the *Church Dogmatics* with a firm reservation. Religion, he says, can never be true in and of itself. Revelation makes this impossible, for "as the self-offering and self-manifestation of God, as the work of peace which God Himself has concluded between Himself and man, revelation is the truth beside which there is no other truth, over against which there is only lying and wrong."[31] Religion can only become true by virtue of the revealed grace of God. It may be affirmed, or denied, by God. Revelation can "adopt" religion and declare it to be true. Religion is, therefore, as much "a creature of grace" as is the justified sinner. And on this analogy, Barth does not hesitate to identify the Christian religion with "true religion."[32]

Grace, though, does not change the character of religion. A religion of grace still does not contain truth within itself and, in this respect, is no different from other religions.

> The decisive thing for the existence of the Church and the children of God and for the truth of their religion . . . is the fact that by the grace of God they live by His grace. That is what makes them what they are. That is what makes their religion true. That is what lifts it above the general level of religious history.[33]

God's free act of grace far exceeds human understanding. We may only begin to comprehend its "concrete significance" when the grace of God is brought into correspondence with Jesus Christ. Through Jesus Christ, the Son of God incarnate and "eternal Object of the divine good pleasure,"

> man has also become the object of the divine good pleasure, not by his own merit or deserving, but by the grace which assumed man to itself in the Son of God. In this One, the revelation of God among men and the reconciliation of man with God has been fulfilled once and for all.[34]

Thus, says Wüstenberg, in the *Church Dogmatics*, the critique of religion set out with such force and eloquence in *The Epistle to the Romans* is transformed into a "revelatory-positive" view of religion, rather than providing, as Bonhoeffer evidently came to believe more plausible, the foundation for a religionless understanding of God. Religion, for Barth, is still an anthropological phenomenon which belongs to our sinful being, but it now "finds a fixed theological place in the doctrine of justification" to the extent that, as Christian, or true, religion, it may be considered justified by revelation.[35]

Criticism of Barth is often prompted by the absolute nature of his claims. But it was not Barth's unyielding, prophetic style of argumentation that troubled Bonhoeffer. Indeed, Bonhoeffer would almost certainly have agreed with Alan Spence that a particular strength of Barth's theology lies in its ability to transport us "from the spiritual barrenness of . . . [nineteenth-century] historicism and subjectivism . . . to a place where God is spoken of with fluency and delight."[36] So long as this kind of positivism supported a negative critique of religion, Bonhoeffer had no reason to quarrel with it. What he objects to in the prison letters is Barth's "turn" from a negative to a positive assessment of religion.

Andreas Pangritz finds evidence of this "turn" already in the second, revised edition of *Romans*[37]—the very book on which Bonhoeffer appears to base his praise of Barth's critique of religion in the prison letters.[38] And it is certainly true that, in *Romans*, religion does not appear in an unrelievedly negative light. It still has a role to play as "the final human possibility."

It takes us as far as we can travel by ourselves and, in doing so, helps us to understand our limitations. There is, however, no suggestion here that religion may be "adopted" by revelation and marked off as "true." Religion seeks, and purports to explore, a path that simply does not exist—a way from human beings to God. It mistakes a wholly human undertaking for something divine and confronts the free grace of God as death does life.

Bonhoeffer seems early to have expressed concerns that Barth's evolving dogmatics constituted a regression from the *Epistle to the Romans*[39]—concerns which Pangritz believes initially to have been only those of "a biblical theologian of liberal orientation" who feared that a much respected colleague had succumbed, quite unnecessarily, to "the structural constraints of theological orthodoxy."[40] The prison letters, however, reveal a more fundamental problem. Barth believes religion to be unavoidable—a perennial fact of life—whereas Bonhoeffer has come to see it as a passing historical phenomenon. More importantly, as Ernst Feil points out, Bonhoeffer is preoccupied with "the question of concreteness, reality, and history" as a problem for theology, and while it may be an overstatement to describe Barth as "irrevocably mired" in an unworldly "absence of history," it could have been the case that he was not able to help Bonhoeffer resolve the question of Christ's claim on "a world come of age" because he was prevented, or so at least Bonhoeffer believed, by a religious "positivism of revelation" from taking the world seriously enough.[41]

The Free Majesty of God

Barth believed contemporary theology—which, for him, was essentially liberal Protestant theology—to have lost its sense of direction. God had been abandoned for anthropology. Barth sought to recover a genuine awareness of God's transcendence, and to ground human experience of the divine in an actual event: in God's act of revelation—the encounter with the Word of God in Jesus Christ. Bonhoeffer strongly approved of Barth's project, but, as Bethge observes, he did not hesitate, "as an ally," to criticize it whenever he felt the need to do so—as, for example, when Barth's stress on "the inaccessibility and free majesty of God" threatened to dispel all serious concern for "humanity's concrete, earthly plight."[42] Bonhoeffer's reservations about Barth's approach to God and the world are thus not confined to the prison letters. They date back to his doctoral and habilitation dissertations, both of which contain criticisms of Barth's uncompromising transcendentalism.

In *Sanctorum Communio*, for example, Bonhoeffer speaks of a Christian love that "loves the real neighbor,"[43] and takes issue with Barth's exegesis of the command to love in *Romans*.[44] In Christ, says Barth, "I am not only one with God, but, because 'with God,' one also with the neighbour." Christian love is only ever a "disclosing of the One in the other" and will perceive in other human beings no more than "the parable of him who is to be loved." Love is still love of "concrete, particular men," but it has no favorites—"no pre-ference for any particular man."[45] Bonhoeffer insists, against Barth, that love "really does love the other, not the One in the other." He challenges Barth's right to affirm the unimportance of the other "'as such' . . . when God commands us to love precisely that person."[46]

Bethge understands Bonhoeffer to have held the *extra calvinisticum* responsible for Barth's tendency to deny "the complete entry of God's majesty into this world."[47] The *extra calvinisticum* is a Lutheran expression referring to the Reformed tradition's insistence on the unqualified supremacy of the divine nature over the human nature of Christ. The Reformed, for their part, interpret the *extra calvinisticum* in line with the dictum *finitum non capax infiniti*, "the finite is incapable of the infinite," which here signifies that "the finite humanity of Christ is incapable of receiving or grasping infinite attributes such as omnipresence, omnipotence, or omniscience."[48] Michael DeJonge observes that, while the *(in)capax* debate is essentially "a sacramental dispute about whether Christ is present in the bread and wine of the Lord's supper," it also has a christological dimension, grounded in divergent Lutheran and Reformed interpretations of the relationship of the divine and human natures, and their attributes, in the person of Christ.[49] The Lutheran *finitum est capax infiniti* corroborates and systematizes two of Luther's deepest convictions: the christological "this man, Jesus, *is* God"; and the sacramental "this *is* my body," which highlights Luther's insistence on the actual, bodily presence of Christ in the sacrament of the Lord's supper. DeJonge describes the christological "is"—which speaks to "the exclusive agency of the person of Christ"—as the heartbeat of Lutheran Christology. "And it is this heartbeat that pulses out into the sacramental 'is'—this is my body—and ultimately into the majestic genus [where the majestic properties of the divine nature are communicated to the human nature of Christ] and the *capax*." DeJonge suspects Barth to have neglected the christological implications of Lutheran fidelity to the concept of sole agency. "The contrast with Bonhoeffer here is strong," he says. "If there is anything about the Lutheran tradition that Bonhoeffer sees with clarity and pursues with abandon, it is the exclusive christological agency of the person of Christ."[50]

In his habilitation thesis, *Act and Being*, Bonhoeffer warns Barth of the dangers of transcendental philosophy and tries "to make him more 'Lutheran.'" Bonhoeffer, says Bethge, wanted Barth to acknowledge the truth of the *finitum capax infiniti*—to accept that "despite everything, God *was* accessible."[51] And nowhere in *Act and Being* is God's accessibility more keenly observed than in the objection raised to a theology built on an exclusively formalistic understanding of the freedom of God. The freedom associated with the unconditioned, self-subsistent God is one thing. It does not touch us. But, in revelation, says Bonhoeffer, it is God's *"given* Word" that is important—"the covenant in which God is bound by God's own action." In revelation, "the freedom of God . . . finds its strongest evidence precisely in that God freely chose to be bound to historical human beings and to be placed at the disposal of human beings. God is free not from human beings but for them. Christ is the word of God's freedom."[52]

Bonhoeffer perfectly understands Barth's affirmation "that power to grow comes always from above and never from below."[53] And, like Barth, he is driven to proclaim God's sovereignty. But whereas the Barth Bonhoeffer knew found it difficult, if not impossible, truly to bring God and the world into intimate relation, Bonhoeffer strove earnestly, and with growing urgency, to do so. While, says Bethge, "the early Barth, desiring to proclaim God's majesty, began by removing him to a remote distance, Bonhoeffer's starting point, inspired by the same desire to proclaim his majesty, brought him into close proximity."[54]

Revelation speaks plainly to Barth, as to Bonhoeffer, of the consummation of God's Word in Jesus Christ. And nowhere is the power of the Word more evident to Barth than in the divine act of resurrection, to which theology must faithfully witness and attest, while yet paying scrupulous attention "to that reserve maintained by the divine over against the human."[55]

> In the Resurrection the new world of the Holy Spirit touches the old world of the flesh, but touches it as a tangent touches a circle, that is, without touching it. . . . Jesus is *declared to be the Son of God* wherever He reveals Himself and is recognized as the Messiah, before the first Easter Day and, most assuredly, after it.[56]

We must not, warns Barth, confuse the *humanitas christi* with the revealing Word of God, but rather bear in mind the Old Testament concept of God's holiness, thereby avoiding "the possibility of having God disclose Himself through man," and otherwise resisting the temptation to raise human beings to the level of God. For Barth, Jesus is essentially a means of divine action: "the power and continuity in which the man Jesus of Nazareth was in fact the revealed Word . . . consisted . . . in the power and continuity of the divine action in this form and not in the continuity of this form as such."[57]

As we shall see when we come later to consider Bonhoeffer's Christology, Bonhoeffer has a rather different sense of God's presence in the world of human experience, and of our relationship to God, which is "no 'religious' relationship to some highest, most powerful, and best being imaginable," but rather "a new life in 'being there for others,' through participation in the being of Jesus."[58]

The Mysteries of the Faith

We have still to consider Bonhoeffer's specific criticism of what he saw as Barth's tendency to treat the various elements of the Christian tradition—"whether it's the virgin birth, the Trinity, or anything else"—as "equally significant and necessary parts" of an undifferentiated whole.[59]

In the *Church Dogmatics*, Barth gives deliberate, careful, and sympathetic attention to the doctrine of the early church, which he regards as "in some sense normative."[60] The alternative, as he sees it, is simply to deplore the muddle of "modern Protestantism" and the loss, "along with the Trinity and the Virgin Birth," of a whole dimension—the dimension of mystery—and its replacement with all sorts of "worthless substitutes," including Nazi fantasies of race and *Führer*.[61]

The issue here is essentially one of emphasis. The mysteries of the Christian faith (prayer, worship, sacraments, creed) are no less important to Bonhoeffer than they are to Barth. It is the risk posed to the mysteries by indiscriminate proclamation that worries him. For Bonhoeffer, sacred theology is a "prayerful kneeling before the mystery of the divine child in the stable." Its only task is "to keep the miracle of God a miracle, to comprehend, defend, and exalt the mystery of God, precisely as mystery."[62] Bonhoeffer understands the historical situation to be no longer such as to allow articles of faith (the virgin birth, for example) to be treated as straightforward matters of public instruction. He reminds us that "[t]here are degrees of cognition and degrees of significance" which demand an "'arcane discipline' . . . through which the mysteries of the Christian faith are sheltered against profanation."[63] The mysteries of the faith lie hidden in the liturgical life of the church and must be preserved there, in the hearts of the worshiping community of Christ, rather than exposed to the incredulity of an increasingly skeptical world.

The critique of Barth's prolix, God-centered dogmatics may also have been influenced by Bonhoeffer's reflections on his own liberal inheritance. Liberal theology, he says in the letter of June 8, 1944, will be overcome only when "the question it asks is really taken up and answered (which is *not* the case with the Confessing Church's positivism of revelation!)."[64] Bonhoeffer was never able fully to set aside the historical-critical issues raised by liberal theology. The Apostles' Creed, he declares, in his lectures on the church in the summer of 1932, "is not adequate for the Protestant Confessio."[65] It leaves too many questions unresolved, including those of liberal theology "and Harnack."[66] As the church-community's only genuine "constitution," the confession of faith must be "completely true," and yet often the language of the Creed itself ("descended into hell," "born of a virgin"[67]) invites skepticism rather than confidence. "The word must be true and clear," not just for the sake of the church-community but also for the sake of those who do not yet believe.[68]

Bonhoeffer returns to this issue in the "Outline for a Book," which he enclosed with one of the last (August 3) of the theological letters from prison. What, he asks, "do we really believe? I mean, believe in such a way that our lives depend on it?" Again, the "problem" of the Apostles' Creed. To ask, "what *must* I believe?" is to ask the wrong question. Barth and the Confessing Church encourage people simply to take refuge in something called the "faith of the Church," rather than to think and to speak up for themselves. "This is why even in the Confessing Church the breezes are blowing less than freely."[69] The church, for Bonhoeffer, is *not* a place of diminished responsibility. Christians must decide what they really believe. Nothing can finally absolve them of the need to be honest with themselves.[70]

Andreas Pangritz believes Bonhoeffer's criticism here to be directed not so much against Barth himself as against conservative Barthians in the Confessing Church such as Hans Asmussen who, as chair of the Berlin Council of Brethren, protested the church's publication of Rudolf Bultmann's Alpirsbach address of June 1, 1941, on demythologizing the Bible. Bultmann had argued that it was unreasonable to expect "modern man" to accept the gospel in its "mythical" setting, which is "simply the cosmology of a pre-scientific age" with nothing "specifically Christian" about it.[71] Myth, said Bultmann, is not in any case intended to be an objective representation of reality. It speaks rather of our dependence on a transcendent power or powers which ground, limit, and control us in ways that permit us to make sense of the world and our place in it. The significance of the mythology of the New Testament "lies not in its imagery but in the understanding of existence which it enshrines." This existential understanding must be reinterpreted in contemporary terms to ensure the continuing relevance and credibility of the Christian message.[72] Asmussen rejected Bultmann's argument as thoroughly unchristian and judged it no more acceptable to Christians for being "presented intelligently and with reason."[73]

Bonhoeffer, by contrast, admired Bultmann's intellectual integrity. He took "great pleasure in the new Bultmann volume" and described the arrogance of its critics as "a real scandal for the Confessing Church."[74] Bonhoeffer, though, is not finally convinced of the merits of Bultmann's demythologization program, which he finds guilty of a typically liberal inclination to reduce Christianity to some so-called essence. This he believes to be a mistake. The New Testament is not "a mythological dressing up of a universal truth, but this mythology (resurrection and so forth) is the thing itself!"[75] Clifford Green argues that Bonhoeffer had long understood "the language of myth, magic and anthropomorphism" to be just as valid a word of God's address to us as "modern, technical and abstract language."[76] In the lectures on Genesis 1–3, published in book form as *Creation and Fall* in 1933, Bonhoeffer says of the myth of the "enchanted garden" at the center of the world that "with these ancient magical images as well as with our technical, abstract images, God must reach out to us, and . . . teach us if we are to become wise."[77]

Barth, for his part, sternly criticizes Bultmann's thesis for failing to recognize the biblically grounded "this-worldly" reality of God in Jesus Christ. The demythologized kerygma, says Barth, simply has nothing to say about "God's having condescended to become this-worldly, objective and . . . datable." It is silent on the cause of faith and "must suppress or even deny the fact that the cross and resurrection of Jesus Christ . . . is the event of our redemption, that it possessed an intrinsic significance of its own, and that only because it has that primary significance has it a derived significance here and now."[78] For Barth, the "mythological" elements of the New Testament are there to show us that our faith "does not depend on some unknown distant deity." Rather, they ground our faith in the crucified and risen Christ "as the one in whom God *first* loved us."[79]

BONHOEFFER'S CRITIQUE OF RELIGION: BARTH AND BEYOND

Bonhoeffer's critique of religion grew naturally out of Barth's theology of revelation and was for a long time predominantly Barthian. It is already visible, in embryo, in *Sanctorum Communio*, where Bonhoeffer declares that Jesus Christ established neither a new religion nor, indeed, a religious community. These were the work of the apostles. The Son of God "brought, established, and proclaimed the reality of the new [God-reconciled] humanity." The picture of a new religion recruiting followers comes from a later time.[80] Wüstenberg argues that, prior to 1927, Bonhoeffer reads Barth "from a revelatory-theological, ecclesiological, and pneumatological perspective that as yet has nothing to do with a critique of religion."[81] In *Sanctorum Communio*, the liberal and the revelatory-theological understanding of religion stand side by side. "Although a critique of religion is prepared, it is not carried through."[82]

Barth's presence is more strongly felt in *Act and Being*, which, in addition to its measured embrace of revelation theology, includes elements of a now more self-conscious critique of religion. The critique of religion here plays a role, for example, in Bonhoeffer's firm rejection of Reinhold Seeberg's concept of the "religious a priori"—a judgment reaffirmed by Bonhoeffer in the prison letters.

Seeberg believes human beings to be open, emotionally and intuitively, to the immediate (i.e., unmediated) experience of God. There is, according to Bonhoeffer's characterization of this position, "a mold in human beings [a religious a priori] into which the divine content of revelation, too, may pour."[83] Revelation thus becomes religion, and genuine transcendence is forsaken for a subjective immediacy, a unity in which the ability truly to distinguish between I and Other (the I and God) is lost.

Bonhoeffer cannot accept this. If, he says, "we are to assume that the compelling ability to receive revelation and, by implication, to believe, is given with this a priori, we have already said too much." We have no innate capacity for divinity. "Natural religion, too, remains flesh and seeks after flesh." True revelation, on the other hand, is utterly transforming. It is God's work in us. "In this matter, there is no ability to hear before the hearing." And it is of course God's "concrete, preached word" that we must hear, as the only way from God to human beings. There is no other "immediateness."[84]

While Seeberg, says Bonhoeffer, would not contest this view of revelation as God's gift of grace or work of faith in us, he is led astray nonetheless by the idea of the "religious a priori," which would make a specific religious quality in humankind, rather than God's Word, "the mediator of the contact between God and human beings."[85]

In *Act and Being*, too, we find Barth's distinction between faith and religion, for while it is true, says Bonhoeffer, that God "'is' only in faith," it is God's self-revelation—"God as such"—that faith reveals. And that is why "faith is something essentially different from religion," and why "genuine transcendentalism" is not to be confused with idealism. "Only faith itself can say whether God 'is' also outside the act of faith. The transcendental approach leaves room for such an I-transcendent being without, however, placing it into the reach of the I."[86]

Bonhoeffer's early postdoctoral years in Berlin, Barcelona, and New York provide abundant evidence of a strong affinity with Barth's revelation theology and early critique of religion. In a sermon on Romans 11:6, which Bonhoeffer gave in March 1928 as vicar to the German Protestant congregation in Barcelona, he describes religion as "the most grandiose and most gentle of all human attempts to attain the eternal from out of the anxiety and restlessness of the heart."[87] It is, however, an attempt that is always doomed to fail, simply because there is no human path to God.

> [I]t is not we who go to God, but God who comes to us. . . . It is God's deed that is important here, God's deed before which all our claims sink. . . . The motives of our morality and our religion have been unmasked; we wanted to be masters of the eternal and now we are its slaves. Only one means of rescue remains, namely, God's path, and that means grace. . . . Not religion, but rather revelation, grace, love; not the path to God, but rather God's path to human beings, that is the sum total of Christianity.[88]

Later that year, and still in Barcelona, Bonhoeffer delivered a lecture on "Jesus Christ and the Essence of Christianity" in which he spoke of God's absolute transcendence, of the chasm which no human initiative can bridge. We have a limited, relative, and essentially anthropomorphic knowledge of God, which yields a view of God that is simply an expression of human desires and needs. Here Bonhoeffer again insists:

> It is not knowledge or morality or religion that leads us to God. . . . [T]here is absolutely no path leading from human beings to God, for such a path is ultimately based on human capabilities. . . . If human beings and God are to come together, there is but one way, namely, the way from God to human beings. Here all human claims are at an end; God alone has the honor.[89]

At Union Theological Seminary in New York, where he spent a year (1930–1931) as a postdoctoral fellow, Bonhoeffer took upon himself the responsibility of explaining Barth's theology to an American audience that was largely unfamiliar with it. In a seminar paper on "The Theology of Crisis," Bonhoeffer expounds Barth's biblically grounded understanding of "God's coming which destroys all human attempts to come, which condemns all morality and religion, by means of which man tries to make superfluous God's revelation." God's new order subverts and replaces everything human that has preceded it. God's work with human beings is not the continuation and perfection of some human religious or moral enterprise but is rather an act of limitation, a combination of God's judgment and God's grace. The faith which allows us frankly to admit our limitations, and to give the glory to God, is a gift from God, "who sets and shows these limits to man." This is what it means to be justified by grace, or faith, alone.[90]

Barth's objective, says Bonhoeffer, is to introduce into theology a category foreign to all religious thinking, "the category of the word of God, of the revelation straight from above, from *outside* of man, according to the justification of the sinner by grace." But theology, as an academic or scholarly discipline, is not well-served by this category, because revelation cannot be grounded scientifically "upon general formal presuppositions of thinking." Theology's only real presupposition is faith, and this forces an acknowledgment of that "great antithesis of the word of God and the word of man, of grace and religion, of a pure Christian category and general religious category, of reality and interpretation."[91]

Bonhoeffer revisits these themes in a series of lectures on contemporary systematic theology given at the University of Berlin in the winter of 1932–1933 "against the background of a question that Karl Barth raised in his 1922 *Letter to the Romans*." And this, of course, is the question of God's Word, of the word that only God can speak. This Word, of judgment and forgiveness, "cuts vertically through human words."[92]

> God speaks this Word anew, again and again, and it should be seized anew, again and again, in faith. . . . God is the way from eternity into time; there is no way from below to above, which is why the way from above to below cannot be proven. It is only faith that proves itself.[93]

Wüstenberg observes that, as the 1930s draw on, and Bonhoeffer's interest in religion (which had been motivated largely by engagement with Barth's theology) is gradually overwhelmed by practical ecclesiastical and political activities, Barth's influence on Bonhoeffer's work likewise declines.[94] But Barth, and especially Barth's early theology, never ceases to be significant for Bonhoeffer. And this is especially true of the critique of religion to be found in the prison letters which, despite repeated criticism of Barth's failure to recognize the need for a religionless understanding of Christianity, is grounded nonetheless in Barth's own most fundamental conviction: the conviction that there is no way from below to above—there is no human path to God.

Meanwhile, Bonhoeffer chanced upon a very different kind of thinking in the nineteenth-century German philosopher Wilhelm Dilthey.

BONHOEFFER AND THE PHILOSOPHY OF LIFE

Wüstenberg rightly draws attention to Dilthey's influence on Bonhoeffer's theological letters from prison. "Metaphysics" and "inwardness," as well as ideas of "autonomy" and "coming of age," which Bonhoeffer had not previously associated with a critique of religion, assume a new and telling significance in Bonhoeffer's prison theology under the influence of Dilthey's philosophical historicism.[95] Wüstenberg suspects that Bonhoeffer may, in fact, first have come across the term "religionless" in Dilthey's *Introduction to the Human Sciences*, with which Bonhoeffer shows some evidence of familiarity in his 1931–1932 winter semester lectures on systematic theology.[96] In this book, Dilthey describes metaphysics as "a historically limited phenomenon,"[97] but "excludes the historical understanding of a religionless condition and of the emergence of a religious condition from it."[98] Bonhoeffer, says Wüstenberg, "critically appropriates" the word "religionless" without excluding it as a historical possibility. Rather, he comes to regard the "religionless condition" as an accomplished historical fact: "The *time of religion* has passed."[99]

The pragmatism of William James, with whose philosophy Bonhoeffer became acquainted at Union Theological Seminary, also helped him to clarify his views on religion. In the report on his year of study there, Bonhoeffer says that he found in pragmatism, and especially in James, "the key to the modern theological language and conceptual forms of liberal enlightened Americans." In pragmatism, philosophy is no longer the quest for "truth," but becomes instead "a positive individual discipline with practical goals." Truth is held hostage to utility, and this has consequences also for theology, where God, too, is considered either an effective truth or no truth at all—"that is, he is either active in the processes of human life or he 'is' not at all."[100] Religion and faith in human progress are here combined "in a virtuoso manner," with each serving to justify the other. In the process, religion is reduced to social ethics.[101] Bonhoeffer could hardly have been expected to approve of a philosophy which based its positive view of religion on God's efficacy rather than on God's reality—and he didn't. But he respected James's scholarship, and valued him as an interlocutor.[102]

James and Dilthey both prioritized life as a key interpretive concept. And it was Dilthey's philosophy of life, which sought to offset the dominance of the natural sciences by emphasizing the more labile influence of history and change on the human condition, that Wüstenberg believes assumed special importance for Bonhoeffer in prison. The prison letters are suffused with a strong sense of the wholeness of life, and phrases such as "polyphony of life" acquire a particular significance for Bonhoeffer as a result of his reading of Dilthey.[103]

Bonhoeffer perhaps never felt more sharply than he did in prison the need to embrace life in its fullness, for as he says in a letter to Eberhard and Renate Bethge written early in 1944:

> I believe we honor God better by knowing everything we value in the life God has given us, and loving and enjoying it to the full, and therefore feeling intensely and honestly the pain of whatever of life's values has been diminished or lost . . . rather than being dulled to what is important in life and therefore also dulled to the pain.[104]

Life and faith are brought into close relationship in the letters and papers from prison and given a christological emphasis. Bonhoeffer expresses this most succinctly in the "Outline for a Book," where he refers to our relationship with God as "a new life in 'being there for others' [*Dasein-für-andere*] through participation in the being [*Sein*] of Jesus."[105] Life and faith are here united in the being [*Sein*] of Jesus Christ. We come, through faith, to "new life" in Jesus Christ. No "religious act" is involved. We are called "not to a new religion but to life."[106]

In what was almost the last letter to reach Bethge from Tegel military prison, Bonhoeffer insists that it is only the assurance we have of Christ's having once shared this earth with us—the assurance that Christ *lived*—that makes our lives meaningful. If, he says,

> the earth was deemed worthy to bear the human being Jesus Christ, if a human being like Jesus lived, then and only then does our life as human beings have meaning. Had Jesus not lived, then our life would be meaningless, despite all the other people we know, respect, and love.[107]

Whereas Bonhoeffer had previously criticized religion primarily from the perspective of faith, in the prison letters "life" assumes a place of central importance for Bonhoeffer's understanding of God's self-revelation in Jesus Christ, and for the critique of religion.

METAPHYSICS, INWARDNESS, PRIVILEGE, AND PARTIALITY

So far in this chapter, I have discussed the influence of Karl Barth's theology on Bonhoeffer's understanding of religion, and briefly outlined the impact on his thought of William James's philosophical pragmatism and Wilhelm Dilthey's historicism and philosophy of life. Now it is time to bring these elements into relation with others which give rise, collectively, to the broader, more self-conscious, critique of religion that comes to flower particularly, but by no means exclusively, in the *Letters and Papers from Prison*.

Bethge observes that Bonhoeffer never really drew Barth's theological concept of religion into relationship with the historical one he (Bonhoeffer) derived from Dilthey.[108] He nonetheless believes that a critique of religion—its fragmentary nature notwithstanding—can be distilled from the "totality of [Bonhoeffer's] thought and action,"[109] and adopts the following classification as a basis for discussion: metaphysics, individualism, partiality, privilege, guardianship, and dispensability.[110]

Green argues that, when Bonhoeffer speaks of religion, he is in fact describing patterns of behavior which have their origin in "a particular psychic posture" of weakness and dependence on the saving power of God.[111] For Green, Bonhoeffer's concept of religion is predominantly "*operational* or behavioral," rather than institutional.[112]

> A "non-religious Christianity," therefore, is not one which repudiates the church and the elements of its common life; it is one that *changes* the psychic posture of Christianity from a religious one to another which can engage the self-understanding and life-style of people who have "come of age."[113]

Consistent with this basic orientation, Bonhoeffer comes to regard religion as essentially "dysfunctional," crisis-driven, otherworldly, episodic, peripheral, self-absorbed, intellectually dishonest, and humiliating.[114]

The two approaches have much in common, but I have used what is essentially Bethge's classification for the purposes of the following discussion, because it seems to me to facilitate a clearer subdivision of the subject matter.

Metaphysics, Individualism, and Inwardness

Metaphysics, individualism, and inwardness are best considered jointly. Bonhoeffer clearly sees them as closely linked and tends himself to group them together. As Bethge points out, the conceptual pairing of metaphysics and individualism/inwardness[115] goes back to the doctoral and habilitation dissertations, for "as Bonhoeffer never tired of showing, in the epistemological transcendence of the metaphysical everything is ultimately 'drawn' into the subject, which ultimately remains alone."[116] Wüstenberg observes, however, that, prior to 1944, Bonhoeffer does not engage with metaphysics and inwardness as means of advancing a critique of religion.[117] They assume this function only in the prison letters as Bonhoeffer, standing as he thought on the threshold of a "completely religionless age," seeks a realistic and appropriate way forward for the Christian understanding of God, a way of talking about God "without religion, that is, without the temporally conditioned presuppositions of metaphysics, the inner life, and so on."[118]

Here, to speak religiously means, for Bonhoeffer, to speak both "metaphysically" (*metaphysisch*) and "individualistically" (*individualistisch*) in ways that reveal a quite unbiblical preoccupation with personal salvation.

> Does [he asks] the question of saving one's soul even come up in the Old Testament? Isn't God's righteousness and kingdom on earth the center of everything? And isn't Rom. 3:24ff. the culmination of the view that God alone is righteous, rather than an individualistic doctrine of salvation?[119]

The Bible, he believes, directs our attention not to some other world but to a proper understanding of this one, "how it is created and preserved, is given laws, reconciled and renewed."[120] What lies "beyond this world" is not something remote from everyday life, but its most solid foundation, "in the biblical [and thoroughly christological] sense of the creation and the incarnation, crucifixion, and resurrection of Jesus Christ."[121] This "God in human form" is neither a metaphysical concept nor an existential one. We can, and indeed must, take Jesus Christ's humanity seriously, without seeing him as the embodiment of some particular, isolated human being. He is rather *the* "human being for others" and, as such, provides us with a radically new understanding of transcendence, where the transcendent is "not the infinite, unattainable tasks, but the neighbor within reach in any given situation."[122] The world then ceases to be, as Kevin Hart suggests, "the site against which we construe transcendence" and becomes instead "the place where we can grasp what transcendence truly is."[123] As Bethge observes, Bonhoeffer "was not thinking in terms of 'immanence-transcendence,' in order to eliminate transcendence in favor of immanence." He wanted instead to replace, with "a genuine transcendence," a metaphysics that now served only to deceive, as a chimerical extension of the world.[124]

Bonhoeffer nonetheless recognized that metaphysically inspired religious formulations had long provided the Christian West with the otherworldly assurances it craved, and that the decline of religion had made its dependents both apprehensive and vulnerable.

> God's being pushed out of the world, away from public human existence, has led to an attempt to hang on to God at least in the realm of the "personal," the "inner life," the "private" sphere. And since each person has a "private" sphere somewhere, this became the easiest point of attack. What used to be the servants' secrets . . . —that is, the intimate areas of life (from prayer to sexuality)—became the hunting ground of modern pastors.[125]

As Green suggests, by directing people to focus principally on their own shortcomings—their very human weaknesses, feelings of guilt, and fears of mortality—religion is anything but transformative and does nothing to nurture "a free and responsible 'existence-for-others.'" It offers no real hope of transcendence but serves only further to entrench those feelings of weakness and dependency in which it is embedded.[126]

Bonhoeffer strongly deplores this kind of exploitation. Should we, he asks, "jump on a few unfortunates in their hour of weakness and commit, so to speak, religious rape [*religiös vergewaltigen*]?"[127] Bonhoeffer does not believe that a person's "essential nature" lies in their "innermost, intimate depths."[128] This idea is wholly foreign to his understanding of human nature, which is thoroughly relational. For Bonhoeffer, a person "exists always and only in ethical responsibility."[129] As such, he consistently rejects, in philosophy and theology, anything and everything that speaks to him of "individualistic social atomism."[130]

Partiality

Bethge traces Bonhoeffer's concern with "partiality"[131] back to a youthful encounter with the German pastor, theologian, and social liberal politician Friedrich Naumann's question "about the extent to which the Christian religion had become a separate area among the other areas of life."[132] Bonhoeffer may also have associated partiality with Seeberg's religious a priori, that "mold in human beings into which the divine content of revelation, too, may pour."[133] And he was, of course, familiar with Barth's characterization of religion as "always a thing in the midst of other things."[134]

As Green observes, symptomatic of religion's partiality is its provincial character; its failure to shape and motivate more than a fragment of life.[135] Bonhoeffer seems already to have been firmly of this view as early as 1928 when, in the lecture he gave in Barcelona on the essence of Christianity, he declares that Christ has "for all practical purposes . . . been eliminated from our lives." He has become "a thing of the church, or of the religiosity of a group of people," whereas, in fact, we truly understand Christ only when "we commit to him in an abrupt either-or." Really to know Christ is to "recognize that he makes crucial claims on our entire lives."[136]

A similar tension, between wholeness and partiality, is evident in the way Bonhoeffer distinguishes between the church and a religious community (*Gemeinschaft*) in the lecture on "The Visible Church in the New Testament," where he describes the coming of the Spirit at Pentecost as "a new creation" in which, instead of a new religion, "a bit of world is created anew." The church is established by an act of God which embraces all of life, and not merely its religious dimension.[137]

> It is a matter not even of the precedence of the religious over the secular . . . but of the precedence of God's actions over both the religious and the secular. Here we find the essential difference between the church and a "religious community. . . ."[138] The "religious community" is concerned with the subordination of the secular . . . to the religious, with dividing life into the religious and the secular, with a hierarchy of values and status.[139]

The church, though, is concerned only with the Word of God, "with actually implementing this new creation from the Spirit."[140]

Here the critique of religion takes a particular ecclesiological form. Unlike religion, the church, if it is really church, is not partial. The church is no human invention, no religious association, but rather the creative act of God, which encompasses "all of life." And its sole function is obedience— "the practical doing of what has been commanded."[141] Barry Harvey rightly believes Bonhoeffer's "deconstruction of religion as a viable theological category" to open the way for the church to reclaim its broader (non-religious) political and social vocation as "the body of Christ."[142]

Again we find a like tension between wholeness and partiality in Bonhoeffer's *Ethics*, where "the good" is said to have its origin "*in the indivisible whole of God's reality*,"[143] and this one reality is "God's reality revealed in

Christ in the reality of the world."[144] The church has thus to come to terms with the fact that the traditional division of reality into opposing divine and mundane realms has been overcome, and that the church can now "only defend its own space by fighting, not for space, but for the salvation of the world."[145] A genuinely Christian sense of responsibility is all-encompassing. It cannot be restricted to some imagined "religious sphere" of life.[146]

In the letters from prison, Bonhoeffer emphasizes the need to avoid thinking of God as simply the "God of the gaps." In science, as in human affairs generally, it is right to describe God, from a religious perspective, as "on the retreat,"[147] "losing ground."[148] But, in these circumstances, to cling to God as a "stopgap"—a placeholder for a temporary lack of understanding—is both disingenuous and bound to disappoint for, as human knowledge expands, God is inevitably pushed ever further away. Honor should rather be given to God not only as we approach "the limits of our possibilities" but also "in the midst of our lives"; not just in suffering, and not just in sin, but in everything we do.[149]

Jesus calls us to a faithful fullness of life, and religion is of no help here because "[t]he 'religious act' is always something partial [*Partielles*], whereas 'faith' is something whole and involves one's whole life."[150]

Deus ex machina

In the opening verse of the prison poem "Christians and Heathens" (*Christen und Heiden*), Bonhoeffer gives a concise account of what he believes to be the religious motive:

People go to God when they're in need,
plead for help, pray for blessing and bread,
for rescue from their sickness, guilt, and death.
So do they all, all of them, Christians and heathens.[151]

All religion, says Bethge, depends on this idea—on the idea of an all-powerful, all-knowing being who can be expected to keep us safe and to answer our ultimate questions.[152] And this, according to Green, makes religion essentially "episodic," crisis-driven, eschatological, and—because it tends to invoke God only as a last resort—finally dishonest.[153] Bonhoeffer is highly critical of this notion of God, which draws strength from human limitations. Religious people speak of God only when they feel they have no other option. Indeed, it seems to Bonhoeffer that "we leave room for God only out of anxiety."[154]

With God now being progressively squeezed out of the world of human experience, theology is at risk of entirely losing its way, having, on the one hand, sought vainly to deny the advance of science and, on the other, "resigned itself to the way things have gone and allowed God to function only as *deus ex machina* in the so-called ultimate questions . . . a solution to life's needs and conflicts."[155] In this situation, anyone who seems to be largely untroubled by, or uninterested in, such questions is presumed to be either "really closed to talking about God" or in a state of denial, requiring assistance. Existential philosophy and psychotherapy have proved (one might imagine largely unintentionally) helpful to the religious zealots in this respect. But if people cannot at last be persuaded "to regard their happiness as disastrous, their health as sickness, and their vitality as an object of despair, then the theologians are at their wits' end."[156]

Bonhoeffer, by contrast, wants to draw our attention to God's presence at the center and heart of life rather than at its margins. He wants to speak of God in fullness of life and human goodness rather than in the shadow of sin and death.[157] This is not to suggest, though, that God is other than the God who is revealed in the life, death, and resurrection of Jesus Christ, or that we are other than those who have been reconciled with God through Jesus Christ. God, "the center of life,"[158] is also the God who has consented "to be pushed out of the world and onto the cross."[159] Whereas the religious person expects God to intervene selectively, with deeds of power, in human affairs, the Bible points instead "toward the powerlessness and the suffering of God." Indeed, the Bible tells us that "only the suffering God can help."[160] The cross of Christ is the promise and the proof of God's love for human beings, and it is this love that lights our way in the world.

Bonhoeffer presents a vivid picture of the suffering God, and of the proper Christian response, in "Christians and Heathens":

People go to God when God's in need,
find God poor, reviled, without shelter or bread,
see God devoured by sin, weakness, and death.
Christians stand by God in God's own pain.[161]

Whereas religious people look to God for relief from life's existential angst, Christians nonetheless understand a genuine relationship with God ultimately to depend on their ability to share in God's own suffering on behalf of all humanity.

Privilege

In the first of the theological letters from prison, as Bonhoeffer reflects on the implications of a religionless world for Christian life, he asks, "How do we go about being 'religionless-worldly' Christians, how can we be ἐκ-κλησία, those who are called out, without understanding ourselves religiously as privileged, but instead seeing ourselves as belonging wholly to the world?"[162] While this, as Bethge notes, is the only specific mention of religious privilege in the letters, we should not underestimate the importance Bonhoeffer attached to this idea. Bethge claims that Bonhoeffer's struggle "to overcome the dangerously privileged character of the Christian religion" in fact determined the whole direction of his life, shaping all his major decisions, including the decision to study theology, his move from the academy to the ministry, and the decision to join the conspiracy against Hitler.[163] While this is, at best, an oversimplification, it is certainly true that Bonhoeffer believed a worldly preoccupation with privilege and power to be incompatible with a Christian life lived in responsible obedience to the Word of God.

In the *Ethics*, Bonhoeffer speaks matter-of-factly about the collapse, in the face of "liberated ratio" and the "discovery of eternal human rights," of a range of previously entrenched tyrannies, including "ecclesiastical claims to power";[164] while, some years earlier, in his lectures on the church, he had criticized the church's careful accommodations to contemporary bourgeois Western culture as a way of preserving a privileged place for itself in an increasingly skeptical world.[165]

Privilege, though, is not to be confused with relationships of authority, which have their proper origin in the commandment of God revealed in Jesus Christ—in "the total and concrete claim of human beings by the merciful and holy God in Jesus Christ."[166] The commandment is in fact *"the sole authorization for ethical discourse."*[167] As such, "the orientation from above to below inherent in the ethical is . . . anything but a sanctioning of privileges."[168] Authority brings responsibility, and is intended not to benefit the officeholder but rather those for whom the office holder assumes responsibility.

The church's responsibility is thus not to dominate but to help and serve.[169] The church can never create a favored place for itself in the world. Only God can do this. It is God who gives the church its *"characteristic place"* as "the place of God himself."[170] The church is to be found only "[w]here the word breaks in."[171] It is, therefore, not the church's responsibility to be always on the "right" side of history. The church is wrong whenever it seeks simply to ensure its own survival as a privileged institution; whenever it fights "only for its self-preservation, as if that were an end in itself."[172] Indeed, the church is really church "only when it is there for others," a willing participant in the everyday lives of ordinary people. It must set the example for those who want to know what "a life with Christ is," and can do this only if it is willing first to confront its own besetting sins of pride, worship of power, envy, and pretense.[173]

There are, Bonhoeffer assures us, no preliminary qualifications required for hearing the Word of God. Paul tells his readers that περιτομή (circumcision) is not a condition for justification. The question today is whether religion is a condition for salvation, and the answer is the same. "Freedom from περιτομή [says Bonhoeffer] is also freedom from religion."[174] And there is, finally, no place for privilege in a Christian witness which attests simply to Jesus Christ as "the one Word of God whom we have to hear, and whom we have to trust and obey in life and death."[175]

Guardianship

As we have seen, Bonhoeffer is strongly critical of those who feel compelled "to persuade this world come of age that it cannot live without 'God' as its guardian."[176] He describes their efforts to undermine human autonomy as "pointless," "ignoble," and "unchristian": pointless, because they seek to turn mature adults back into children; ignoble, because they prey on people's fears and weaknesses; and unchristian, because they confuse God's self-revelation in Jesus Christ with a passing expression of human religiosity.[177] They provide false refuge for "'the last of the knights' or a few intellectually dishonest people" who cling to the worn-out vestiges of religion,[178] and for the small number of self-preoccupied, intellectual "degenerates" (*Degenerierten*) who are otherwise prone to existential despair.[179] Christians are called not to the peace of some remote heavenly sanctuary, or to hide the world's godlessness behind the veil of religion, or, indeed, to "save the church as an institution of salvation,"[180] but rather to live free of "false religious obligations and inhibitions"[181] as "religionless-worldly" Christians[182] in an autonomous world come of age.[183]

CONCLUSION

Bonhoeffer's views on religion owe much to the early theology of Karl Barth. Barth enabled him to distinguish faith from religion and convinced him of the futility of all human efforts to initiate the encounter with God. Barth was able to demonstrate to Bonhoeffer's satisfaction that, with the coming of Christ, religion had been made redundant. From the vantage point of the cross, it was reasonable to conclude that religion, "as a particular aspect of human behaviour . . . [had been] taken out of the way."[184] For some years, as a student and as an academic, Bonhoeffer made Barth's critique of religion his own. But when, in prison and facing possible execution for treason, Bonhoeffer was prompted to draw those famously radical religionless conclusions, he was critical of Barth's failure to precede him.

Bonhoeffer is moved, on several occasions in the prison letters to Bethge, to express a strong personal distaste for religion. He senses "how an opposition to all that is 'religious'" is growing in him. He is not, he says, "religious by nature," and yet thinks constantly "of God, of Christ." Life, authenticity, freedom, and mercy mean everything to him. It is "the religious clothes they wear" that make him "so uncomfortable."[185]

Bonhoeffer's unfailing confidence in the reality of God's self-revelation, his life as a dissenting pastor in Nazi Germany, and his sense of an increasingly invincible Western secularism lead him to identify certain ways of thinking and acting as characteristic of that vain, religious reaching out to God to which Barth first drew his attention. What remains for Bonhoeffer, when these things are set aside, is simply God's Word to human beings. This is God's gift to us. In this gift is fullness of life and faith, in Christ. And it is this very specific vision of "new life in 'being there for others,'" through participation in the being of Jesus"[186] that encourages Bonhoeffer to step out in a direction that Barth never took—in the direction of a new, religionless form of Christianity, appropriate to life with Christ in a religionless age.

Bethge correctly calls attention to an important distinction underlying Bonhoeffer's critique of religion. For Bonhoeffer, the "age of Jesus" and the "age of religion" are two very different things, and there is no reason to think of the former as coming to an end. Bonhoeffer's priority "is always Jesus and the way in which he is present to us." Religion simply fails to see him. Indeed, Jesus is the very antithesis of religion. Jesus does not ask us to embrace complex forms of thought and behavior. He is gregarious, hospitable, and vulnerable. He is not tempted by the lure of the *deus ex machina* but instead worships God "with his life." He prefers the company of outcasts to that of the privileged classes and, perhaps most importantly, he frees us to find our own responsible answers to life's questions "through his own powerlessness, which shames and utterly convinces us."[187]

Bonhoeffer does not fear the approach of a religionless age. The collapse of religion, properly understood, need have no adverse implications for faith in God's self-revelation in Jesus Christ. Quite the opposite is true in fact. Through *faith* in Jesus Christ, we are called not to *religion* but to *life*. Thus, with religion, as he sees it, effectively out of the way, we now turn our attention to the heart of Bonhoeffer's theology, to his Christology, as we begin to explore Bonhoeffer's response to the challenge of finding new ways of proclaiming God's Word, of serving Christ and furthering his work of love, in a religionless world.

NOTES

1. Wüstenberg, *A Theology of Life*, 30.
2. Wüstenberg, *A Theology of Life*, 27.
3. Christoph Schwöbel, "'Religion' and 'Religionlessness,'" in *Mysteries in the Theology of Dietrich Bonhoeffer*, ed. Kirsten Busch Nielsen, Ulrik Nissen, and Christiane Tietz (Göttingen: Vandenhoeck and Ruprecht, 2007), 165.
4. *Letters and Papers*, DBWE 8: 363.
5. *Letters and Papers*, DBWE 8: 364.
6. *Letters and Papers*, DBWE 8: 363–64 (April 30, 1944), 373 (May 5, 1944), 428–29 (June 8, 1944).
7. *Letters and Papers*, DBWE 8: 373.
8. *Letters and Papers*, DBWE 8: 429.
9. Karl Barth, *The Epistle to the Romans*, trans. Edwyn C. Hoskyns (London: Oxford University Press, 1968), 231.
10. Barth, *Romans*, 238.
11. Barth, *Romans*, 240. Torrance argues that no other theologian since the Reformation "has applied justification by grace alone so radically and daringly to human theologizing as Karl Barth." The truth, for Barth, is never to be found in ourselves. We must always "look for it beyond ourselves in God." Thomas F. Torrance, *God and Rationality* (Edinburgh: T&T Clark, 1997), 68.
12. Barth, *Romans*, 242.
13. Barth, *Romans*, 250.
14. Barth, *Romans*, 268–69.
15. Barth, *Romans*, 233.
16. Barth, *Romans*, 269.
17. Barth, *Romans*, 234.
18. Barth, *Romans*, 332. "The Grand Inquisitor" is the title of a prose poem, narrated by Ivan to his brother Alyosha, in Dostoevsky's novel *The Brothers Karamazov*. Set in sixteenth-century Seville, the poem tells of a brief, very public appearance by Christ at the height of the Spanish Inquisition, and of his prompt arrest and incarceration by the Grand Inquisitor, who tells him that he has neither the right to return nor to add anything to the words he spoke 1,500 years ago. According to the Grand Inquisitor, only a small number of human beings are able to cope with the freedoms of faith and conscience that Christ gives them. The remainder would be happier if Christ had succumbed to the temptations of Satan, thereby providing conclusive proof of his (Christ's) readiness to sustain, amaze, and rule over them. People generally want to be spared the knowledge of good and evil; the anxiety of making free decisions for themselves. They want to be spared the curse of personal responsibility. The church has assumed these intolerable burdens on humanity's behalf. It has taken a long time—many centuries—to sort out the mess Christ left behind, and the church will brook no further intervention by him. Only those who understand the value of complete submission are happy. "Then," says the Grand Inquisitor,

we shall give them the quiet humble happiness of weak creatures such as they are by nature.... Yes, we shall set them to work, but in their leisure hours we shall make their life like a child's game, with children's songs and innocent dance. Oh, we shall allow them even sin.... We shall tell them that every sin will be expiated, if it is done with our permission, that we allow them to sin because we love them, and the punishment for these sins we take upon ourselves. And we shall take it upon ourselves, and they will adore us as their saviours who have taken on themselves their sins before God.

Fyodor M. Dostoevsky, *The Brothers Karamazov*, trans. Constance Garnett (London: Heron Books, 1967), 253–72.

19. Barth, *Romans*, 392.
20. Barth, *Romans*, 334–35.
21. Bethge, *Dietrich Bonhoeffer*, 872.
22. Bethge, *Dietrich Bonhoeffer*, 75.
23. Martin Rumscheidt, "The Formation of Bonhoeffer's Theology," in *The Cambridge Companion to Dietrich Bonhoeffer*, ed. John de Gruchy (New York: Cambridge University Press, 1999), 64.
24. *Letters and Papers*, DBWE 8: 364. Barth, for his part, found the prison letters both stimulating and enigmatic. He was not sure what to make of the "positivism of revelation" which Bonhoeffer professed to find in him but was nonetheless ready to concede that he may sometimes have expressed himself "positivistically." Karl Barth, "From a Letter to Superintendent Herrenbrück," in *World Come of Age. A Symposium on Dietrich Bonhoeffer*, ed. Ronald Gregor Smith (London: Collins, 1967), 90.
25. Andreas Pangritz, *Karl Barth in the Theology of Dietrich Bonhoeffer*, trans. Barbara and Martin Rumscheidt (Grand Rapids: Eerdmans, 2000), 73.
26. Pangritz, *Barth in Bonhoeffer*, 71.
27. *Act and Being*, DBWE 2: 194. Erich Seeberg's *Luthers Theologie: Motive und Ideen*. Vol. 1, *Die Gottesanschauung* (Göttingen, 1929) is included in the bibliography of literature used by Bonhoeffer.
28. Ebeling, *Word and Faith*, 99.
29. Barth, *Romans*, 255.
30. Wüstenberg, *A Theology of Life*, 62–65.
31. Karl Barth, *Church Dogmatics I.2*, trans. G. W. Bromiley, G. T. Thomson, and Harold Knight (London: T&T Clark, 2009), 128.
32. Barth, *Church Dogmatics I.2*, 128.
33. Barth, *Church Dogmatics I.2*, 148.
34. Barth, *Church Dogmatics I.2*, 148–49.
35. Wüstenberg, *A Theology of Life*, 64.
36. Alan Spence, *Christology: A Guide for the Perplexed* (London: T&T Clark, 2008), 128.
37. Pangritz, *Barth in Bonhoeffer*, 94.
38. *Letters and Papers*, DBWE 8: 429. Pangritz credits Bonhoeffer with keeping, "rather, to the early version of Barth's critique of religion as expressed in the first edition of *Romans*." Pangritz, *Barth in Bonhoeffer*, 93. There is, however, no evidence to suggest that Bonhoeffer was familiar with the first edition. It was the revised edition

he consulted when he came to write *Sanctorum Communio*, and it is the revised edition to which he refers approvingly in the *Letters and Papers from Prison*.

39. Bethge, *Dietrich Bonhoeffer*, 76. Bethge quotes from a letter sent to Bonhoeffer by a friend, Richard Widmann, early in 1926, in which Widmann offers a defense of Barth in response to criticism which has not survived in its original form: "'You once mentioned that you deplored Barth's relapse into servitude in these *Dogmatics*—that he takes anxious care . . . to follow in the footsteps of the dogmaticians of ancient times. I do not regard this reactionary gesture as wrong.'"

40. Pangritz, *Barth in Bonhoeffer*, 16.

41. Ernst Feil, *The Theology of Dietrich Bonhoeffer*, trans. Martin Rumscheidt (Philadelphia: Fortress Press, 1985), 176–77.

42. Bethge, *Dietrich Bonhoeffer*, 75.

43. *Sanctorum Communio*, DBWE 1: 169.

44. This discussion was deleted from the published version of the dissertation but is included as a footnote in DBWE 1: 169–70.

45. Barth, *Romans*, 495–96.

46. *Sanctorum Communio*, DBWE 1: 170. Bonhoeffer here draws on Rudolf Bultmann for support, citing his *Jesus and the Word*:

> Whatever of kindness, pity, mercy, I show my neighbor is not something that I do for God . . . ; the neighbor is not a sort of tool, by means of which I practice the love of God. . . . As I can love my neighbor only when I surrender my will completely to God's will, so I can love God only while I will what [God] wills, while I really love my neighbor.

Rudolf Bultmann, *Jesus* (Berlin: Deutsche Bibliotek, 1926). English translation: *Jesus and the Word*, trans. Louise Pettibone Smith and Erminie Huntress Lantero (New York: Scribner, 1962, 1989), 115.

47. Bethge, *Dietrich Bonhoeffer*, 134.

48. Richard A. Muller, *Dictionary of Latin and Greek Theological Terms* (Grand Rapids: Baker Books, 1985), 111.

49. Michael P. DeJonge, *Bonhoeffer's Reception of Luther* (Oxford: OUP, 2017), 48.

50. DeJonge, *Luther*, 67.

51. Bethge, *Dietrich Bonhoeffer*, 133. Unlike Bethge, DeJonge believes Bonhoeffer ultimately to reject the Lutheran *capax*, while continuing to affirm the particular christological and sacramental qualities it encapsulates. For Bonhoeffer, "thinking about Christ must begin with the present person of Christ rather than the two natures." DeJonge, *Luther*, 73. As Bonhoeffer says in the Christology lectures, "from the presence of Christ arises the twofold certainty that he is both human being and God." "Lectures on Christology," DBWE 12: 312. The present person of Christ is our starting point. Anything we may subsequently choose to infer regarding his humanity and divinity will have this as its premise. Bonhoeffer believes the Lutheran doctrine of the *genus majestaticum*, and the *capax* which followed it, effectively to turn this argument on its head. As DeJonge explains,

[i]t begins with the idea that a human body is locally confined and the idea that divine nature is omnipresent before using the logic of the communication of attributes to cobble together a Christ whose human body is capable of multi-presence. This Lutheran attempt to secure Luther's insistence on the sacramental presence in fact betrays it by undermining the person-oriented "who" form of christological thinking appropriate to it.

Bonhoeffer thus "affirms Luther's *est* but rejects the majestic genus and the *capax* that developed to support it." DeJonge, *Luther*, 73–74.

52. *Act and Being*, DBWE 2: 90–91.

53. Karl Barth, *The Word of God and the Word of Man*, trans. Douglas Horton (New York: Harper Torchbooks, 1957), 324.

54. Bethge, *Dietrich Bonhoeffer*, 134.

55. Barth, *Word of God*, 287.

56. Barth, *Romans*, 30.

57. Karl Barth, *Church Dogmatics I.1*, trans. G. W. Bromiley (London: T&T Clark, 1975), 323.

58. *Letters and Papers*, DBWE 8: 501.

59. *Letters and Papers*, DBWE 8: 373.

60. Barth, *Church Dogmatics I.1*, Preface, xiii.

61. Barth, *Church Dogmatics I.1*, Preface, xiv.

62. Dietrich Bonhoeffer, "Meditation on Christmas, December 1939," in *Theological Education Underground: 1937–1940*, ed. Victoria J. Barnett (Minneapolis: Fortress Press, 2012), DBWE 15: 528–29.

63. *Letters and Papers*, DBWE 8: 373.

64. *Letters and Papers*, DBWE 8: 430–31.

65. Dietrich Bonhoeffer, "Lecture Course: The Nature of the Church (Student Notes)," in *Ecumenical, Academic, and Pastoral Work: 1931–1932*, ed. Victoria J. Barnett, Mark S. Brocker, and Michael B. Lukens (Minneapolis: Fortress Press, 2012), DBWE 11: 314.

66. "Nature of the Church," DBWE 11: 313. Pangritz believes this to be an allusion to the "Apostles' Creed controversy" of 1892 in which Bonhoeffer's teacher, the church historian "Adolf von Harnack argued the liberal case against the dogma of the virgin birth in particular." Pangritz, *Barth in Bonhoeffer*, 112.

67. In the lectures on Christology, from the summer of 1933, Bonhoeffer describes the doctrine of the virgin birth as opaque and largely unhelpful. He urges us not to speak of God "becoming human [das Menschwerden]," because this is a "how" question, "to be found in the old doctrine of the virgin birth," which is not clearly attested in the Bible. We should speak rather of the God who "became human [der Menschgewordene]," of the God who "became like us." In other words, our focus should be not on the process, or means, of incarnation, but rather on its implications. "Lectures on Christology," DBWE 12: 354–55.

68. "Nature of the Church," DBWE 11: 313.

69. *Letters and Papers*, DBWE 8: 502.

70. *Letters and Papers*, DBWE 8: 503.

71. Rudolf Bultmann, "New Testament and Mythology," in *Kerygma and Myth: A Theological Debate*, ed. Hans-Werner Bartsch (London: SPCK, 1972), Vol. I, 3.

72. Bultmann, in Bartsch, Vol. I, 11.
73. Cited in Pangritz, *Barth in Bonhoeffer*, 78.
74. Dietrich Bonhoeffer, *Conspiracy and Imprisonment: 1940–1945*, ed. Mark S. Brocker (Minneapolis: Fortress Press, 2006), DBWE 16: 260–61.
75. *Letters and Papers*, DBWE 8: 430.
76. Clifford J. Green, "Bonhoeffer's Quest for Authentic Christianity: Beyond Fundamentalism, Nationalism, Religion and Secularism," in *Dietrich Bonhoeffer's Theology Today: A Way between Fundamentalism and Secularism?* ed. John W. de Gruchy, Stephen Plant, and Christiane Tietz (Gütersloh: Gütersloher Verlagshaus, 2009), 337.
77. Dietrich Bonhoeffer, *Creation and Fall*, ed. John W. de Gruchy (Minneapolis: Fortress Press, 2004), DBWE 3: 82.
78. Karl Barth, "Rudolf Bultmann – An Attempt to Understand Him," in Bartsch, Vol. II, 109.
79. Barth, in Bartsch, Vol. II, 110.
80. *Sanctorum Communio*, DBWE 1: 152–53.
81. Wüstenberg, *A Theology of Life*, 34.
82. Wüstenberg, *A Theology of Life*, 38.
83. *Act and Being*, DBWE 2: 57.
84. *Act and Being*, DBWE 2: 58.
85. *Act and Being*, DBWE 2: 58. The "religious a priori" recalls the "father" of modern (liberal) theology, Friedrich Schleiermacher, who believed every human being "is born with the religious capacity as with every other, and . . . if only that communion between a person and the universe . . . is not blocked and barricaded, then religion would have to develop unerringly in each person according to his own individual manner." Friedrich Schleiermacher, *On Religion*, trans. Richard Crouter (Cambridge: Cambridge University Press, 1996), 59. Religion, for Schleiermacher, is essentially a state of mind—what Bonhoeffer describes as "the most subjective and comprehensive consciousness of human beings." Dietrich Bonhoeffer, "The History of Twentieth-Century Systematic Theology (Student Notes)," in *Ecumenical, Academic, and Pastoral Work*, DBWE 11: 185. Christianity is then "only anthropology," as Ludwig Feuerbach believed. Feuerbach, says Bonhoeffer, "was Schleiermacher's most consistent pupil, but he regarded as an illusion what for Schleiermacher was an unproved assumption." "20th Century Systematic Theology," DBWE 11: 185.
86. *Act and Being*, DBWE 2: 93.
87. Dietrich Bonhoeffer, "Sermon on Romans 11:6, Barcelona, Oculi, March 11, 1928," in *Barcelona, Berlin, New York*, DBWE 10: 482. "But if it is by grace, it is no longer on the basis of works, otherwise grace would no longer be grace (Rom. 11:6)."
88. "Sermon on Romans 11:6," DBWE 10: 483.
89. Dietrich Bonhoeffer, "Jesus Christ and the Essence of Christianity," in *Barcelona, Berlin, New York*, DBWE 10: 353.
90. Dietrich Bonhoeffer, "Seminar Paper: The Theology of Crisis and Its Attitude toward Philosophy and Science," in *Barcelona, Berlin, New York*, DBWE 10: 466–67. The Theology of Crisis, Dialectical Theology, and (Barth's) theology of revelation are kindred terms. I have generally depended on "theology of revelation"

to convey, as clearly and economically as possible, the sense of a biblically grounded theology which attributes all sure knowledge of God exclusively to God's self-revelation in Jesus Christ.

91. "Theology of Crisis," DBWE 10: 467–68.

92. Dietrich Bonhoeffer, "Lecture: Review and Discussion of New Publications in Systematic Theology (Student Notes)," in *Berlin*, DBWE 12: 192.

93. "New Publications in Systematic Theology," DBWE 10: 192. In lectures given the previous winter, Bonhoeffer employs the Barthian formula "Deus dixit" (God has spoken) to describe "the beginning of all genuine theological thinking." "20th Century Systematic Theology," DBWE 11: 231. "[O]nly from the revelation itself do we know God as the absolute beginning of self-revelation in Jesus Christ." God speaks to us only in "the Word, Jesus, preaching. We would know nothing about God if God did not come in this way." And this is the mystery of God. Religion cannot explain it. There is no getting behind God. We must "begin with God's own beginning set for us," and "we must each receive it as told to us." "20th Century Systematic Theology," DBWE 11: 230–1.

94. Wüstenberg, *A Theology of Life*, 57.

95. Wüstenberg, *A Theology of Life*, 83.

96. "20th Century Systematic Theology," DBWE 11: 184, 211.

97. Wüstenberg, *A Theology of Life*, 74. Wüstenberg here cites Wilhelm Dilthey, *Gesammelte Schriften 1: Einleitung in die Geisteswissenschaften* (1922); partial English translation *Introduction to the Human Sciences*, ed. R. A. Makkreel and Frithjof Rodi, in *Wilhelm Dilthey: Selected Works*, vol. 1 (Princeton: Princeton University Press, 1989), 182 (in the English translation).

98. Wüstenberg, *A Theology of Life*, 74. Wüstenberg here cites Dilthey, *Einleitung*, 138 (in the German edition).

99. Wüstenberg, *A Theology of Life*, 75.

100. "Report on My Year of Study at Union Theological Seminary in New York, 1930/31," in *Barcelona, Berlin, New York*, DBWE 10: 310–11.

101. "Report on Year of Study in New York," DBWE 10: 311.

102. At Union Theological Seminary, Bonhoeffer quickly sensed a need to familiarize himself with American philosophy as "a prerequisite for any fair assessment of [American] theology." Eugene William Lyman, professor of philosophy of religion, "was very willing to accommodate this wish, and for one afternoon every two weeks I was able to discuss with him the salient philosophical literature I had prepared beforehand. We began with pragmatism. I read almost the entire philosophical works of William James, which really captivated me." "Report on Year of Study in New York," DBWE 10: 310.

103. *Letters and Papers*, DBWE 8: 393–94; Wüstenberg, *A Theology of Life*, 117. We shall see in the following chapter that such phrases also owe much to Bonhoeffer's renewed sense in prison of the Old Testament's faithful embrace of the world.

104. *Letters and Papers*, DBWE 8: 266.

105. *Letters and Papers*, DBWE 8: 501.

106. *Letters and Papers*, DBWE 8: 482.

107. *Letters and Papers*, DBWE 8: 515.

108. Bethge, *Dietrich Bonhoeffer*, 877.

109. Bethge, *Dietrich Bonhoeffer*, 872.
110. Bethge, *Dietrich Bonhoeffer*, 873–77.
111. Green, *Theology of Sociality*, 262.
112. Green, *Theology of Sociality*, 262.
113. Green, *Theology of Sociality*, 263.
114. Green, *Theology of Sociality*, 263–65.
115. Bonhoeffer uses these terms—"individualism" (*Individualismus*) and "inwardness" (*Innerlichkeit*)—to describe what he believes to be a peculiarly "religious" preoccupation with the anxious, isolated self.
116. Bethge, *Dietrich Bonhoeffer*, 874.
117. Wüstenberg, *A Theology of Life*, 76.
118. *Letters and Papers*, DBWE 8: 364.
119. *Letters and Papers*, DBWE 8: 372–73. In Rom. 3:24–26, Paul speaks of God's gift of justification "through the redemption that is in Christ Jesus." God, says Paul, "did this to show his righteousness, because in his divine forbearance he had passed over the sins previously committed; it was to prove at the present time that he himself is righteous and that he justifies the one who has faith in Jesus."
120. *Letters and Papers*, DBWE 8: 372–73.
121. *Letters and Papers*, DBWE 8: 373.
122. *Letters and Papers*, DBWE 8: 501.
123. Kevin Hart, "Bonhoeffer's 'Religious Clothes': The Naked Man, the Secret, and What We Hear," in *Bonhoeffer and Continental Thought*, ed. Brian Gregor and Jens Zimmermann (Bloomington: Indiana University Press, 2009), 187.
124. Bethge, *Dietrich Bonhoeffer*, 873.
125. *Letters and Papers*, DBWE 8: 455.
126. Green, *Theology of Sociality*, 265.
127. *Letters and Papers*, DBWE 8: 363.
128. *Letters and Papers*, DBWE 8: 456.
129. *Sanctorum Communio*, DBWE 1: 48.
130. *Sanctorum Communio*, DBWE 1: 33.
131. In this book, the word "partiality" is used consistently to signal a particular limitation of religion—its confinement to a *part* or fragment of life.
132. Bethge, *Dietrich Bonhoeffer*, 875. Bonhoeffer seems first to have read Naumann's *Briefe über Religion* while still at school. According to Bethge, he never forgot, and was always challenged by, Naumann's description of the gulf between Christian belief and practice: "All the biddings of the Gospel merely hover like distant, white clouds of aspiration over the real conduct of our time." F. Naumann, Letter 19 in *Briefe über Religion*, 7th ed. (1917), 61. Cited in Bethge, *Dietrich Bonhoeffer*, 42–43.
133. *Act and Being*, DBWE 2: 57.
134. Barth, *Romans*, 231.
135. Green, *Theology of Sociality*, 263. We may recall, in this connection, Ebeling's observation that people now are at most partly religious. They are religious only "in the religious province of their being, whereas for the rest over broad stretches of their life their existence is in fact as non-religious as any." Ebeling, *Word and Faith*, 132. Harvey describes religion as caught up in a now largely secular process

of cultural engineering—the division of culture into "autonomous value spheres (science, religion, morality, art)"—by means of which religion, "as a private facet of human experience," becomes a mechanism for confining faith to a particular space "within the contours and dynamics of modernity." Barry A. Harvey, "A Post-Critical Approach to 'Religionless Christianity,'" in *Theology and the Practice of Responsibility: Essays on Dietrich Bonhoeffer*, ed. Wayne Whitson Floyd Jr. and Charles Marsh (Valley Forge, PA: Trinity Press International, 1994), 39, 47. Bonhoeffer's critique of religious "partiality" may thus be described as the rejection of a peculiarly modern strategy for supervising "the distinctively Christian practice of everyday life." Harvey, "A Post-Critical Approach to 'Religionless Christianity,'" in Floyd and Marsh, 55.

136. "Essence of Christianity," DBWE 10: 342.

137. Dietrich Bonhoeffer, "Lecture: The Visible Church in the New Testament," in *Theological Education at Finkenwalde*, DBWE 14: 441–42.

138. The difference here is essentially one of attitude or approach rather than a material difference of institution.

139. "Visible Church," DBWE 14: 442.

140. "Visible Church," DBWE 14: 442.

141. "Visible Church," DBWE 14: 442.

142. Harvey, "A Post-Critical Approach to 'Religionless Christianity,'" in Floyd and Marsh, 55.

143. *Ethics*, DBWE 6: 53.

144. *Ethics*, DBWE 6: 58.

145. *Ethics*, DBWE 6: 64.

146. *Ethics*, DBWE 6. 239.

147. *Letters and Papers*, DBWE 8: 406.

148. *Letters and Papers*, DBWE 8: 426.

149. *Letters and Papers*, DBWE 8: 406–7.

150. *Letters and Papers*, DBWE 8: 482.

151. *Letters and Papers*, DBWE 8: 460.

152. Bethge, *Dietrich Bonhoeffer*, 876.

153. Green, *Theology of Sociality*, 263–64.

154. *Letters and Papers*, DBWE 8: 366.

155. *Letters and Papers*, DBWE 8: 450. Bonhoeffer elsewhere describes these "so-called ultimate questions" as "the universal human questions about death, suffering, and guilt." *Letters and Papers*, DBWE 8: 406.

156. *Letters and Papers*, DBWE 8: 450.

157. *Letters and Papers*, DBWE 8: 366–67, 406.

158. *Letters and Papers*, DBWE 8: 406.

159. *Letters and Papers*, DBWE: 479.

160. *Letters and Papers*, DBWE 8: 479.

161. *Letters and Papers*, DBWE 8: 461. The poem concludes with a comprehensive assurance of God's saving grace: "God goes to all people in their need/fills body and soul with God's own bread/goes for Christians and heathens to Calvary's death/ and forgives them both." *Letters and Papers*, DBWE 8: 461.

162. *Letters and Papers*, DBWE 8: 364.
163. Bethge, *Dietrich Bonhoeffer*, 876.
164. *Ethics*, DBWE 6: 117–18.
165. "Nature of the Church," DBWE 11: 276–78.
166. *Ethics*, DBWE 6: 378.
167. . . . although it does not itself belong to the subject matter of ethics. Nor should we think of the commandment of God as something "timeless and generally valid as opposed to being historical and temporal." It is not, says Bonhoeffer, "the principle as opposed to its application, not the abstract as opposed to the concrete, not the indeterminate as opposed to the determinate. If it were anything of the kind, it would have ceased to be the commandment of *God*"—because it would then be up to us to decide what, if anything, in practice, to do with it. *Ethics*, DBWE 6: 378.
168. *Ethics*, DBWE 6: 374.
169. *Letters and Papers*, DBWE 8: 503.
170. "Nature of the Church," DBWE 11: 279.
171. "Nature of the Church," DBWE 11: 281.
172. *Letters and Papers*, DBWE 8: 389.
173. *Letters and Papers*, DBWE 8: 503.
174. *Letters and Papers*, DBWE 8: 365–66.
175. Article 1 of the German Confessing Church's primary confession of faith (the Barmen Theological Declaration of May 1934), drafted mainly by Karl Barth. Cited in William Werpehowski, "Karl Barth and Politics," in *The Cambridge Companion to Karl Barth*, ed. John Webster (Cambridge University Press, 2000), 229–30. Bonhoeffer did not attend the Barmen Synod but kept subsequently to the understanding of the church and its mission set out in the Declaration. Haddon Willmer, "Costly Discipleship," in de Gruchy, *Cambridge Companion*, 174.
176. *Letters and Papers*, DBWE 8: 426–27.
177. *Letters and Papers*, DBWE 8: 427.
178. *Letters and Papers*, DBWE 8: 363. De Gruchy understands Bonhoeffer to mean, by "last of the knights," that "traditional 'Christianity' and its representatives seem to belong to a lost era." *Letters and Papers*, DBWE 8: 363, ed. fn. 13.
179. *Letters and Papers*, DBWE 8: 427.
180. *Letters and Papers*, DBWE 8: 500.
181. *Letters and Papers*, DBWE 8: 480.
182. *Letters and Papers*, DBWE 8: 364.
183. Bethge's final category, "dispensability," which treats religion as "a historically conditioned and transitory form of human expression" (*Letters and Papers*, DBWE 8: 363), is considered at length in chapter 1.
184. Barth, *Romans*, 233.
185. *Conspiracy and Imprisonment*, DBWE 16: 329.
186. *Letters and Papers*, DBWE 8: 501.
187. Bethge, *Dietrich Bonhoeffer*, 878.

Chapter 3

Religionless Christianity in Its Christological Context

The concept of a religionless Christianity appears in just a handful of letters smuggled out of Tegel military prison in the spring and summer of 1944. All are addressed to Eberhard Bethge, who finds in them convincing evidence of "a decisive new beginning in April 1944." Bethge does not mean to suggest by this that Bonhoeffer's earlier thinking must now be considered redundant.

> On the contrary, it is part of the origin of the new. The building blocks are there and are being used. But the old arrangement of these building blocks has been altered, and there is clearly an extension of the theme that is tantamount to a change in theme. Bonhoeffer himself thought he was pursuing a completely new path.[1]

Ernst Feil justly describes Bonhoeffer's theology as a unity within which there is "development and unfolding." We are thus obliged to draw on the whole of it for a comprehensive understanding of Bonhoeffer's theological reflections in prison.[2]

It is also the case, though, that no extended discussion of religionless Christianity is possible without an appreciation of what Bonhoeffer meant by the term when he came to introduce it in 1944. We will, therefore, first examine the "new" theology which emerges, in somewhat hesitant form, from the prison letters, before attempting to trace the path that leads to it.

As we saw in the previous chapter, there is in the prison letters a consolidation and intensification of the critique of religion. Bonhoeffer is now convinced that religion is doomed to disappear and believes he can substantiate this claim from both a systematic and a historical point of view. Religion is doomed systematically because, no matter how much sympathy one may have for the goal to which it aspires—for the desire to engage with God on human terms—it is always finally shown to be a vain reaching out to God from below. And it is doomed historically, as a time-bound, "transitory form of human expression,"³ whose end is now fast approaching in the West.

Indeed, Bonhoeffer is convinced that we live, to all intents and purposes, already in a godless world, and must not try "to cover up its godlessness somehow with religion."⁴ He is likewise convinced that such a profound cultural shift demands a radical Christian response. If religion is just a garment worn by Christianity—and changed from time to time—what then might Christianity look like without it? Can a person be both Christian and religionless? "How can Christ become Lord of the religionless as well?"⁵ Bonhoeffer's theological letters (and what has survived of his papers) from prison are the only record we have of his all-too-brief engagement with these questions, but they provide nonetheless compelling glimpses of what he believed to be realistic and appropriate ways of addressing them.

A THOROUGHLY CHRISTOCENTRIC THEOLOGIAN

There is broad agreement among scholars that Bonhoeffer was a thoroughly christocentric theologian, whose sense of Christ's presence in the world grew steadily deeper over the years. The keynote of Bonhoeffer's life and theology, says Feil, is Christ and the "world come of age."⁶ Bonhoeffer's preoccupation with "the event of God's becoming human in Jesus Christ" meant, for him, that all theology must in essence be Christology.⁷ Charles Marsh, too, speaks of Bonhoeffer's "sweeping, uncompromising christocentrism,"⁸ and Ralf Wüstenberg warns that anyone who "fails to see Bonhoeffer's christological centre" misinterprets him "in the larger sense, even and especially with regard to the notion of non-religious interpretation."⁹

Indeed, Christopher Holmes is critical of what he believes to be the absence of a doctrine of God in Bonhoeffer's theology. For Bonhoeffer, "the first premise of all theology [is] that God, out of mercy freely given, truly became a human being."¹⁰ Absent from this approach, says Holmes, is "talk of the processions of Son and Spirit from the Father in God's life as the ground of their missions and the principle of their intelligibility."¹¹ Holmes insists that Christology is "derivative" of theology and believes Bonhoeffer's christological preoccupation to discourage "recognition of Christology's foundation and first premise: God."¹² Bonhoeffer evidently does not share this view. As far as he is concerned, Christ is "the very Word of God" and Christology, as "doctrine, speaking, the word about the Word of God," becomes, "[f]rom outside," the very "center of knowledge." As such, it "stands alone," pointing only to "the transcendence of its object."¹³

Bonhoeffer did not lack Lutheran Trinitarian sensibilities, but he never produced anything resembling a comprehensive Christian, or church, dogmatics, and I think it safe to say that a "doctrine of the processions and missions of Son and Spirit—understood along Augustinian and Thomistic lines"[14] was simply not on his theological radar. It should, perhaps, also be observed in this context that Bonhoeffer was not inclined to dwell, in abstraction, on God's perfections. This was essentially because he did not think Christians could really be expected to relate to them in any meaningful way. Holmes himself draws attention to the outline for a Trinity Sermon (1936) in which Bonhoeffer makes this clear, posing the question, "What good does a God do us who is in eternity and is stronger than the majesty of the world, stronger than sin and death?" This God, says Bonhoeffer, "does not concern us. How can such a God help us? Does this God inquire after me?" But God says, "I am the Lord *your* God. The God who was from the beginning ... is with me, next to me, for me, in me. ... God is not distant but rather close at hand. What a splendid gospel this is: 'I am *your* God!'"[15]

Holmes accepts that, for Bonhoeffer, "God *is* an event, 'the God who became human,'" and he has no problem with this. In fact, something of real importance is achieved here, "a kind of discipline ... the discipline of remembering that it is *God* who acts for us and for our salvation." Holmes, like Bonhoeffer, does not want to be confined to some idea of God but rather to speak "of the one who delivered his people from bondage in Egypt and raised Jesus from the dead." But he wants also "to speak of God as one whose perfect life is revealed in these acts, not conflated with them," and it would seem, from his own description of what this requires (a doctrine of God's life and of the Trinity), that he must do it without Bonhoeffer.[16]

THE NEW THEOLOGY

Andreas Pangritz discerns in the question "Who is Jesus Christ?" "the *cantus firmus* of Bonhoeffer's theological development from the beginning to the end."[17] And it is the "who" question that grounds the new theology to which we are introduced in the prison letters. In his initial ruminations on the possibility of a religionless Christianity, Bonhoeffer tells Bethge that he is troubled constantly by the question, "what is Christianity, or who is Christ actually for us today?"[18] He then goes on to speak with assurance of the approach of "a completely religionless age," and begins to reflect on Christian life in a religionless world. How, he asks, do we speak of God in the absence of religion? What does it mean to talk about God in a "worldly" way? "How do we go about being 'religionless-worldly' Christians?" Are Christians ready to abandon their sense of religious privilege, and to commit themselves "wholly to the world?"[19]

I have already observed that Bonhoeffer sees no point, and no merit, in striving to convince a world which has so clearly reached its majority "that it cannot live without God as its guardian."[20] On the contrary, he believes this coming of age can potentially bring Christians to a more authentic understanding of their condition.

> God would have us know that we must live as those who manage their lives without God. The same God who is with us is the God who forsakes us (Mark 15:34!).[21] The same God who makes us to live in the world without the working hypothesis of God is the God before whom we stand continually. Before God, and with God, we live without God. God consents to be pushed out of the world and onto the cross; God is weak and powerless in the world and in precisely this way, and only so, is at our side and helps us. Matt. 8:17[22] makes it quite clear that Christ helps us not by virtue of his omnipotence but rather by virtue of his weakness and suffering![23]

It is this tempered, but still confronting, sense of God's absence as a form of God's presence that distinguishes Christianity from all religions, for whereas religion "directs people in need to the power of God in the world" (to God as *deus ex machina*), the Bible reveals its antithesis. It reveals "the powerlessness and the suffering of God."[24] We find that "only the suffering God can help."[25]

The conviction that God suffers is of critical importance to Bonhoeffer. Suffering and God, he says elsewhere, "is not a contradiction but rather a necessary unity; for me the idea that God himself is suffering has always been one of the most convincing teachings of Christianity."[26] It is God who cries out and dies—for us—on the cross. God knows exactly what it is like to live in a world without God. As Wolfgang Huber observes, "the cross is the place with respect to which it is not a self-contradiction to say: 'Before God and with God we live without God.'"[27] And it is precisely our coming of age—this flourishing of human autonomy, which has served to overturn a fallacious idea of God—that "frees us to see the God of the Bible, who gains ground and power in the world by being powerless."[28]

This is clearly not a religious view of the world but neither is it a secular, or despairing, one. The world is not other than we find and know it to be. In such a world, we can no more expect God to spare us the personal and historical consequences of our, and others', actions than we can expect to avoid the other natural vicissitudes of mortal, biological life. We are instead called "to share in God's suffering at the hands of a godless world,"[29] and can do this only by living thoroughly worldly lives. This does not mean to be "religious in a certain way."[30] We must rather abandon all thoughts of self-transformation and throw ourselves "completely into the arms of God."[31] This yielding is not, however, an act of surrender to some higher power. Indeed, it is not what Bonhoeffer would call a religious action at all. He is rather describing a Christlike, self-emptying love, born of faith and confidence in God's unfailing grace. This act of love includes, in its context, the prospect of suffering, and the promise of life but, importantly, no otherworldly hope of salvation. And this is precisely what Bonhoeffer means by "this-worldliness" (*Diesseitigkeit*). He means "living fully in the midst of life's tasks, questions, successes and failures, experiences, and perplexities." He means letting go of our personal preoccupations and focusing instead on the suffering of God in the world. Then, he says, "one stays awake with Christ in Gethsemane."[32] We must learn to be "the human being Christ creates in us" by allowing ourselves "to be pulled into walking the path that Jesus walks, into the messianic event, in which Isa. 53 is now being fulfilled!"[33]

As Peter Frick observes, Bonhoeffer here firmly repudiates Friedrich Nietzsche's critique of Christian unworldliness. Bonhoeffer and Nietzsche may both be said to affirm this-worldly life "in all its manifestations," but whereas for Nietzsche the affirmation is "the end in itself," for Bonhoeffer it is a badge of Christian discipleship—"the hallmark of following Christ, whose reality brings about on this earth the very groundedness and life-affirmation that Zarathustra announces."[34]

In a letter to his brother-in-law, Rüdiger Schleicher, written in 1936, Bonhoeffer makes a distinction—consistent with his understanding of the difference between religion and revelation—between those people who decide for themselves where God is to be found, and those who leave the decision to God. If, he says,

> it is I who says where God is to be found, then I will always find a God there who in some manner corresponds to me, is pleasing to me, who is commensurate with my own nature. But if it is God who says where he is to be found, then it will probably be a place that is not at all commensurate with my own nature and that does not please me at all. This place . . . is the cross of Jesus.[35]

As Gaylon Barker puts it, "[f]or Bonhoeffer, what we must live without is not God *per se*, but our caricatures of God."[36]

Bonhoeffer finds a firm biblical anchor for Christian worldliness in the Old Testament. In December 1943, he tells Bethge that he is spending more time with the Old Testament than with the New, and that he now understands the need to strike a better balance between the two.

> Only when one knows that the name of God may not be uttered may one sometimes speak the name of Jesus Christ. Only when one loves life and the earth so much that with it everything seems to be lost and at its end may one believe in

the resurrection of the dead and a new world. . . . And only when the wrath and vengeance of God against God's enemies are allowed to stand can something of forgiveness and the love of enemies touch our hearts. Whoever wishes to be and perceive things too quickly and too directly in New Testament ways is to my mind no Christian.[37]

The Old Testament reveals a people in awe of God and in love with life in all its imperfection. This should be our example. The way to the new world lies through this one, and we must not overlook the significance of the journey.[38]

Elsewhere, Bonhoeffer stresses the importance of reaching a proper understanding of the role of redemption in Judaism and Christianity. In the Old Testament, the Jewish experience of redemption is essentially historical, temporal: "Israel is redeemed out of Egypt so that it may live before God, as God's people on earth." The Christian experience—which is the experience of the risen Christ—is generally thought to be different. The resurrection gives rise to a "genuine religion of redemption" which, in keeping with other redemption myths, looks forward to a new and perfect life beyond death.[39]

But is this, Bonhoeffer asks, really the essence of the New Testament proclamation? He does not think so and believes the Christian hope of resurrection to serve another purpose, by transforming attitudes to life on earth.

> Unlike believers in the redemption myths, Christians do not have an ultimate escape route out of their earthly tasks and difficulties into eternity. Like Christ . . . they have to drink the cup of earthly life to the last drop, and only when they do this is the Crucified and Risen One with them, and they are crucified and resurrected with Christ.[40]

Redemption myths, says Bonhoeffer, "arise from the human experience of boundaries," but Christ takes hold of people in the midst of their lives.[41] In Jesus Christ, every human being is reconciled with God, and human life is celebrated as a multidimensional whole. Never, says Bonhoeffer, do we see Jesus questioning a person's health, or strength, or good fortune. Why otherwise would he have restored the sick to health and given strength back to the weak? "Jesus claims all of human life, in all its manifestations, for himself and for the kingdom of God."[42]

In a meditation on his favorite psalm, written on his return to Germany following a second, and soon abandoned, visit to the United States in the summer of 1939, Bonhoeffer stresses the importance of understanding that life is a gift from God and that it is not, as such, a means to an end but rather "fulfillment in itself." When life is regarded as a means to an end, "[t]hen the goal, the good, is sought in the hereafter" and the goodness of life itself is denied.[43] "This-worldliness must not be abolished ahead of its time," he tells Bethge, in the letter of June 27, 1944.[44]

Bonhoeffer concedes, in his reflections on Psalm 119, that life is finite and brief, and that we are pilgrims and sojourners on the earth, with no strong support in people or in things. We have nonetheless

> to submit to the laws of [our] shelter. The earth that feeds me has a right to my work and my strength.... I owe it faithfulness and thanksgiving.... I should not close my heart ... to the tasks, pains, and joys of the earth, and I should wait patiently for the divine promise to be redeemed, but truly wait for it, and not rob myself of it in advance, in wishes and dreams.[45]

Bonhoeffer does not give up on heaven, but he thinks it wrong—indeed unchristian—to divert ourselves with thoughts of another world until we have fully satisfied the demands of this one.

Bonhoeffer's determination to distance himself from every form of shallow piety, including those religious people whose presence made him so uncomfortable as to be virtually incapable of speech,[46] is evident, too, in his praise of the Song of Solomon's inclusion in the Bible. This, he believes, nullifies the argument that Christianity is "about tempering one's passions." Where, he asks, "is there any such tempering in the Old Testament?" Where the *cantus firmus*—here, the love of God—is plain to see, a counterpoint—in this case, earthly love—can "develop as mightily as it wants."[47]

The key to understanding the mode of God's presence in the world is Jesus Christ. A genuine experience of God is to be found only in the encounter with Jesus Christ, "the human being for others." Our relationship with God is thus not a "religious" connection to "some highest, most powerful and best being imaginable,"[48] but rather "a new life in 'being there for others,' through participation in the being of Jesus."[49] And this gives rise to a similarly genuine experience of transcendence which, at least in this context, is neither boundless nor remote but simply "the neighbor within reach in any given situation." Anyone may live a transcendent, and yet thoroughly worldly, life by participating in the being of Jesus, in his "becoming human," his cross, and resurrection.[50] Bethge believes the phrase "the human being for others,"[51] now so intimately associated with Bonhoeffer's late theology, to describe "an ethical impulse" which thwarts both the religious inclination to reject the world and the ecclesial predisposition to dominate it, and which "finally praises Jesus with words that are soaked in experience."[52]

The church, too, is church "only when it is there for others." The church must set the example for life with Christ by forsaking property, power, and pride, and by rededicating itself to the service of humanity.[53] In every respect, as Bonhoeffer knew from his own involvement during the 1930s in the ecumenical peace movement in Europe, and in the German Protestant church struggle (*Kirchenkampf*) between the *Deutsche Christen* and the Confessing Church, the church had largely failed the test of these turbulent times. As the decade wore on, Bonhoeffer became increasingly disillusioned with the European churches' flagging commitment to peace, and with his own Confessing Church's all too frequent failure to stand up for Christ in the face of Nazi tyranny and brutality.

Already, in the *Ethics*, Bonhoeffer had accused the church of being a silent witness to "oppression, hatred, and murder," and of failing to come to the aid of "the weakest and most defenseless brothers and sisters of Jesus Christ."[54] The church, he said, had sought only to keep itself safe, and to secure its material interests,[55] and had become, by its silence, "guilty for the loss of responsible action in society." In this way, it had facilitated the state's own "falling away from Christ."[56]

Now, in the *Letters and Papers from Prison*, Bonhoeffer describes the German Protestant churches as pusillanimous and bent solely on preserving their brand of Christianity as religion for pious, inward-looking souls.[57] As such, and given its overwhelming preoccupation with its own survival, the Confessing Church

> has become incapable of bringing the word of reconciliation and redemption . . . to the world. So the words we used before must lose their power, be silenced, and we can be Christians today in only two ways, through prayer and in doing justice among human beings. All Christian thinking, talking, and organizing must be born anew, out of that prayer and action.[58]

And all true Christian prayer and action springs from just one source, from Jesus Christ, who encompasses everything that we may reasonably "expect or beg of God."[59] This is not the God of the religious imagination. We have rather to "immerse ourselves again and again, for a long time and quite calmly, in Jesus's life, his sayings, actions, suffering, and dying in order to recognize what God promises and fulfills."[60] Through Jesus Christ we are drawn into the very presence of God and into new life with God, including the certainty that "in suffering lies hidden the source of our joy" and "in dying the source of our life," which comes with this understanding.[61]

CONSISTENCY AND CONTINUITY IN BONHOEFFER'S THEOLOGY

The key elements of Bonhoeffer's new theology are not themselves new. As Bethge observes, "[t]he building blocks are there and are being used."[62] But, in 1944, with Bonhoeffer in prison and facing possible execution, they now stand in a somewhat different arrangement. The new look is important and must be seen in its own light, but to ignore its provenance is to risk a serious misunderstanding of what Bonhoeffer means, even provisionally, by religionless Christianity, and to overlook a wealth of clarifying detail. The mode of God's presence in the world (which is the encounter with Jesus Christ), the idea that "only the suffering God can help," the promise of new life in "being there for others" through participation in the being of Jesus—all this is grounded firmly in Bonhoeffer's earlier theology, and especially in the vision of Jesus Christ as fully human *and* wholly God that suffuses it.

What follows is a selective account of Bonhoeffer's theological journey. It highlights elements of Bonhoeffer's thinking which seem to me to presage, and indeed to make possible, the emergence of his prison theology. Prominent among them are Bonhoeffer's intensely relational concept of person, his understanding of transcendence, his idea of freedom, the notion of vicarious representative action, the emphasis on conformity to Christ, the concept of Christ *pro me* and *for others*, and his overarching vision of one reality in Christ.

Christ Existing as Church-Community

Bonhoeffer completed his doctoral dissertation, *Sanctorum Communio*, in July 1927, when he was just twenty-one. In this "theological study of the sociology of the church,"[63] the emphasis is on ecclesiology rather than Christology, but there are already signs of Christ's emergence as the fulcrum of Bonhoeffer's theology. In *Sanctorum Communio*, the church's claim to be God's church-community is presented as "a reality of revelation" which can be grasped only from the inside, in faith, by its members.[64] Revelation here takes the form of "Christ existing as church-community" (*Christus als Gemeinde existierend*), which is synonymous with Paul's "indicative, 'you are the body of Christ.'"[65] The church is the expression of God's "new will and purpose" for redeemed humanity,[66] and Christ's relation to it is twofold. He gives the church both an eternal and a temporal character. In Christ, as God's self-revelation, the church is already complete; there is nothing more to do; "time is suspended." But there is still a church "to be built within time upon Christ as the firm foundation."[67] This is the Holy Spirit at work in the word of the church-community, which "has no other content than the fact of Christ."[68] Jesus Christ is always and everywhere a real, spiritual presence for the church, presiding over its historical unfolding.[69] And the church is Christ's "presence on earth, for it has his word." As such, it can be understood only as "a movement from above to below," and in no other way.[70]

The young Bonhoeffer is thus led to adopt an exclusive definition of community with God. Human beings, he says, have access to God only through Christ, and "Christ is present only in his church-community . . . *therefore community with God exists only in the church.*"[71]

Elsewhere in *Sanctorum Communio*, Bonhoeffer shows that he is both sensitive to and a little uncomfortable with the theological implications of this view. While, he says, on the one hand, it would seem that the church, "as Christ's presence in the world," might reasonably expect to be the place of salvation—a salvation available only to believers—the "recognition that the gift of God's boundless love has been received without any merit would, on the other hand, make it seem just as impossible to exclude others from this gift and this love." Bonhoeffer believes the most compelling reason for accepting the idea of *apocatastasis* (the Greek term for the doctrine of the salvation by grace of all creatures) to be a shared Christian sense of responsibility for bringing sin into the world, and thus "of being bound together with the whole of humanity in sin."[72]

In *Sanctorum Communio*, Bonhoeffer first establishes his ethic of responsibility in relation to the concept of person and, in doing so, offers "a fundamental refutation of individualistic social atomism."[73] We cannot testify, he says, to "*the real existence of other subjects by way of the purely transcendental category of the universal.*"[74] There is no purely cognitive way to the other. Rather, we must begin with an experience of duality, "the absolute duality of God and humanity,"[75] which gives rise, as Clifford Green describes it, to "the theological axiom that the human person always exists in relation to an Other, namely God, and that human relations are in some way analogies of this fundamental relation."[76]

This allows Bonhoeffer to argue that a person[77] truly "exists always and only in ethical responsibility."[78] I have my being only in relation to a You, because only by accepting (or rejecting) the claim of a You do I assume (or seek to avoid) responsibility.[79] The worldly "being for others" of the prison letters is already making its presence felt here, in the ecclesial theology of Bonhoeffer's doctoral dissertation. It is to be found elsewhere in Bonhoeffer's early theology, too, in the 1932–1933 winter semester lectures on Genesis 1–3, where he describes freedom as a "being-free-for-the-other"[80] and, perhaps most vividly, in the sermons as, for example, when Bonhoeffer tells his congregation in Barcelona that they come face-to-face with Jesus Christ in every human encounter:

> [T]he other person, this enigmatic, impenetrable You, is God's claim on us; indeed, it is the holy God in person whom we encounter. . . . I am for you, and you are for me God's claim, God himself; in this recognition, our gaze opens to the fullness of divine life in the world.[81]

It will be evident that the fashioning of ethical persons conscious of responsibility is not, for Bonhoeffer, something that human beings simply do for one another.

> *God or the Holy Spirit joins the concrete You; only through God's active working does the other become a You to me from whom my I arises. In other words,*

every human You is an image of the divine You. You-character is in fact the essential form in which the divine is experienced; every human You bears its You-character only by virtue of the divine.[82]

Jens Zimmermann contends that, in the incarnation, transcendence "is structured ontologically as being-there-for-the-other."[83] Yet anyone who reads only Bonhoeffer's *Letters and Papers from Prison*, where he describes transcendence as Jesus's "being-for-others" and "the transcendent" as "the neighbor within reach in any given situation,"[84] could still perhaps be forgiven for losing sight of its divine origin. Here, in his doctoral thesis, Bonhoeffer's understanding of transcendence is already firmly anchored in the notion of a genuine other, a "concrete You," but it is, first and foremost, the "You of God" of which he speaks—the "You of God . . . who here becomes visible in the concrete You of social life."[85] Only "through God's active working" does a genuine other become truly (i.e., externally) present for me. It is the "divine You" that creates the "human You," becoming in the process, for every I, its essential experience of the transcendent—its assurance of a real outside. As Christiane Tietz observes, "Only the other, who really comes from the outside, who really is *extra me*, interrupts the circle of the I and lets the I experience its boundaries."[86]

Consistent with Bonhoeffer's concept of personhood, we also meet for the first time in *Sanctorum Communio* the "life-principle of the new humanity," vicarious representative action (*Stellvertretung*),[87] which has its origin and archetype in Jesus Christ. A guiltless Jesus takes on the sins of the world and is punished for them.[88] In and through him, we are restored to new life with God.

> While the old humanity consists of countless isolated units—each one an Adam . . . the new humanity is entirely concentrated in the one single historical point, Jesus Christ, and only in Christ is it perceived as a whole. For in Christ, as the foundation and the body of the building called Christ's church-community, the work of God takes place and is completed.[89]

Vicarious representative action is, at this stage, essentially a theological rather than an ethical concept—a form of the satisfaction theory of atonement but one which places the emphasis on God's love rather than God's wrath.[90] Indeed, Christ's action as vicarious representative is God's gift of love to us—the gift that makes us whole and sustains us—and may be emulated only in Christ's church-community, where the structural "being-with-each-other" and responsible "acting-for-each-other" of the members of the church-community together constitute "the specific sociological nature of the community of love."[91]

Daniel Migliore, drawing on the work of Dorothee Sölle, suggests that traditional statements of satisfaction theory generally fail to distinguish properly between a "substitute" and a "representative." While the act of substitution belongs to "the impersonal world of replaceable things," the act of representation is always something personal. "A representative stands in for us, speaks and acts for us, without simply displacing us." A representative does not relieve us of responsibility, and the atoning work of Christ is better understood as "an act of personal representation . . . than a work of mechanical substitution."[92] This distinction is helpful here, and consistent also with Bonhoeffer's later understanding of Christian action as springing from the unity of God and the world in Jesus Christ, a unity which "exists solely in the person of Jesus Christ, in whom God became human, acting in vicarious representative responsibility [stellvertretende Verantwortung] and entering out of love for the real human being into the guilt of the world."[93]

The Limits of Reflection

Much of Bonhoeffer's early academic work must, as Wayne Floyd suggests, "be understood as a journey to discover an adequate barrier or resistance to the power of the intellect to try to comprehend all of reality."[94] On this journey, Bonhoeffer drew on the resources of Continental philosophy as well as theology. Floyd emphasizes Bonhoeffer's competence in philosophy, in which he took a keen interest first at high school and later as an undergraduate at Tübingen and Berlin universities.

Bonhoeffer is careful, though, not to confuse philosophy with theology. In his inaugural lecture at the University of Berlin, he describes the nature of philosophical inquiry as essentially self-enclosed. In philosophy, the human being "understands himself [solely] on the basis of his possibilities in self-reflection." Theology accepts the results of philosophical inquiry, but "interprets them in its own fashion as the thinking of the *cor curvum in se* [the heart turned in on itself]." In theology, the question about the human being, if it is to be taken seriously, can be asked only in the presence of God. "That is, the human being is torn completely out of himself, drawn as a whole person before God, and here the question about the human being becomes serious precisely because it no longer includes its own answer." Instead, God provides the answer "completely freely and completely anew."[95]

Bonhoeffer nonetheless acknowledges, in the seminar presentation he gave on Barth's theology at Union Theological Seminary in New York, that theology uses "certain general forms of thinking" and that it "has those forms in common with philosophy."[96] Philosophy may also sometimes be of direct benefit to theology. The critical philosophy of Immanuel Kant proved especially fruitful for Barth, and for Bonhoeffer himself. In Kant, says Bonhoeffer, Barth "finds expressed the critic of thinking upon thinking, here he sees man considered not in his full possession of transcendence but in the eternal act of referring to transcendence, man not in boundlessness, but in limitation." Although Barth recognizes that philosophy can never finally overcome the egocentric boundlessness of systematic thinking, he appreciates Kant's attempt to leave room for transcendent reality by imposing a rational limit to human understanding. He uses Kantian terminology "to express the eternal crisis of man, which is brought upon him by God in Christ and which is beyond all philosophical grasp." God is known only in God's self-revelation, in the "pure act of referring to God." Theology and philosophy, on the other hand, are both products of reflection, "which God does not enter." They differ though in that

> theology at least knows of an act of God, which tears man out of his reflection into an actus directus toward God. Here man knows himself and God not by looking into himself, but by looking to the word of God, which tells him that he is sinner and justified, which he never before could understand.[97]

Bonhoeffer is thus convinced that we can never arrive at a reliable knowledge of reality through philosophical reflection alone. Thought, whether systematic or critical, remains self-enclosed. Only God can break through the closed circle of the self, from the outside. Only revelation can place us truly "into reality."[98] And revelation requires a way of thinking that recognizes revelation's historical particularity, while at the same time knowing itself, as thought, to be something other than the ontological reality it comprehends.[99] But just how are we to understand this? What does it mean to speak of God's self-revelation in Jesus Christ—to speak of "the being of revelation"[100]—in this way?

The Being of Revelation

In his postdoctoral thesis, Bonhoeffer seeks to reach a genuinely theological understanding of the problem of act and being. It is, he says,

> a question of the "objectivity" of the concept of God and an adequate concept of cognition, the issue of determining the relationship between "the being of God" and the mental act which grasps that being. In other words, the meaning of "the being of God in revelation" must be interpreted theologically, including how it is known, how faith as act, and revelation as being, are related to one another and, correspondingly, *how human beings stand in light of revelation.*[101]

Bonhoeffer thus sets out to describe what Floyd calls "a theology of consciousness" which reflects the Reformation understanding of the *cor curvum in se* as the beginning of human sinfulness—the principal cause of our turning away from God and each other.[102] What is needed to make room for revelation is a theological epistemology, or philosophy of knowledge, that places the object of knowledge, whether divine or human, safely beyond the controlling reach of the knower[103]—a way of thinking which, as Floyd describes it, gives life to transcendental philosophy's own necessarily flawed endeavors "to think critically rather than systematically, its attempts to articulate a genuine . . . dialectics of Otherness."[104]

In *Act and Being*, Bonhoeffer seeks to expound a "genuine transcendentalism" and its correlate, a "genuine ontology," with reference to Kant's distinction between the transcendental unity of apperception (our self-conscious ordering of the various elements of experience) and the *Ding-an-sich*, the thing-in-itself (which lies always outside or beyond our experience). Floyd believes a genuine transcendental philosophy and a genuine ontology to be possible for Bonhoeffer only when a relationship is maintained between the act of thinking "*and* something transcendent to thought—ontologically distinct from the thinking subject—neither of which 'swallows up' the other."[105] This requires a dialectical form of thinking that is able to sustain "both thought—understood to be always 'in reference to' but not totally able to grasp reality in its entirety—and the ontological resistance of authentic otherness itself—both act and being."[106] It must be able to accommodate both the transcendental act of faith and the ontological being of revelation. The only alternative is systematic and totalizing thinking ("idealism,"[107] for Bonhoeffer) which is of no value to theology because it apprehends "*neither* the true act of thinking-within-limits (the goal of genuine transcendental philosophy) *nor* the nature of the being of what-is-thought, yet remains beyond-thought—something transcendent (the goal of genuine ontology)."[108]

Bonhoeffer argues that a "*genuine* ontology" requires an object of knowledge—a genuine Other—that "challenges and limits" the I; that resists being drawn into the I as a contingent object of cognition. Indeed, "the object of knowledge must so stand over against the I that it is free from becoming known." It does not depend on the I, whose being and existing it precedes in every respect. Knowledge is suspended in "a being-already-known."[109]

This, as Floyd says, is why the concept of revelation is so important for Bonhoeffer—"it names that situation of openness, where reality is always and only to be understood 'in reference to' the thinking subject, whose process of thought is ontologically 'suspended' in being that it has not created."[110] It demands the recognition that human existence is always already a "being in." The reality of revelation is the reality of our being already in Christ, where life plays out in manifold "acts of existence."[111] We have our being in Christ, in whom "alone is unity and wholeness of life,"[112] and can speak, in this context, of a genuine ontology and a genuine transcendentalism only if we define "being in" in such a way that human knowing, "encountering itself in that which is," is able simply to accept the being of existing things without seeking to press them into its service.[113]

The Christian revelation is present wherever Christ is present, in Christ's church, and happens for the community of faith in the proclamation of Christ's death and resurrection.[114] Revelation is not to be thought of individualistically but is always related to community, just as human beings are never simply individuals but always a part of society. Thus, the being of revelation may be regarded as the community "constituted and formed by the person of Christ [*Christus als Gemeinde existierend*] and in which individuals already find themselves in their new existence."[115] Indeed, it is Christ who gives human beings their personhood. Through him, other human beings

> are moved out of the world of things—to which they, as still something-existing, continue to belong—and into the social sphere of persons. Only through Christ does my neighbor meet me as one who claims me in an absolute way from a position outside my existence.[116]

Freedom for Others

Of critical significance for the worldly, other-centered theology of the prison letters is the understanding of divine and human freedom set out in *Act and Being*, and in the 1932–1933 winter semester lectures on Genesis 1–3, published subsequently as *Creation and Fall*. In *Act and Being*, Bonhoeffer writes of "God's coming out of God's own self" in the Word of revelation, by which "God is bound by God's own action."[117] In God's own free decision "to be bound to historical human beings," Bonhoeffer finds a substantial, rather than purely formal,[118] means of understanding God's freedom. "God is free not from human beings but for them," and to this God attests in Jesus Christ. God is present "not in eternal non-objectivity," but "'haveable,' graspable in the Word within the church."[119]

In *Creation and Fall*, Bonhoeffer considers the nature of human freedom. If, he says, we believe that, in human beings, God has created God's own image—that "[h]umankind differs from the other creatures in that God is in humankind as the very image of God in which the free Creator looks upon the Creator's own self "[120]—then it follows that human beings, like God, are free, for "[o]nly in that which is itself free could the free Creator behold the Creator."[121] And as God is free not from but for human beings, so is their freedom a freedom only *for* the other.[122]

> Freedom is not a quality a human being has; it is not an ability, a capacity, an attribute of being. . . . [I]t is a relation and nothing else. To be more precise, freedom is a relation between two persons. Being free means "being-free-for-the-other," because I am bound to the other.[123]

It makes no more sense to speak of freedom "in itself" (*an sich*)[124] than it does to speak of the person in him or herself (of the I without the You).[125]

Again we are reminded of the intrinsically social and ethically responsible nature of human existence. Our creatureliness, Bonhoeffer says, is no more a quality, capacity, or attribute of being than human freedom is, and "can be defined in simply no other way than in terms of the existence of human beings over-against-one-another, with-one-another, and in-dependence-upon-one-another."[126] As such, the "image that is like God" is to be understood not as an *analogia entis* (an analogy of being "in which human beings, in their existence in-and-of themselves . . . could be said to be like God's being") but as an *analogia relationis* (an analogy of relationship "which God has established" and "in which human beings are set").[127]

This, however, is not the world with which most of us are familiar. Human life cannot be defined solely in terms of altruistic sociality. Ours is a fallen existence. In the language of Genesis, we have tasted the fruit of the forbidden tree—the tree of the knowledge of good and evil—which stands at the center of the garden of Eden and, in doing so, have transgressed "the boundary at the center" of human existence.

Bonhoeffer here makes an important distinction between the boundary "at the center" and the boundary "on the margin." Whereas the boundary on the margin signals the furthest reach of human possibilities at a given historical point in time, the boundary at the center "is the limit of human *reality*, of human *existence as such*." Human beings can generally be expected to push the boundary on the margin, with a view to its indefinite extension. But if they truly understand the nature of that other boundary, they will know that "the whole of existence, human existence in every possible way that it may comport itself, has its limit."[128]

Humankind now stands in the center, where it cannot stand. It acknowledges no limit (what it does not yet know, it will know), and lives alone, out of its own resources. Humankind is *sicut deus* (like God).[129] It has no further need of God.

Bonhoeffer has previously made this point in *Act and Being*, where—in sharp contrast to his ethically responsible concept of person—he places particular emphasis on the isolation of the human being *sicut deus*, on the *cor curvum in se*. "Human beings have torn themselves loose from community with God," and with one another. They now stand alone in a world of their own, in which "other human beings have sunk into the world of things." God is reduced to the standing of "a religious object," while human beings assume the roles of "creator and lord." In this situation, it is inevitable that they should "begin and end with themselves in their knowing."[130]

Bonhoeffer returns to this theme in *Discipleship*, where he writes of the restoration in Christ of the image of God that was once in Adam. "In Adam, God sought to observe this image with joy, as the culmination of God's creation." But, while Adam might reasonably have been expected to preserve, in "gratitude and obedience . . . his secret of being creature and yet God-like," he desired instead "to become what, from God's perspective, he already was. That was the fall. Adam became 'like God'—sicut deus—in his own way. Having made himself into a god, he now no longer had a God."[131]

In *Creation and Fall*, Bonhoeffer paints a vivid picture of the gulf between a life lived in the image of God and one lived *sicut deus*, and of Christ's redemptive role in restoring human beings to new life and wholeness before God:

> Imago dei—humankind in the image of God in being for God and the neighbor, in its original creatureliness and limitedness; sicut deus—humankind like God in knowing out of its own self about good and evil, in having no limit and acting out of its own resources . . . in its being alone. Imago dei—bound to the word of the Creator and deriving life from the Creator; sicut deus—bound to the depths of its own knowledge of God. . . . Imago dei—the creature living in the unity of obedience; sicut deus—the creator-human-being who lives on the basis of the divide . . . between good and evil. Imago dei, sicut deus, agnus dei—the human being who is God incarnate, who was sacrificed for humankind sicut deus, in true divinity slaying its false divinity and restoring the imago dei.[132]

A life lived in the image of God is a whole life, compassionate, humble, and obedient to God; while the life of the human being who has become "like God" is a fragmented and lonely life, a sham, and a conceit. Fallen humanity is sovereign lord of "its own mute, violated, silenced, dead, ego-world [*Ichwelt*],"[133] from which only the crucified and risen Christ can redeem it.[134] Those who "thirst for life" are raised up anew with the resurrected Christ.[135] They no longer see themselves as both creature and creator but know themselves instead to be truly God's creatures in Christ.

Fully Human, Wholly God

Bonhoeffer's Christology comes to full expression in a series of lectures given at the University of Berlin in the summer of 1933. He begins by emphasizing the paradoxical nature of his inquiry. Christology, he says, can only point to the transcendence of its object. The divine Logos appears to us in the shape of a human being whose transcendence is grounded firmly in presupposition and is not subject to proof. No other approach is possible. The transcendent can only ever be "the prerequisite for our thinking, never the proof. For as an object providing proof it would no longer be the transcendent."[136]

Teaching about Christ begins then most appropriately in humble silence. "The silence of the church is silence before the Word. In proclaiming Christ, the church falls on its knees in silence before the inexpressible."[137] The church thus affirms both God's revelation and the limits of human understanding.

Christ is the very Word, the Logos of God, and this Logos is a person, a real human being. "This human person is the transcendent."[138]

Christology is concerned with just one question, the question "who are you?"[139] The answer to this question is not accessible to critical thought. It is given only in God's self-revelation. The question can only really be asked in the church, by those who already have the answer, by those who accept the validity of Christ's claim to be the Word of God.[140] It is a question asked of Christ by those who believe in him, "the question of faith: 'Who are you? Are you God's very self?'"[141] The question "who" expresses "the otherness of the other," and obliges us to accept that, in the O/other, we have reached the boundary of our existence. Unlike the "how" question, which is always an intellectual act of domestication or confinement ("Tell me *how* you exist, tell me *how* you think, and I'll tell you who you are"), the "who" question "interrogates the very existence of the one asking it." It is truly the question of transcendence.[142]

> Transcendence is the boundary of the being that has been given to me. . . . If the "who" question is the only question I ask that goes beyond my own being, then this is the only question that asks about transcendence and existence. The "who question" cannot be answered by human beings themselves. Even existence cannot provide the answer, because the existence of a human being cannot go beyond its own limits but remains entirely within its own frame of reference and mirrors itself to itself.[143]

Bonhoeffer's understanding of the true "otherness of the other"—of a genuine transcendence to which we have access, essentially and originally, through faith in God's self-revelation in a unique human being—allows him to speak confidently of Jesus Christ as wholly human and wholly God in an appropriately "Chalcedonian sense," where thinking begins not with the two natures (the divinity and humanity) of Christ, considered separately, "but rather with the fact that Jesus Christ is God."[144] The Chalcedonian formula reaches beyond conceptual forms. It embraces paradox not as the dubious solution to unresolved puzzles but as a means of expressing God's mystery and transcendence. Here, "the fact of the God-human stand[s] as the presupposition." Only in this way "do we begin to know who God is."[145]

Jesus is "the God who became human as we became human."[146] Nothing human is absent in him. And this human being is God "not in a divine nature," and indeed in no tangible way, "but rather God in our faith alone."[147] God's *"vertical Word from above"* neither adds anything to nor subtracts anything from Jesus Christ, "but rather qualifies this entire human being as God."[148] As such, we should not speak of Jesus Christ as we might of the *idea* of some all-powerful and omniscient God, but rather of "his birth in a manger and of his cross."[149] In his humiliation on the cross, we see "a dying human being, despairing of God." And still we say of this person, "this is God."[150]

The Present Christ

Bonhoeffer, says DeJonge, manifests a thoroughly Lutheran concern with Christ's presence. "There is no thinking from Christ towards Christ's presence."[151] Christ's presence is "Christ's way of being."[152]

Jesus Christ is present to the church, in space and time, in the one whole person of the God-human. The risen Christ is still the human Jesus. He can be present to us only because he is human, and eternally with us only because he is God. No other explanation of Christ's contemporary presence is possible. We are separated from the historical Jesus by the passage of time, and from God by God's timelessness. Neither can truly be said to exist for us in isolation. They are inseparable. "God in his timeless eternity is *not* God. Jesus Christ in his humanity, limited in time, is *not* Jesus Christ. Instead, in the human being Jesus Christ, God is God. Only in Jesus Christ is God present."[153] Jesus Christ is present as word, sacrament, and church-community; and he is present in the strictly person-oriented sense of Luther's christological and sacramental "*est*" statements ("this man, Jesus, *is* God," and "this *is* my body"), rather than as sign or symbol. He *is* the preaching, the sacraments, the one whole body, the very life of the church.[154]

But this, for Bonhoeffer, is still not a sufficient explanation of Jesus's ability to be present always and everywhere to those who believe in him. Again, the question is not *how* do we know this, but rather *who* is this person, and "by virtue of what personal ontological structure is Christ present to the church?"[155] The answer to this question lies in the "*pro me*" form of the person of Christ, and in Bonhoeffer's characteristic emphasis on relationship. "The being of Christ's person is essentially relatedness to me," and this "*pro me*" is no incidental, or otherwise transient, quality or effect of Christ's presence in the world. This is "who" Christ is. Bonhoeffer can think of Jesus Christ "only in existential relationship" as "the one present in the church-community *pro me*."[156] It is both "useless" and "godless" to contemplate "Christ-in-himself . . . precisely because Christ is not there in-himself, but rather is there for you."[157]

Christ the Mediator

The place of Jesus Christ in Bonhoeffer's theology is captured perfectly in the image of Christ the mediator. As the "one Lord . . . through whom are all things and through whom we exist" (1 Cor. 8:6), Christ is the mediator of every creaturely relationship with the Creator. He stands in my place, where

I should but cannot stand. In him, I acknowledge my limit, and find my new center. Christ is the instrument of my redemption in a fallen world, my judge, and my justification.

History dwells meanwhile in restless expectation of a messiah and fails consistently to fulfill its own corrupt messianic promises. But in Christ

> the messianic expectation of history is crushed as well as fulfilled. It is crushed because its fulfillment is hidden. It is fulfilled because the Messiah has truly come. The meaning of history is swallowed up in an event that takes place in the deepest desolation of human life, on the cross.[158]

In the natural world, too, Christ finds a lost and guilty creature caught between servitude and redemption. Christ is "the new creation" who lifts "the curse of God upon Adam's field" and redeems "the enslaved creation . . . into hope."[159]

Bonhoeffer insists that to speak of Christ as the center of human existence, of history, and of nature is no mere theological abstraction, and, furthermore, that to distinguish between these three is, in practice, impossible. There are not three centers, but only one, for human existence encompasses both history and nature. Christ, as the one who "stands in my place, in my behalf before God, *pro me*," does this for the whole of God's creation. He is the bridge between two worlds—the old, fallen world, which is coming to an end, and God's new world, which is now beginning.[160]

The Historical Jesus

Bonhoeffer judged liberal theology, and the historical-critical approach to biblical studies with which it is associated, to have come full circle. Having proceeded on the assumption that it was both possible and necessary to distinguish between the Jesus of the Synoptic Gospels and the Christ of Paul, liberal theology was eventually forced to conclude that the two are in fact inseparable. "It did not prove possible to write a historically credible biography of Jesus."[161] Liberal theology, says Bonhoeffer, came to an end with William Wrede and Albert Schweitzer, the fruits of their research having served, on the one hand, to undermine liberal theology's conviction that "Jesus is someone other than the Christ," and, on the other, to demonstrate that we can only hope to understand the New Testament in its historical context if we take its own thesis—that Jesus is Lord—seriously.[162]

But this new understanding of the nature of the relationship between history and dogmatics brings with it new uncertainties. There is still more than enough of the liberal theologian in Bonhoeffer for him to be persuaded that Christian dogmatics cannot finally do without the Jesus of history, and that Christianity will not survive unless it can be sure that the present Christ and the historical Jesus are one.[163] "If this were not so," says Bonhoeffer, "then we would have to say with Paul that our faith would be in vain, for then the substance of our church would be taken away."[164] History, though, no longer yields such certainties, and Bonhoeffer is led to secure the required assurance of the historical integrity of the person of Jesus Christ by subordinating history to faith.

He begins by transforming an apparent weakness into a strength. "Absolute certainty about a historical fact is *in itself* not to be had," and would be insufficient in any case. To satisfy the assertions of dogmatics, history must be simultaneously past and present, and this is made possible only by faith in the miracle of the resurrection. We have access to the historical Jesus only "through the Word by which Christ resurrected bears witness to himself."[165] Apart from this, history's verdict on Christ's existence is of no importance.

Bonhoeffer may, perhaps, have aspired to preserve for history a more solid place in Christology if he had said what he apparently meant: that scholarship is necessarily constrained by the fact that the historical Jesus is still largely present and accessible, to theology and to history, *only* from a post-resurrection New Testament perspective; and that we have ultimately to decide for ourselves what this leads us to believe about him.

The Humiliated Christ

That the God-human, Jesus Christ, chooses freely to enter "the world of sin and death," and to conceal himself there "as a beggar among beggars, an outcast among outcasts . . . a sinner among sinners," presents a challenge to Christology.[166] If, says Bonhoeffer, Jesus had not claimed to be the Son of God, or, conversely, if he had worked miracles on demand, people would perhaps have been more likely to follow him, and less likely to condemn him. But they would still have failed to comprehend God's purpose, for if Jesus, when asked whether he was the messiah, had replied by performing a miracle, then he could not have been a human being like us, because "at the decisive moment an exception would have been made."[167]

It is Christ's humiliation that makes "faith in God become human" possible. Only when I am ready to stake my life on the God who has hidden God's self in Jesus Christ can I really be said to believe in God.[168] The church, too, must approach the humiliation of Christ as a practical matter of fact rather than of principle. The church has no need to call attention either to its lowliness or to its power but should instead be ready to receive, new each day, God's will for it in Christ.[169]

In the Christology lectures, his last as a university academic, given shortly after Hitler's rise to power, Christ's presence at the heart of Bonhoeffer's theology is secured.

Discipleship

Bonhoeffer's celebrated reflections on Christian discipleship and the experience of life in purposeful Christian community are contained in two of his most popular works, *Discipleship* and *Life Together*. They are the product of a particular place and time—the Confessing Church's underground seminary near Finkenwalde, which Bonhoeffer directed from July 1935 until it was closed by the Gestapo in September 1937—and have a certain monastic quality which is not to be found in Bonhoeffer's later work but which contributes nonetheless importantly to it.

Bonhoeffer finds, in Mark's account of Levi's decision to follow Christ—"As he was walking along, he saw Levi son of Alphaeus sitting at the tax booth, and he said to him, 'Follow me.' And he got up and followed him" (Mark 2:14)—a fitting description of the nature of Christian discipleship. It is the obedient deed. Jesus Christ, the Son of God, calls, and Levi follows. Nothing heralds the call, and nothing follows it, other than "the obedience of the called."[170] The disciples are compelled by a mysterious power to leave everything behind, "to 'step out' of their previous existence . . . to 'exist' in the strict sense of the word." They are now "bound to Jesus Christ alone."[171] This act of simple obedience is "death to the old self."[172] It is the love of Christ that lives in the disciples, and they live only in him, and in their brothers and sisters as those to whom Jesus comes.

The emphasis in *Discipleship* is on conformity to Christ. This is not something that human beings can achieve for themselves. We cannot remake ourselves in God's image. Rather, in Jesus Christ, "God has created anew the divine image on earth,"[173] and it is this image of God—the form of the crucified and risen Christ—which "seeks to take shape within us" (Gal. 4:19).[174] God's purpose and will for us is that human beings in their entirety (body, soul, and spirit) should bear, and be, the image of God on earth.[175]

Bonhoeffer takes up this theme again in the *Ethics*, where he refers to our being drawn into the form of Jesus Christ not by our own efforts and aspirations—"Christian people do not form the world with their ideas"—but by Jesus Christ himself, as we are conformed by Christ "to the one who has become human."[176] Here the emphasis is on the truly human rather than on the *imago dei*. God became human not that we might become divine, but that we should become "human before God."[177] There is no question, though, of "forcing people to submit to an ideal, a type, or a particular image of the human." Human freedom is not compromised. Rather, to be conformed to Christ means simply to be the person "we really are."[178] Christ, as the God who became human, is always "one and the same," but he takes form "in real human beings, and thus in quite different ways."[179]

In *Discipleship*, Bonhoeffer tells Christians that it is by suffering for Christ's sake that "Christ himself attains visible form within his community."

In this way, they are delivered from the isolating effects of sin. They become truly a part of the whole of humanity, which is borne by him. As such, they too now bear, as followers of Christ and brothers and sisters of all human beings, "the troubles and the sins of all others." The life of the disciple, says Bonhoeffer, is in fact "a life in the image and likeness of Christ's death" (Phil. 3:10; Rom. 6:4f.). Those, however, in whom Christ takes form will share not only in Christ's passion but also in his glorification, as they grow in "perfection in the form of likeness to the image of the Son of God."[180]

All this is possible only where Christ is present, in the church. There is no solitary path to salvation. The church-community is the new human being, "Christ himself,"[181] and it is the Holy Spirit who creates this community, by bringing Christ to individuals, and by gathering individuals into the church. The church-community—as the place of Christ's continuing presence in the world—is the body of Christ; but the risen Christ is Spirit and is present to his church only in this way. Christ now lives in those who believe in him. His life has become their life.[182]

In one of the prison letters, Bonhoeffer recalls a time when he believed he could perhaps come to faith by living "something like a saintly life. I suppose [he says] I wrote *Discipleship* at the end of this path. Today I clearly see the dangers of that book, though I still stand by it."[183] The emphasis in *Discipleship* is on a visible act of separation from the world.[184] But there is also here, as in his earlier work,[185] evidence of a universality in tension with particularity that paves the way for the greater this-worldliness of the *Ethics* and the prison letters; as, for example, when Bonhoeffer writes, "It is true that all human beings as such are 'with Christ' as a consequence of the incarnation, since Jesus bears the whole of human nature. His life, death, and resurrection are thus real events which involve all human beings."[186] And yet, Christians are with Christ "in a special sense."[187]

Life Together

In the Christology lectures and in *Discipleship*, Bonhoeffer describes Christ as the sole mediator of our relationships with God and one another.[188] In *Life Together*, he takes up this theme again. Here, Christ frees us from the demands of a self-centered love that seeks only to bind others to itself. He does this by standing between me and every other, thereby liberating me from the desire to construct for the other a form of my own making. He helps me understand that "God did not make others as I would have made them," or place them under my control. Rather, God has given me the gift of other people "so that I might find the Creator by means of them."[189] We have no cause to interfere with the freedom enjoyed by others. We have simply to accept, affirm, and delight in "the reality of the other's creation by God."[190]

One Reality

It is at most a very short step from Christ the mediator and center of life to a christocentric vision of reality as a whole. And Bonhoeffer takes this step when he tells us that "[i]n Jesus Christ the reality of God has entered into the reality of the world." The answers to all our questions about God and the world are now "enclosed in this name."[191]

Bonhoeffer observes that Christian ethics has traditionally divided reality into opposing realms, "one divine, holy, supernatural, and Christian; the other worldly, profane, natural, and unchristian."[192] Reality is split, and it is the job of Christian ethics to establish an appropriate relationship between the parts—between the realm of grace and the realm of nature. This, says Bonhoeffer, has been accomplished in different ways at different times. For example, "[i]n the high scholastic period the natural realm was subordinated to the realm of grace [whereas i]n pseudo-Lutheranism the autonomy of the orders of this world is proclaimed against the law of Christ."[193] Christ is inevitably diminished by dividing reality. In a divided reality, there will clearly be one or more realities "outside the reality of Christ" to which we have access independently of him. No matter how important we may judge reality in Christ to be, it is always a reality beside others.[194]

Bonhoeffer wants to replace the image of a divided reality with one that is "just as simple and plausible"[195]—the image of "*the one realm of the Christ-reality [Christuswirklichkeit], in which the reality of God and the reality of the world are united.*"[196] There is in truth no other reality. There is only the reality that is given with God's revelation in Christ. Thus, it is no longer possible to "speak rightly of either God or the world without speaking of Jesus Christ."[197]

Peter Dabrock describes the *Christuswirklichkeit* (this "*Gottes* 'Wirklichkeit' in Jesus Christ") as "an irrefutable, personally experienced 'Anspruch' to believers to regard the reality of the world in the *light* of reconciliation." Dabrock leaves *Anspruch* untranslated but clearly understands it at least potentially to encompass an appeal, claim, or demand that "precedes all traditional interpreted constitutions of reality"; while God's revelation is assumed to incorporate the semantic fields of light *and* communication. This "calling 'Anspruch'" engenders "a constant yet fruitful disquiet over against all attempts at exact orientation"—against "all attempts to exaggerate and claim penultimate [contingent] things as ultimate things." Our confidence in the Word should lead us to "distance ourselves from all assumed claims of explaining the world in definite terms."[198] Dabrock reminds us that, even for Christians, the *Christuswirklichkeit* is not objective reality. It is, phenomenologically speaking, a (no matter how personally convincing) construal, a product of the mutual interactions of experience and interpretation. As Dabrock says, "[R]eality neither runs out into the unrelated, unstructured plenitude of data nor exists as a descending function of an *a priori ideatum*."[199]

Bonhoeffer is careful not to press the one reality image to such an extreme as to lose all sense of difference between God and the world. Christian and worldly preoccupations, the supernatural and the natural, the holy and the profane, revelation and reason are each very different from the other but they cannot stand in isolation. "[T]hey behave toward each other polemically, and precisely therein witness to their common reality, their unity in the Christ-reality."[200] In Christ, we are privileged to share one reality with God and, as Marsh suggests, this shared reality, "mediated by Christ alone," insulates us against our own "self-mediated" conceptions of what reality should be.[201]

Two Kingdoms

Bonhoeffer's essentially theological views on the nature of reality draw selectively on traditional Lutheran approaches to social order, and on his own historical experience. Of particular significance in this context is Bonhoeffer's understanding of Luther's two kingdoms doctrine, and its implications not only for the concept of one reality, or realm, in Christ but also for the relationship between church and state.

Green believes Luther's doctrine of the two kingdoms to give "too much authority and autonomy" to the state and "too little responsibility and initiative in corporate life" to the Christian.[202] Bonhoeffer, he argues, was able to transcend two kingdoms thinking by placing the ego, transformed by Christ, rather than the conscience, consumed by guilt, at the heart of soteriology. Thus, when Christ transforms "the strong ego ... corrupted by power ... into the strong ego which serves others," he changes the nature of the "relationship between the Christian and politics, the church and the state." The church enters the political arena.[203]

DeJonge, though, contends that Green, and others, have been misled by a way of thinking which has its origins in the German history of religions school (*Religionsgeschischtliche Schule*), and specifically in Ernst Troeltsch—a way of thinking which, with the very able support of Reinhold Niebuhr, came to dominate twentieth-century American "interpretations of Luther's social ethics in general and his two-kingdoms thinking in particular."[204] While Luther, according to DeJonge, used two kingdoms language expansively to describe both "the twofold way in which God relates to the world through preservation and redemption, and the twofold form of Christian existence that is oriented both to God and others,"[205] the Troeltsch-Niebuhr line of thinking led to a narrowly dualistic understanding of the two kingdoms, and to their more or less exclusive association with the concepts of church and state.

Bonhoeffer's own understanding of the divine ordering of relations between church and state draws substantially on Luther's two kingdoms doctrine, but his sense of duality is carefully nuanced. In the lectures on "The Nature of the Church," Bonhoeffer emphasizes not only the respective autonomy of church and state but also God's sovereignty over both ("God's word has power also over the state"), as well as the church's duty to defend itself against encroachment by the state ("[o]bedience to the state exists only when the state does not threaten the word").[206] The state's autonomy is circumscribed. A year later, in his Christology lectures, Bonhoeffer says of the two kingdoms, "As long as Christ was on earth, he alone was the kingdom of God. Since he was crucified, it is as if his form [Gestalt] is broken into the right hand and the left hand of God. He can now be recognized only in twofold form, as church and state."[207] Christ is present in *both* church and state, and properly so only if both church *and* state remain true to him. The state is justified by Christ but not unconditionally. "A state that threatens the proclamation of the Christian message negates itself," and the church is then obliged to do everything it can (it may, in some circumstances, even "seize the wheel" of the state itself) to turn this situation around.[208]

In the *Ethics*, too, Bonhoeffer describes the relationship between church and state in the language of the two kingdoms.

> There are two kingdoms [Zwei Reiche], which . . . must never be mixed together, yet never torn apart: the kingdom of the proclaimed word of God and the kingdom of the sword, the kingdom of the church and the kingdom of the world. . . . The sword can never bring about the unity of the church and faith; preaching can never rule the peoples. But the lord of both kingdoms is God revealed in Jesus Christ. . . . The bearers of both of these offices are accountable to God.[209]

Christ is the source of all true unity, both in and outside the church. Only through and in him do all things come, and remain, together. As DeJonge observes, "there is nothing in this 1940 account that differentiates it substantially from the earliest two-kingdoms account in 'The Nature of the Church' from 1932."[210] Green revisits, but does not modify, his own understanding of Bonhoeffer's two kingdoms thinking in the introduction to the *Ethics*, where he writes that, having posited a single God-world reality in Christ, Bonhoeffer then "proceeds to a vigorous polemic against thinking in 'two realms.'"[211] DeJonge allows that Green here correctly identifies the importance of Bonhoeffer's critique of the "pseudo-Lutheran division of reality into two realms or two spheres," but that he appears simultaneously to overlook the distinction Bonhoeffer makes between realms (*Räume*) and kingdoms (*Reiche*).[212]

The words *Raum* and *Reich* are not interchangeable. Bonhoeffer, as we have seen, understands two realms thinking to divide reality into hostile spheres (one holy and one profane), and thus to reckon with "realities outside the reality of Christ." As long, says Bonhoeffer, as Christ and the world are conceived as opposing realms (*Räume*), we must choose between two equally unsatisfactory alternatives: "either we place ourselves in one of the two realms, wanting Christ without the world or the world without Christ . . . [o]r we try to stand in the two realms at the same time, thereby becoming people in eternal conflict."[213]

We must not, though, confuse two realms thinking (which Bonhoeffer believes should now make way for the one realm of the *Christuswirklichkeit*) with Luther's two kingdoms, where the freedom of the one to proclaim God's Word and of the other to preserve law and order is in each case subject to God's overriding sovereignty and has no otherwise unchanging character of its own. Bonhoeffer did not "transcend" Luther's two kingdoms thinking, but he did reject its "pseudo-Lutheran" applications. Bonhoeffer consistently understood the two kingdoms (as church and state) each to enjoy a qualified autonomy, and a conditional legitimacy, based on mutually reinforcing commitments to live by the cross of Christ.

Vicarious Representative Action

I have previously described the concept of vicarious representative action (*Stellvertretung*) in its christological-ecclesiastical context. In the *Ethics*, we meet it again, embedded now in a much more complex, ambiguous, and thoroughly worldly milieu. It is still christological, but no longer functions, as it does in *Sanctorum Communio*, exclusively to describe a virtuous life in loving church-community.[214]

In the *Ethics*, *Stellvertretung* is bound up with the *Christuswirklichkeit*, with the Christ-centered unity of God and the world, and "the already accomplished reconciliation of the world with God." Vicarious representative action is responsible action taken on behalf, and for the love, of all human beings.[215] Bonhoeffer dismisses as a fiction the notion of the "ethical isolation of the individual."[216] We live rather in the ethical situation of encounter, which necessarily entails accepting responsibility for other people. Responsible action is worldly action, risked in faith and freely undertaken. There is no appeal to principles, to people, to history, or indeed to anything that could compromise the responsible actor's freedom of decision.[217] Responsible action takes place "in the twilight that the historical situation casts upon good and evil" and, as responsible actors, we must decide "not simply between right and wrong, good and evil, but between right and right, wrong and wrong."[218] This means that we can never be sure we have done the right thing, because we have effectively renounced any claim to possess, as a human competence, "an ultimately dependable knowledge of good and evil."[219] But we are not without support and guidance, for "[t]he deed that is done, after responsibly weighing all circumstances in light of God's becoming human in Christ, is completely surrendered to God the moment it is carried out."[220] Discernment, says Bonhoeffer, "arises from the knowledge of being preserved, held, and guided by the will of God. . . . And daily it seeks anew to solidify this knowledge in concrete living." It does not question the "unity that has been regained in Jesus. Instead, it presupposes it, and yet must gain it ever anew."[221] We must try to discern God's will for each occasion and, having done this to the best of our ability, place our trust in Christ, and our hope in God's forgiveness.

As responsible human beings, we are both bound and free: bound *to* other human beings and to God; and free *for* them. We are bound by the requirement to act both responsibly and contextually; and (unavoidably) free to choose the actions for which we will be held accountable![222] True responsibility, Bonhoeffer insists, must have this ambiguous quality. To emphasize only obedience would be to reduce responsibility to "Kant's ethic of duty"; while to make freedom wholly sovereign could lead only to "a romantic ethic of genius." Each of these approaches affirms itself and requires no further justification. Responsible human beings, on the other hand, are justified "neither by their bond nor by their freedom, but only . . . [by] the One who has placed them in this—humanly impossible—situation and who requires them to act."[223]

Responsible life, says DeJonge, "holds together . . . the critique of life in the name of the good and the performance of the good in the context of life."[224] Neither a simple, pseudo-Lutheran affirmation of the status quo nor a simple, radical, or "enthusiastic" rebellion from it will suffice, for we now live "stretched between the Yes and the No."[225] God's will is revealed only in God's Word, which comes new to us each day. It is not to be deduced from ethical or religious principles. Or is it in fact the case, Bonhoeffer asks himself in the course of a Meditation on Psalm 119, written in the winter of 1939–1940, that "I already live so much by the skeleton of my own principles that perhaps I would no longer even sense it were God one day to withdraw his living commandment from me?"[226]

A PROGRESSIVELY MORE INCLUSIVE THEOLOGY

Bethge traces the roots of Bonhoeffer's new theology all the way back to his early Christology, and notes, in this context, a change in the nature of Christ's claim on the world. By the time we come to the prison letters, "the one-sided cry of 'the world for Christ,'" so evident in *Discipleship*, has found a counterpoint in "Christ for the world."[227] The church, says Bethge, as the place where Christ is present, had long monopolized Bonhoeffer's attention, but now the world assumes new importance as "the sphere of the regnum Christi."[228] Feil also speaks of a turn to the world, again facilitated by a change in Bonhoeffer's christological emphasis, whereby the Christ "for us" of the lectures on Christology becomes the Christ "for others" of the prison letters.[229]

In his doctoral dissertation, the young Bonhoeffer makes his initial position clear in a syllogism. Community with God, he says, "exists only through Christ, but Christ is present only in his church-community, and *therefore community with God exists only in the church.*"[230] It logically follows that anyone who is not in the church has no real life with Christ.[231] There is, though, always a tension in Bonhoeffer's work between this rigorous Christian exclusiveness, rooted in ecclesiology, and a more accommodating inclusiveness, embedded in Christology. We see this, for example, even in *Discipleship* where Bonhoeffer says that Christ "has restored the image of God for all who bear a human countenance,"[232] and that no one is excluded from the presence of Christ, "since Jesus bears the whole of human nature." Yet Christians are with Christ "in a special sense" because they have come to know him as Immanuel, "God with us."[233]

Bonhoeffer does not seek formally to resolve the tension between his conventionally exclusive ecclesiology and his progressively more inclusive Christology until he comes to write the *Ethics*, by which time he is ready to adopt a more nuanced approach to the relationship between Christ, his church, and the rest of humanity. There we read, "The human being, accepted, judged, and awakened to new life by God—this is Jesus Christ, this is the whole of humanity in Christ, this is us."[234] While this sentiment is not new, he now goes on to give it a more explicitly inclusive character. "In Christ the form of humanity was created anew. What was at stake was not a matter of place, time, climate, race, individual, society, religion, or taste, but nothing less than the life of humanity, which recognized here its image and its hope."[235] To understand this properly, we must look to the body of Jesus Christ, to "the one who became human, was crucified, and is risen," wherein all human beings, without exception, are reconciled and united with God.[236]

> There is no part of the world, no matter how lost, no matter how godless, that has not been accepted by God in Jesus Christ and reconciled to God. Whoever perceives the body of Jesus Christ in faith can no longer speak of the world as if it were lost, as if it were separated from God. . . . The world belongs to Christ, and only in Christ is the world what it is. . . . Everything would be spoiled if we were to reserve Christ for the church. . . . Christ has died for the world, and Christ is Christ only in the midst of the world.[237]

Bonhoeffer here favors us with a strikingly clear, simple, yet comprehensive account of the place occupied by Jesus Christ in the Christian universe. The world belongs to Christ and Christ to the world. Through him, all creation is reconciled with God. No one and nothing is lost. No one is excluded from Christ's all-inclusive work of redemption.

Bonhoeffer seeks to balance the competing claims of Christian exclusiveness and inclusiveness with reference to the apparently contradictory statements in Matthew 12:30 ("Whoever is not for me is against me") and Mark 9:40 ("Whoever is not against us is for us"). These sayings "belong together, one as the exclusive claim . . . and the other as the all-encompassing claim . . . of Jesus Christ." In isolation, the first "leads to fanaticism and sectarianism," and the second "to the secularization and capitulation of the church." Together, however, they reveal, in the exclusive confession of Christ as Lord, the true "breadth," or inclusiveness, of Christ's lordship.[238]

Bonhoeffer's understanding of Christ's presence and place in the world broadens and deepens over time, losing in the process much of its early ecclesial rigidity. In Jesus Christ, the God who became human embraces human nature in its totality. Through Jesus Christ, all humanity—and, indeed, all creation—is reconciled with God. Bonhoeffer is able finally to accept, and to assimilate, the idea of *apocatastasis*, which troubled him in his youth as he wrote the final pages of *Sanctorum Communio*.

But there remains a huge problem of ignorance and forgetfulness. Christ is Lord of all creation, but most of his creatures do not recognize him. His form is still to be discerned only in the church, whose function it will always be to proclaim God's revelation to the world. Bonhoeffer now sees though that the church may only be called the body of Christ "because in the body of Jesus Christ *human beings per se* . . . have really been taken on."[239] The church "bears the form that . . . is meant for all people"[240] and is obliged to address the whole of humanity in this light—in the light of the form which humanity "has already received, but which it has not grasped and accepted, namely, the form of Jesus Christ that is its own."[241]

CONCLUSION

In the new theology of the *Letters and Papers from Prison*, Bonhoeffer, as John de Gruchy observes, is looking for a way of speaking about "the God of Jesus Christ" without having to depend on a religious worldview which is no longer viable.[242] He wants to know how God intends to sustain God's self-revelation—to know "who" Christ is—in a world that has come to believe it has no further need of God. To this end, Bonhoeffer, having previously affirmed the unity of God and the world in the one reality of Jesus Christ, now seeks to ground his christological understanding not in God's power but in Christ's powerlessness and self-emptying love.

In a remarkable series of letters, smuggled out of a military prison at intervals during the spring and summer of 1944, Bonhoeffer provides us with a preliminary sketch of his concept of religionless Christianity. He begins with a restatement of the "who" question: "who is Christ actually for us today?"—a question now made more urgent by the approach of "a completely religionless age."[243]

In "this world that has come of age,"[244] what has always been true has now become inescapable for Christians. The powerful God of religion is not to be found in Jesus Christ. In him, they are drawn not to the *deus ex machina* but rather to "an event that takes place in the deepest desolation of human life, on the cross."[245] Christians must free themselves of the delusion that God is the answer to life's "so-called ultimate questions";[246] that God represents a last, secure refuge from life's uncertainties. Their hope lies not in the almighty God of religion but in the crucified God of the Bible "who gains ground and power in the world by being powerless." God *is*, for Christians, the encounter with Jesus Christ. No other genuine experience of God is possible for them. As such, they are called "to share in God's suffering at the hands of a godless world,"[247] and can do this only by living thoroughly worldly lives. Faith is participating in the being of Jesus, in his "becoming human," his cross, and resurrection.[248] In his "being for others" is their being for others, in the act of following him.

We cannot, of course, be sure where Bonhoeffer would have taken these ideas if he had survived the war, for as he says of the "Outline for a Book," in the last of the prison letters to Bethge, "it has all been so little discussed that it often comes out too clumsily."[249] But we certainly have a better idea of where the new theology is likely to have led him when account is taken of his broader theology. And this gives me confidence that Bonhoeffer would have abandoned neither the radical christocentrism nor the rejection of "individualistic social atomism"[250] which serves essentially to define the whole of his theology, and which so clearly shapes his concepts of revelation, person, freedom, responsibility, and one reality in Christ. Much of this, as will be seen in chapter 6, fits easily into a more substantial account of religionless Christianity than is available to us in the *Letters and Papers from Prison*.

In addition, however, to the selective embrace of continuities in Bonhoeffer's theology, we have also to take account of the considerably more inclusive view of Christ's place in the world that emerges, particularly, in the *Ethics*. While it is still the case in the *Ethics* that, although Jesus "bears the whole of human nature,"[251] only the church is likely to recognize him,[252] the language of inclusiveness is more robust and assured than it is in Bonhoeffer's earlier writings. The world now belongs to Christ and Christ to the world. No one is excluded from Christ's work of redemption,[253] and the church can only truly proclaim Christ "as the one in whom God has [already] bodily taken on [all] humanity."[254]

Bonhoeffer raises some important questions about the possible future shape and direction of a religionless Christianity in his initial reflections on the implications for Christianity of "a complete absence of religion."[255] How, he asks, might Christians speak "in a worldly way about God?"[256] "Is there such a thing as a religionless Christian?" "How can Christ become Lord of the religionless as well?"[257] It is quite possible that Bonhoeffer, with thoughts pouring out of him in this quite unguarded letter to his closest friend, understands himself to be asking much the same question in various ways; but he isn't. He is asking three different ones. The first is the question of nonreligious interpretation. How do Christians "talk about God—without religion?"[258] Do they need a new language among themselves, or only for outsiders? The second question focuses on the integrity of belief. Can faith really be separated from religion? Is it possible for a Christian to abandon the intellectual, emotional, symbolic, and practical trappings of religion, and remain true to Christ? The third question is truly the question of inclusiveness. There is, as Bonhoeffer says, "no explaining the mystery that only a part of humanity recognizes the form of its savior."[259] This has always been the case, and it is hard to imagine the Lordship of Christ becoming more, rather than less, obvious to people in a religionless world. But then perhaps a genuinely religionless form of Christianity would allow the light of Christ to shine more brightly than ever, including in those "lost" and "godless" parts of the world which have yet to comprehend the form of Jesus Christ which already belongs to them.

These, as I have said, are different questions, but they are by no means unrelated. And all depend, to a significant degree, on the approach taken to the first question—the question of (nonreligious) interpretation—to which I now turn.

NOTES

1. Bethge, *Dietrich Bonhoeffer*, 860.
2. Feil, *The Theology of Dietrich Bonhoeffer*, 54–55.
3. *Letters and Papers*, DBWE 8: 363.
4. *Letters and Papers*, DBWE 8: 480.
5. *Letters and Papers*, DBWE 8: 363.
6. Feil, *The Theology of Dietrich Bonhoeffer*, xv.
7. Feil, *The Theology of Dietrich Bonhoeffer*, 67.
8. Charles Marsh, *Reclaiming Dietrich Bonhoeffer* (New York: Oxford University Press, 1994), 103.

9. Wüstenberg, *A Theology of Life*, xiv.
10. "Lectures on Christology," DBWE 12: 338.
11. Christopher R. J. Holmes, "Beyond Bonhoeffer in Loyalty to Bonhoeffer: Reconsidering Bonhoeffer's Christological Aversion to Theological Metaphysics," in *Christ, Church and World: New Studies in Bonhoeffer's Theology and Ethics*, ed. Michael Mawson and Philip G. Ziegler (London: Bloomsbury T&T Clark, 2016), 36.
12. Holmes, "Beyond Bonhoeffer in Loyalty to Bonhoeffer: Reconsidering Bonhoeffer's Christological Aversion to Theological Metaphysics," in Mawson and Ziegler, 40.
13. "Lectures on Christology," DBWE 12: 301.
14. Holmes, "Beyond Bonhoeffer in Loyalty to Bonhoeffer: Reconsidering Bonhoeffer's Christological Aversion to Theological Metaphysics," in Mawson and Ziegler, 38.
15. Dietrich Bonhoeffer, "Outline on Exodus 20: 2–3 (Student Notes) as a Sermon for Trinity Sunday," in *Theological Education at Finkenwalde*, DBWE 14: 636.
16. Holmes, "Beyond Bonhoeffer in Loyalty to Bonhoeffer: Reconsidering Bonhoeffer's Christological Aversion to Theological Metaphysics," in Mawson and Ziegler, 35.
17. Pangritz, "Who Is Jesus Christ, For Us, Today?" in de Gruchy, *Cambridge Companion*, 134. *Cantus firmus*: "In a polyphonic composition, the primary, steady voice to which the other voices relate." *Letters and Papers*, DBWE 8: 394, ed. fn. 7.
18. *Letters and Papers*, DBWE 8: 362. This is not of course a new question. As Barker reminds us, it is asked of every generation of believers. The Christian life is "always more than a reflection on and adherence to a set of principles or doctrines. The confession of faith leads to a life of discipleship. And because the way Christ is identified in the mind and heart of the believers affects their view of the world and approach to the world, that question is particularly important." H. Gaylon Barker, *The Cross of Reality: Luther's Theologia Crucis and Bonhoeffer's Christology* (Augsburg Fortress, Publishers, 2015), 418–19.
19. *Letters and Papers*, DBWE 8: 364.
20. *Letters and Papers*, DBWE 8: 426–27.
21. "At three o'clock Jesus cried out with a loud voice, 'Eloi, Eloi, lema sabachthani?' which means, 'My God, my God, why have you forsaken me?'" (Mark 15:34).
22. "This was to fulfill what had been spoken through the prophet Isaiah, 'He took our infirmities and bore our diseases'" (Matt. 8:17, referring to Isa. 53:4).
23. *Letters and Papers*, DBWE 8: 478–79.
24. *Letters and Papers*, DBWE 8: 479.
25. *Letters and Papers*, DBWE 8: 479. Hall finds in Bonhoeffer a twentieth-century exponent of Luther's theology of the cross (*theologia crucis*), which sees in Christ's passion not "a substitutionary sacrifice on the part of the one good man who in this way placates a wrathful God, but rather . . . *God* suffering in solidarity with alienated humanity." Douglas John Hall, "Dietrich Bonhoeffer and the Ethics of Participation," www.ucalgary.ca/christchair/files/christchair/Hall_D.Bonhoeffer.PDFfile (accessed April 26, 2017), 7. Green compares Luther's suffering God with Bonhoeffer's sense of Christ's powerlessness. As, he says, Luther's *theologia crucis* "was in

part a polemic against the *theologia gloriae* of scholasticism, so Bonhoeffer's 'weak Christ' is a polemic against the 'power God' of religion." Green, *Theology of Sociality*, 271. Barker believes Bonhoeffer's christocentrism inevitably to give expression to a *theologia crucis*. We know God only "in and through Jesus Christ. And the key to understanding Jesus Christ for us lies in the cross. At the cross all human schemes and plans are brought to naught." The cross is God's way to us. There is no other way. "If we want to find God, we must go to where God has chosen to place himself." Barker, *Cross of Reality*, 420.

26. *Conspiracy and Imprisonment*, DBWE 16: 284.
27. Wolfgang Huber, "Bonhoeffer and Modernity," in Floyd and Marsh, 13.
28. *Letters and Papers*, DBWE 8: 479–80. De Gruchy observes that to speak of God's powerlessness "is shocking to our normal sensibilities of divinity. But no more than when Paul told the Corinthian church that Christ crucified is the power of God at work in human life and the world" (1 Cor. 1:23–25). Such language, he suggests, "radically challenges the human will to power" which gives rise, ineluctably, to violence. In the violence of the cross, and against its human perpetrators, "the mystery of God's power and wisdom is revealed as unfathomable love." John W. de Gruchy, *Led into Mystery* (London: SCM Press, 2013), 127.
29. *Letters and Papers*, DBWE 8: 480.
30. *Letters and Papers*, DBWE 8: 480.
31. *Letters and Papers*, DBWE 8: 486.
32. *Letters and Papers*, DBWE 8: 486.
33. *Letters and Papers*, DBWE 8: 480.
34. Peter Frick, "Nietzsche and Bonhoeffer," in *Bonhoeffer's Intellectual Formation*, ed. Peter Frick (Tübingen: Mohr Siebeck, 2008), 192, 198.
35. *Theological Education at Finkenwalde*, DBWE 14: 168.
36. H. Gaylon Barker, "Without God, We Live with God. Listening to Bonhoeffer's Witness in Today's Public Square," in de Gruchy, Plant, and Tietz, 163.
37. *Letters and Papers*, DBWE 8: 213.
38. *Letters and Papers*, DBWE 8: 213–14.
39. *Letters and Papers*, DBWE 8: 447.
40. *Letters and Papers*, DBWE 8: 447–48. Bonhoeffer, says Hall, "assumes that the Christian community can only learn what it may have to *bring* to the world's healing by first participating in the suffering that is actually present." Hall, "Bonhoeffer and the Ethics of Participation," 14. This-worldliness is characteristic of Luther's (and Bonhoeffer's) *theologia crucis*. "It is really about God's abiding commitment to the world." Hall, "Bonhoeffer and the Ethics of Participation," 8. The classical expression of the theology of the cross is to be found in Paul ("We proclaim Christ crucified . . ." 1 Cor. 1–2), but, says Hall, there is a "greater background" to this tradition to be discerned in the Hebraic prophetic consciousness of divine pathos, in the recognition that God suffers because God's creatures suffer. The *theologia crucis* sees the *passio Christi* as historically continuous with Hebraic divine pathos, and thus "unites the testimony of Israel and the Church in a way that ecclesiastical triumphalism [or *theologia gloriae*] has never done." Hall, "Bonhoeffer and the Ethics of Participation," 6. Bonhoeffer well understood the critical significance of this link for his times. He says in the *Ethics*, for example: "The historical Jesus Christ is the continuity of our

history. . . . Jesus Christ was the promised Messiah of the Israelite-Jewish people. . . . Western history is by God's will inextricably bound up with the people of Israel, not just genetically but in an honest, unceasing encounter. . . . Driving out the Jew(s) from the West must result in driving out Christ with them, for Christ was a Jew." *Ethics*, DBWE 6: 105.

41. *Letters and Papers*, DBWE 8: 448.
42. *Letters and Papers*, DBWE 8: 450.
43. Dietrich Bonhoeffer, "Meditation on Psalm 119," in *Theological Education Underground*, DBWE 15: 519.
44. *Letters and Papers*, DBWE 8: 448.
45. "Meditation on Psalm 119," DBWE 15: 522.
46. *Letters and Papers*, DBWE 8: 366.
47. *Letters and Papers*, DBWE 8: 394.
48. *Letters and Papers*, DBWE 8: 501.
49. *Letters and Papers*, DBWE 8: 501. The phrase "being for others" has strong Lutheran roots. Bainton, in his life of Martin Luther, claims the heart of Luther's ethic to reside in the conviction that "a Christian must be a Christ to his neighbor." Bainton quotes Luther's *On the Freedom of the Christian Man*: "I will give myself as a sort of Christ to my neighbor as Christ gave himself for me." Luther thus understands Christians to live not for themselves but for love of Christ and other people. Roland H. Bainton, *Here I Stand: A Life of Martin Luther* (Nashville: Abingdon Press, 1978), 231.
50. *Letters and Papers*, DBWE 8: 501.
51. *Letters and Papers*, DBWE 8: 501.
52. Bethge, *Dietrich Bonhoeffer*, 886.
53. *Letters and Papers*, DBWE 8: 503–4.
54. *Ethics*, DBWE 6: 139.
55. *Ethics*, DBWE 6: 140.
56. *Ethics*, DBWE 6: 141. Elsewhere in the *Ethics*, Bonhoeffer gives a remarkable description of the appalling consequences of succumbing to a Nazi view of the world. Here,

"[n]othing is fixed, and nothing holds on. . . . Events of world-historical significance, along with the most terrible crimes, leave no trace behind in the forgetful soul. . . . What is quiet, lasting, and essential is discarded as worthless. . . . [T]he foundation of historical life—trust in all its forms—is destroyed. Because truth is not trusted, specious propaganda takes over. Because justice is not trusted, whatever is useful is declared to be just."

All that remains is "fear of nothingness," in the face of which people are ready to surrender everything: "their own judgment, their humanity, their neighbors. Where this fear is exploited without scruple, there are no limits to what can be achieved." *Ethics*, DBWE 6: 129–31.

57. *Letters and Papers*, DBWE 8: 500.
58. *Letters and Papers*, DBWE 8: 389.
59. *Letters and Papers*, DBWE 8: 514. As the Roman Catholic theologian Nicholas Lash says so eloquently: "It is . . . *Jesus* who is confessed to be God's Word made flesh; it is his life, and history, and destiny, that speak to us, inviting our response.

There is no other word in God but this one Word which finds fully focused form and expression, in the created order, in the history of the Crucified. Nothing, therefore, is to be gained by attempting, as it were, to listen to something else, to listen 'beyond' Jesus, for some other word than that which he is said to be." Nicholas Lash, *Holiness, Speech and Silence: Reflections on the Question of God* (Aldershot, HR: Ashgate Publishing Limited, 2004), 76.

60. *Letters and Papers*, DBWE 8: 515.

61. *Letters and Papers*, DBWE 8: 515.

62. Bethge, *Dietrich Bonhoeffer*, 860.

63. *Sanctorum Communio* is sub-titled: *A Theological Study of the Sociology of the Church*.

64. *Sanctorum Communio*, DBWE 1: 127.

65. *Sanctorum Communio*, DBWE 1: 141. The translators of the first volume of the definitive German edition of Bonhoeffer's writings (*Dietrich Bonhoeffer Werke, Band 1*) found his use of the noun *Gemeinde* (community) as a theological term for the church especially challenging. In his introduction to the English-language edition, Green says that Bonhoeffer essentially meant by *Gemeinde*, "Christ present as *sanctorum communio*." As such, it provides "the theological norm for 'church.'" Green continues: "When Bonhoeffer says, 'the church [*Kirche*] is Christ existing as *Gemeinde*,' this does not mean that an institution calling itself church defines where Christ is communally present. On the contrary, it is not a church organisation that defines Christ, but Christ who defines the church. In other words, it is precisely where, and only where, 'Christ-exists-as-*Gemeinde*' that we find the 'church' (*Kirche*)." Green stresses the later practical significance of this distinction for Bonhoeffer in the context of the *Kirchenkampf* (church struggle) against National Socialism. A church is not "church" simply because it might look like one, complete with clergy, congregations, scripture, laws, and traditions. The church is to be found only where Christ is truly "present in communal word and sacrament." But if, on the one hand, Bonhoeffer wished to avoid "making the community of Christ a creature or function of the church institution," he was just as concerned not "to sever the *Gemeinde Christi* from the empirical, institutional church with all its faults." Christ cannot be separated from his church. (There is, for Bonhoeffer, "*no relation to Christ in which the relation to the church [Kirche] is not necessarily established as well.*" *Sanctorum Communio*, DBWE 1: 127.) Bonhoeffer, says Green, clearly "does not regard *Gemeinde* as a theological term for a Christocentric community and *Kirche* as merely a sociological term for describing an empirical, religious institution." The two words must be related theologically. Thus, while some earlier translators of Bonhoeffer have used "church" and others "community" for *Gemeinde*, the translators of *Dietrich Bonhoeffer Werke, Band 1* have used the two in tandem. In *Sanctorum Communio*, the term "church-community" is employed theologically to underscore the communal nature of the *sanctorum communio*, while also calling attention to the connection between *Gemeinde* and its sociological equivalent, *Gemeinschaft*. Moreover, "it links by translation the words *Kirche* and *Gemeinde*, so that Bonhoeffer's intention to define and constitute the former by the latter is honoured." Clifford J. Green, Introduction, *Sanctorum Communio*, DBWE 1: 14–16.

66. *Sanctorum Communio*, DBWE 1: 141.
67. *Sanctorum Communio*, DBWE 1: 153.
68. *Sanctorum Communio*, DBWE 1: 161.
69. *Sanctorum Communio*, DBWE 1: 139.
70. *Sanctorum Communio*, DBWE 1: 209.
71. *Sanctorum Communio*, DBWE 1: 158.
72. *Sanctorum Communio*, DBWE 1: 286–87.
73. *Sanctorum Communio*, DBWE 1: 33.
74. *Sanctorum Communio*, DBWE 1: 45.
75. *Sanctorum Communio*, DBWE 1: 49.
76. *Sanctorum Communio*, DBWE 1: 50, ed. fn. 56.
77. Bonhoeffer distinguishes between the *metaphysical* concept of "the individual," which is defined "without mediation" (i.e. thought to exist in and of itself), and the intrinsically *ethical* concept of "person," which is based, necessarily, "on ethical-social interaction." *Sanctorum Communio*, DBWE 1: 50.
78. *Sanctorum Communio*, DBWE 1: 48.
79. *Sanctorum Communio*, DBWE 1: 50, 54. Later, in *Act and Being*, Bonhoeffer acknowledges what is for him, and from a theological point of view, a serious flaw in the I-You argument—an argument which draws substantially on the dialogical personalism of the philosopher Eberhard Grisebach. Grisebach, says Bonhoeffer, correctly saw that "[o]ne way or another, every system blends reality-truth-I into one; it arrogates to itself the power to understand and to have disposition over reality." But reality cannot in fact be systematized, captured, or confined in this way. It can only ever be "'experienced' in the contingent fact of the claim of the 'others.' Only what comes from 'outside' can direct people to their reality, their existence. In 'taking on' the 'claim of the other,' I exist in reality, I act ethically." *Act and Being*, DBWE 2: 87. While, however, the dialogical approach (and any theology which establishes itself on this foundation) may indeed recognise the claim of the neighbor as a valid, though still self-enclosed, ethical claim on our attention, it has no capacity to recognise the real "from outside" which gives rise to it. No, says Bonhoeffer, "the 'from outside' is perceived alone in what in the first place enables human beings to understand the 'from outside' adequately, namely in revelation through faith." *Act and Being*, DBWE 2: 89. As Bonhoeffer says in his inaugural lecture: "What is really new in Grisebach's position is that he cannot conceive the human being apart from the concrete other person. This position clearly expresses the will to overcome every sort of individualism, that is, any restricting of the I only within itself. Grisebach manages to do this, however, only by absolutizing the You in the place of the I and attributing to it a status belonging only to God. Hence the I posits the other as absolute, acknowledges that other as its concrete, absolute boundary only to have its own absolute essence ultimately returned to it through [the] absolute You [which it posits and could just as easily relativize]." Dietrich Bonhoeffer, "Inaugural Lecture: The Anthropological Question in Contemporary Philosophy and Theology," in *Barcelona, Berlin, New York*, DBWE 10: 398–99.
80. *Creation and Fall*, DBWE 3: 63.
81. "Sermon on Matthew 28:20," DBWE 10: 494–95.

82. *Sanctorum Communio*, DBWE 1: 54–55.

83. Jens Zimmermann, "Dietrich Bonhoeffer and Martin Heidegger: Two Different Visions of Humanity," in Gregor and Zimmermann, 124.

84. *Letters and Papers*, DBWE 8: 501.

85. *Sanctorum Communio*, DBWE 1: 55.

86. Christiane Tietz, "The Role of Jesus Christ for Christian Theology," in Mawson and Ziegler, 16.

87. *Sanctorum Communio*, DBWE 1: 147. Green, in an editorial footnote to the *Ethics*, describes *Stellvertretung* as "taking the place, *Stelle*, and thus standing in for, *Vertretung*, another, representing them, acting on their behalf and for their sake." *Ethics*, DBWE 6: 257, ed. fn. 41. *Stellvertretung* appears as "deputyship" in some earlier translations of *Ethics* but is translated "vicarious representative action" in the critical English edition. DeJonge sees in this word an expression of Bonhoeffer's conviction that there is in fact no such person as the completely isolated ethical individual, "for if ethical action is always in some way action also for others, then all ethical action has the character of *Stellvertretung*." DeJonge, *Luther*, 244. Responsible action, says Bonhoeffer, is vicarious representative action, and "[n]obody can altogether escape responsibility. . . . [E]ven those who are alone live as vicarious representatives." *Ethics*, DBWE 6: 257–58. Stassen emphasises the essentially compassionate nature of *Stellvertretung*. Vicarious representative action is not just a matter of representing others (in some formal or symbolic manner), of stepping in for them, or of taking their place. It is also, and more importantly, an empathetic entering into the very lives of others, and signifies as such a deliberate decision to see the world through others' eyes and willingly to assume its burdens on their behalf. Glen Harold Stassen, *A Thicker Jesus: Incarnational Discipleship in a Secular Age* (Louisville, KY: Westminster John Knox Press, 2012), 152–53, 219.

88. *Sanctorum Communio*, DBWE 1: 155–56.

89. *Sanctorum Communio*, DBWE 1: 146.

90. Jesus dies "a criminal," but it is "vicarious representative love [that] triumphs on the criminal's cross, obedience to God triumphs over sin, and thereby sin is actually punished and overcome." *Sanctorum Communio*, DBWE 1: 156.

91. *Sanctorum Communio*, DBWE 1: 191.

92. Daniel L. Migliore, *Faith Seeking Understanding*, 2nd ed. (Grand Rapids: Eerdmans, 2004), 184–85.

93. *Ethics*, DBWE 6: 238.

94. Wayne Whitson Floyd, "Kant, Hegel and Bonhoeffer," in Frick, 95–96.

95. "The Anthropological Question," DBWE 10: 399–400.

96. "Theology of Crisis," DBWE 10: 468.

97. "Theology of Crisis," DBWE 10: 473–74.

98. *Act and Being*, DBWE 2: 89–90.

99. Wayne Whitson Floyd, Introduction, *Act and Being*, DBWE 2: 17.

100. *Act and Being*, DBWE 2: 107–8.

101. *Act and Being*, DBWE 2: 27–28.

102. Floyd, Introduction, *Act and Being*, DBWE 2: 7.

103. Floyd, Introduction, *Act and Being*, DBWE 2: 8.

104. Floyd, Introduction, *Act and Being*, DBWE 2: 19.
105. Floyd, Introduction, *Act and Being*, DBWE 2: 10.
106. Floyd, "Kant, Hegel and Bonhoeffer," in Frick, 102.
107. Bonhoeffer believed Hegel and his successors to have attempted to overcome "the ontological resistance" of the thing-in-itself by including it in "the movement of consciousness." Floyd, "Kant, Hegel and Bonhoeffer," in Frick, 86. "In the very moment when the Idealists pushed away the 'Ding an sich,'" says Bonhoeffer, "Kant's critical philosophy was destroyed.... Kant had tried to limit human thinking, in order to establish it anew. But Hegel saw that limits only can be set from beyond these limits. That means applied to Kant, that his attempt to limit reason by reason presupposes that reason must have already passed beyond the limits before it sets them.... Thinking as such is boundless, it pulls transcendental reality into its circle." "Theology of Crisis," DBWE 10: 472.
108. Floyd, Introduction, *Act and Being*, DBWE 2: 12.
109. *Act and Being*, DBWE 2: 107.
110. Floyd, "Kant, Hegel and Bonhoeffer," in Frick, 103.
111. *Act and Being*, DBWE 2: 108–9.
112. *Act and Being*, DBWE 2: 134.
113. *Act and Being*, DBWE 2: 109. Bonhoeffer credits one philosopher, Martin Heidegger, with succeeding, where others had so manifestly failed, in the hermeneutical task of forging a credible bond between act and being. Heidegger, says Bonhoeffer, understood Descartes, and those who followed him, to have paid too little attention to the *sum* in the philosophical proposition *cogito, ergo sum* ("I think, therefore I am"). Thought does not "produce its world for itself." As *Dasein* (being there; presence), it always has a temporal-historical location. *Act and Being*, DBWE 2: 70. While being is for Heidegger essentially *Dasein*, "Dasein is spirit [here understood as mind or consciousness] in its historicity. This Dasein must go beyond idealism and inquire about its ontological structure, for in this way only can light be shed on the meaning of being in general. Therefore being has priority over thought, and yet being equals Dasein, equals understanding of being, equals spirit." *Act and Being*, DBWE 2: 71. Heidegger, as Zimmermann explains, "comes closest among Bonhoeffer's philosophical interlocutors to realizing the ancient theological insight that being precedes reflection without sacrificing the transcendence of the human spirit." Zimmermann, "Dietrich Bonhoeffer and Martin Heidegger: Two Different Visions of Humanity," in Gregor and Zimmermann, 111. Heidegger fails nonetheless to evolve, from Bonhoeffer's perspective, an ontology suitable for "a genuinely theological conception of human knowledge." Zimmermann, "Dietrich Bonhoeffer and Martin Heidegger: Two Different Visions of Humanity," in Gregor and Zimmermann, 112. In Heidegger's philosophy, says Bonhoeffer, the anxious human being, summoned by conscience, "takes his guilt [the nullity of his life] upon himself and orients himself towards the most unconquerable of all forces—death. He draws death into his life and lives a being toward death." In this way, the human being overcomes death's character as boundary "and so attains not the end but rather the completion, the wholeness of Dasein." The hermeneutical circle is not broken. "The person remains alone, understanding himself from himself." Here again the question has become the answer; "it

has no ultimate seriousness." "The Anthropological Question," DBWE 10: 396–97. Heidegger thus "falls short . . . of real transcendence, of the exteriority Bonhoeffer deems necessary for genuine self-understanding." Zimmermann, "Dietrich Bonhoeffer and Martin Heidegger: Two Different Visions of Humanity," in Gregor and Zimmermann, 113.

114. *Act and Being*, DBWE 2: 110.
115. *Act and Being*, DBWE 2: 113.
116. *Act and Being*, DBWE 2: 127.
117. *Act and Being*, DBWE 2: 90.
118. i.e., the eternal freedom of God in aseity.
119. *Act and Being*, DBWE 2: 90–91.
120. *Creation and Fall*, DBWE 3: 63–64.
121. *Creation and Fall*, DBWE 3: 61–62.
122. For Bonhoeffer, it is this thoroughly relational "freedom for" that draws God into God's creation. "Because God in Christ is free for humankind, because God does not keep God's freedom to God's self, we can think of freedom only as a 'being free for. . . .'" Created freedom signifies, etc "—and it is this that goes beyond all God's previous acts and is unique . . .—that God's self enters into God's creation." *Creation and Fall*, DBWE 3: 63.
123. *Creation and Fall*, DBWE 3: 62–63.
124. *Creation and Fall*, DBWE 3: 62.
125. *Sanctorum Communio*, DBWE 1: 50, 54.
126. *Creation and Fall*, DBWE 3: 64.
127. *Creation and Fall*, DBWE 3: 64–65.
128. *Creation and Fall*, DBWE 3: 86.
129. *Creation and Fall*, DBWE 3: 115.
130. *Act and Being*, DBWE 2: 134, 137.
131. *Discipleship*, DBWE 4: 281–82. There is a further, late critique of the *sicut deus* in *Ethics*, where Bonhoeffer distinguishes between "shame" (as an appropriate reminder of our disunion with God and one another) and "conscience" (as both the sign and means of addressing internal schism). Conscience, he says, portrays the relationship with God and other people as an autonomous property of the self. "Conscience claims to be the voice of God and the norm for relating to other people." Human beings thus "become the judge of God and others, just as they are their own judge." *Ethics*, DBWE 6: 307–8.
132. *Creation and Fall*, DBWE 3: 113.
133. *Creation and Fall*, DBWE 3: 142.
134. *Creation and Fall*, DBWE 3: 145.
135. *Creation and Fall*, DBWE 3: 146.
136. "Lectures on Christology," DBWE 12: 301.
137. "Lectures on Christology," DBWE 12: 300.
138. "Lectures on Christology," DBWE 12: 301.
139. "Lectures on Christology," DBWE 12: 302.
140. "Lectures on Christology," DBWE 12: 303.
141. "Lectures on Christology," DBWE 12: 302.

142. "Lectures on Christology," DBWE 12: 303.
143. "Lectures on Christology," DBWE 12: 305.
144. "Lectures on Christology," DBWE 12: 350.
145. "Lectures on Christology," DBWE 12: 352–53.
146. "Lectures on Christology," DBWE 12: 353.
147. "Lectures on Christology," DBWE 12: 354.
148. "Lectures on Christology," DBWE 12: 353–54.
149. "Lectures on Christology," DBWE 12: 354.
150. "Lectures on Christology," DBWE 12: 355–56.
151. DeJonge, *Luther*, 75.
152. "Lectures on Christology," DBWE 12: 322.
153. "Lectures on Christology," DBWE 12: 313. Later, in the *Ethics*, Bonhoeffer stresses the critical importance of the God-human for the integrity of the Christian concept of person. "Jesus Christ is the human being and God in one." He is the ground of our self-understanding, and of our knowledge of God. Without him, we would know neither God nor other people. "There is no human being as such, just as there is no God as such; both are empty abstractions. Human beings are accepted in God's becoming human and are loved, judged, and reconciled in Christ, and God is the God who became human. So there is no relation to other human beings without a relation to God, and vice versa." *Ethics*, DBWE 6: 253–54.
154. Christ *is* the Word of God, and "[t]his Christ who is the Word in person is present in the word of the church or as the word of the church. His presence is, by nature, his existence as preaching. His presence is not power or the objective spirit of the church-community out of which it preaches, but rather his presence is preaching." "Lectures on Christology," DBWE 12: 317. Christ *is* the sacrament: "Jesus exists in such a way that he is the one who is present in the sacrament *existentialiter*. His being the sacrament is not a particular desire he expresses nor a characteristic, but rather he exists by nature as sacrament in the church." "Lectures on Christology," DBWE 12: 322. And Christ *is* the church-community: "[T]he church-community *is* the body of Christ . . . in reality. The concept of the body as applied to the church-community is not a functional concept referring to members but is instead a concept of the way in which the Christ exists who is present, exalted, and humiliated." "Lectures on Christology," DBWE 12: 323.
155. "Lectures on Christology," DBWE 12: 314.
156. "Lectures on Christology," DBWE 12: 314.
157. "Lectures on Christology," DBWE 12: 314.
158. "Lectures on Christology," DBWE 12: 325.
159. "Lectures on Christology," DBWE 12: 327.
160. "Lectures on Christology," DBWE 12: 327. Bonhoeffer speaks also of Jesus's role as mediator in the context of the call to discipleship, where "Jesus' call itself . . . breaks the ties with the naturally given surroundings in which a person lives . . . [and binds] the person immediately to himself. . . . Because the whole world was created by him and for him (John 1:3; 1 Cor. 8:6; Heb. 1:2), he is the sole mediator in the world. . . . So people called by Jesus learn that they had lived an illusion in their relationship to the world. The illusion is immediacy. . . . There is no way from us to

others than the path through Christ, his word, and our following him." *Discipleship*, DBWE 4: 93–96.

161. "Lectures on Christology," DBWE 12: 328.

162. "Lectures on Christology," DBWE 12: 328–29. William Wrede, a New Testament scholar at the University of Breslau, published *The Messianic Secret* in 1901. In this influential book, Wrede argues that we are bound to misunderstand the gospels when we see them as historical rather than as early community-driven expressions of faith. He contends that the author of Mark's Gospel has Jesus urge others to keep his messianic identity a secret not as a way of avoiding early arrest, or of managing popular expectations, but because there were still people around who remembered Jesus as a man who made no such claims. Albert Schweitzer's *Quest of the Historical Jesus* appeared in 1906. He concludes that previous "life of Jesus" scholars had neglected the Jesus of history (Schweitzer's doomed eschatological prophet) in favor of fictions of their own design with which they, and other modern Europeans, were more comfortable. Historical Jesus studies continued after Schweitzer but attracted less interest, partly, as Powell points out, because Schweitzer had "made it difficult for any scholar who followed him to avoid the stigma of bias," and partly as a consequence of the work of theologians like Rudolf Bultmann, who argued that, while we must be able to have confidence in the historical existence of Jesus, the biographical details of his life were relatively unimportant. It was "the Christ of faith" alone that mattered to theology. Mark Allan Powell, *Jesus as a Figure in History*, 2nd ed. (Louisville, KY: Westminster John Knox Press, 2013), 17–18. The quest for the historical Jesus was given new impetus in the 1950s by scholars such as Ernst Käsemann, a former student of Bultmann's, in Germany, and Norman Perrin in the United States, and continues to this day. Unlike their predecessors, contemporary Jesus scholars are now inclined to view their discipline "not as a fitful chronicle of stops and starts [Old Quest, New Quest, Third Quest] but as a progressive process of often insightful exploration" stretching back more than two hundred years. Powell, 24. Bonhoeffer's assessment of the situation in 1933 was nonetheless, in its historical context, and from his own post-liberal and christological perspective, a reasonable one.

163. "Lectures on Christology," DBWE 12: 329.
164. "Lectures on Christology," DBWE 12: 328.
165. "Lectures on Christology," DBWE 12: 330.
166. "Lectures on Christology," DBWE 12: 356.
167. "Lectures on Christology," DBWE 12: 358.
168. "Lectures on Christology," DBWE 12: 358.
169. "Lectures on Christology," DBWE 12: 360.
170. *Discipleship*, DBWE 4: 7.
171. *Discipleship*, DBWE 4: 58–59.
172. *Discipleship*, DBWE 4: 152.
173. *Discipleship*, DBWE 4: 284.
174. *Discipleship*, DBWE 4: 285. "My little children, for whom I am again in the pain of childbirth until Christ is formed in you . . ." (Gal. 4:19).
175. *Discipleship*, DBWE 4: 282–83.
176. *Ethics*, DBWE 6: 93–94.

177. *Ethics*, DBWE 6: 96.
178. *Ethics*, DBWE 6: 94.
179. *Ethics*, DBWE 6: 99.
180. *Discipleship*, DBWE 4: 285–86. "I want to know Christ and the power of his resurrection and the sharing of his sufferings by becoming like him in his death" (Phil. 3:10). "Therefore we have been buried with him by baptism into death, so that, just as Christ was raised from the dead by the glory of the Father, so we too might walk in newness of life. For if we have been united with him in a death like his, we will certainly be united with him in a resurrection like his" (Rom. 6:4–5).
181. *Discipleship*, DBWE 4: 219.
182. "[I]t is no longer I who live, but it is Christ who lives in me" (Gal. 2:20).
183. *Letters and Papers*, DBWE 8: 486.
184. "The followers are the visible community of faith; their discipleship is a visible act which separates them from the world—or it is not discipleship. And discipleship is as visible as light in the night, as a mountain in the flatland." *Discipleship*, DBWE 4: 112–13. Again, says Bonhoeffer, in calling the disciples "Jesus demanded a *visible act of obedience*. . . . The break with the world which has taken place in Christ . . . must become externally visible through active participation in the life and worship of the church-community." *Discipleship*, DBWE 4: 210. Bonhoeffer insists nonetheless (with reference to Matthew 7:13–14: "Enter through the narrow gate . . .") that "[i]t is not the faith community which separates itself from others." The Word does this for them. "The call separates a small group, those who follow, from the great mass of the people. The disciples are few and will always be only a few. This word of Jesus cuts off any false hope of their effectiveness. Disciples should never invest their trust in numbers." *Discipleship*, DBWE 4: 175–76.
185. See, for example, the discussion of *apocatastasis* in *Sanctorum Communio*, DBWE 1: 286–87.
186. *Discipleship*, DBWE 4: 217. Bonhoeffer affirms the patristic doctrine of *anhypostasia*, which emphasizes the general humanity of Jesus. "God became human. This means God took on the whole of our sick and sinful human nature, the whole of humanity which had fallen away from God. It does not mean, however, that God took on the individual human being Jesus. The entire gospel message can be understood properly only in light of this crucial distinction." *Discipleship*, DBWE 4: 214.
187. *Discipleship*, DBWE 4: 217.
188. "Lectures on Christology," DBWE 12: 324–27; *Discipleship*, DBWE 4: 93–96.
189. Dietrich Bonhoeffer, *Life Together*, ed. Geffrey B. Kelly (Minneapolis: Fortress Press, 2005), DBWE 5: 95.
190. *Life Together*, DBWE 5: 101.
191. *Ethics*, DBWE 6: 54–55.
192. *Ethics*, DBWE 6: 56.
193. *Ethics*, DBWE 6: 56–57. Bonhoeffer uses the term "pseudo-Lutheran" to describe what he believes to be distortions of Luther's teaching, especially, in his own time, by those "pseudo-Lutheran" theologians who sought to draw God into the service of the Nazi state.

194. *Ethics*, DBWE 6: 57.
195. *Ethics*, DBWE 6: 66.
196. *Ethics*, DBWE 6: 58.
197. *Ethics*, DBWE 6: 54.
198. Peter Dabrock, "Responding to 'Wirklichkeit': Reclaiming Bonhoeffer's Approach to Theological Ethics between Mystery and the Formation of the World," in Nielsen, Nissen, and Tietz, 62, 67, 77.
199. Dabrock, "Responding to 'Wirklichkeit': Reclaiming Bonhoeffer's Approach to Theological Ethics between Mystery and the Formation of the World," in Nielsen, Nissen, and Tietz, 58.
200. *Ethics*, DBWE 6: 59.
201. Marsh, *Reclaiming Bonhoeffer*, 106.
202. Green, *Theology of Sociality*, 288.
203. Green, *Theology of Sociality*, 290.
204. DeJonge, *Luther*, 100.
205. DeJonge, *Luther*, 83.
206. "Nature of the Church," DBWE 11: 332.
207. "Lectures on Christology," DBWE 12: 326–27.
208. Dietrich Bonhoeffer, "The Church and the Jewish Question," in *Berlin*, DBWE 12: 365.
209. *Ethics*, DBWE 6: 112.
210. DeJonge, *Luther*, 125.
211. Clifford J. Green, Introduction, *Ethics*, DBWE 6: 20.
212. DeJonge, *Luther*, 129.
213. *Ethics*, DBWE 6: 57–58.
214. *Sanctorum Communio*, DBWE 1: 191.
215. *Ethics*, DBWE 6: 238.
216. *Ethics*, DBWE 6: 220.
217. *Ethics*, DBWE 6: 283.
218. *Ethics*, DBWE 6: 284.
219. *Ethics*, DBWE 6: 284.
220. *Ethics*, DBWE 6: 225.
221. *Ethics*, DBWE 6: 323.
222. *Ethics*, DBWE 6: 257.
223. *Ethics*, DBWE 6: 288.
224. DeJonge, *Luther*, 244.
225. *Ethics*, DBWE 6: 251.
226. "Meditation on Psalm 119," DBWE 15: 523.
227. Bethge, *Dietrich Bonhoeffer*, 856.
228. Bethge, *Dietrich Bonhoeffer*, 717.
229. Feil, *The Theology of Dietrich Bonhoeffer*, 95–96.
230. *Sanctorum Communio*, DBWE 1: 158.
231. *Sanctorum Communio*, DBWE 1: 161.
232. *Discipleship*, DBWE 4: 285.
233. *Discipleship*, DBWE 4: 217.

234. *Ethics*, DBWE 6: 92. Marsh believes Bonhoeffer's *Ethics* to reveal "the shifting assumptions of a chastened believer." While no less christocentric than Bonhoeffer's earlier writings, "it is more open to Christ's presence in persons, places, and movements outside the church." Charles Marsh, *Strange Glory: A Life of Dietrich Bonhoeffer* (New York: Vintage Books, 2015), 313.
235. *Ethics*, DBWE 6: 96.
236. *Ethics*, DBWE 6: 66–67.
237. *Ethics*, DBWE 6: 67.
238. *Ethics*, DBWE 6: 344.
239. *Ethics*, DBWE 6: 96–97.
240. *Ethics*, DBWE 6: 97.
241. *Ethics*, DBWE 6: 98.
242. John W. de Gruchy, Introduction, *Letters and Papers from Prison*, DBWE 8: 23.
243. *Letters and Papers*, DBWE 8: 362.
244. *Letters and Papers*, DBWE 8: 426.
245. "Lectures on Christology," DBWE 12: 325.
246. *Letters and Papers*, DBWE 8: 427.
247. *Letters and Papers*, DBWE 8: 480.
248. *Letters and Papers*, DBWE 8: 501.
249. *Letters and Papers*, DBWE 8: 518.
250. *Sanctorum Communio*, DBWE 1: 33.
251. *Discipleship*, DBWE 4: 217.
252. *Ethics*, DBWE 6: 96.
253. *Ethics*, DBWE 6: 67.
254. *Ethics*, DBWE 6: 403.
255. *Letters and Papers*, DBWE 8: 363.
256. *Letters and Papers*, DBWE 8: 364.
257. *Letters and Papers*, DBWE 8: 363.
258. *Letters and Papers*, DBWE 8: 364.
259. *Ethics*, DBWE 6: 96.

Chapter 4

Nonreligious Interpretation

"How do we talk about God—without religion?"¹ Bonhoeffer was keenly aware that, if Christianity was to make the transition to a religionless age, it would have to change not only the way it thought about itself but also the way it talked about itself. Christianity, if it was to mean anything to people who "simply cannot be religious anymore,"² would require a suitably worldly—a nonreligious—interpretation.³

In the "Outline for a Book," which Bonhoeffer sent to Eberhard Bethge in August 1944, he suggests that "the interpretation of biblical concepts . . . (Creation, fall, reconciliation, repentance, faith, *vita nova*, last things)" should reflect a new understanding of the human experience of transcendence, which is the experience of "'being there for others,' through participation in the being of Jesus."⁴ An earlier letter describes "repentance, faith, justification, rebirth, and sanctification" as in need of worldly reinterpretation "in the Old Testament sense," and in the sense of the incarnation (John 1:14).⁵

Bonhoeffer, though, is not inclined to rush into this task. As Ernst Feil points out, he is clearly sensitive to the "problem of language," but sees the introduction of new words as no answer to the challenge posed by now "empty" phrases.⁶ In a letter written in March 1940 to Roberta Ruth Stahlberg, Bonhoeffer readily acknowledges the importance of finding the right words for the church's work of proclamation. Words can be overused, misused, misprized, or outworn. But there is nothing to be gained by simply excising words like "cross," "sin," and "grace" from the Christian vocabulary. We might, perhaps, replace the cross with the guillotine, but this gets us nowhere, "because it was a cross on which Jesus died." Or we could, perhaps, substitute a "feed trough" for a "manger," but this expression, too, would provide at most temporary relief from vapidity. On the whole, Bonhoeffer thinks it best to retain "the simple language of the Bible," because what really "matters is the depth from which [the words] come and the context in which they stand."[7]

Bonhoeffer wants to find new ways of understanding existing concepts, without diminishing the normative value of the concepts themselves. But he is in no position to set firm parameters. He simply cannot know how far this journey might take him, and others, in the future. He is sure, though, as he says in that now-famous passage from "Thoughts" on the day of baptism of his godson, Dietrich Bethge, that the day will come when people will again be called to speak the Word of God

> in a new language, perhaps quite nonreligious language, but liberating and redeeming like Jesus's language, so that people will be alarmed and yet overcome by its power—the language of a new righteousness and truth, a language proclaiming that God makes peace with humankind and that God's kingdom is drawing near.[8]

Here Bonhoeffer speaks eloquently of being "thrown back all the way to the beginnings of our understanding," and is driven to conclude that "what it means to live in Christ and follow Christ . . . is so difficult and remote that we hardly dare speak of it anymore."[9] Bonhoeffer, says Ralf Wüstenberg, is now sure that the existing religious language of the church has lost all meaningful connection with the gospel, from which it follows that nonreligious language should be able to tell us "what it means to live in Christ and follow Christ."[10] Wüstenberg believes the "Thoughts" of May 1944 to "issue directly" into the "Outline for a Book" of August 1944, and to "reach their final goal there,"[11] in Jesus, "the human being for others."[12] Nonreligious interpretation must therefore be chiefly concerned with the place of Jesus Christ in a world come of age, and with the significance of the gospel message for contemporary everyday life.

Wüstenberg follows Gerhard Ebeling in focusing the discussion on Christology, which is as critical to the understanding of Bonhoeffer's approach to nonreligious interpretation as it is to any other aspect of his theology. For Ebeling, a strong christological foundation is one of nonreligious interpretation's three defining characteristics.[13] Bonhoeffer's faith in Jesus Christ is unshakeable. "Jesus Christ has met him," and Bonhoeffer knows himself to belong in that place where God and the human being have become one. The challenge is to express this conviction in language that is both "liberating and redeeming"—in language that provides a responsible and credible answer to the question of Christ's contemporary identity.[14] Nonreligious interpretation must also be "concrete" and consistent with "the indivisible complex of all that concerns me and the ways in which I can be expected to recognize it as concerning me."[15] And it must be comprehensible to nonbelievers, for "the proclaimed word seeks to effect faith," but should not "presuppose" it.[16] The criterion for effective proclamation must be the nonbeliever's ability to grasp what is said. The church, says Ebeling, seems largely to have forgotten this. By allowing the believing congregation to determine the efficacy of proclamation, the church has made the Word of God unintelligible to those outside. Faith has become the prerequisite for hearing the Word, rather than its effect. In this situation, nonreligious interpretation, as Ebeling sees it, heralds a return to "first principles, of finding new, stammering words for the Word of God, of a groping rediscovery of what Christian faith really means."[17]

Bonhoeffer sets out tentatively on this path. In one of the letters from prison, he equates "repentance" with "ultimate honesty,"[18] while in another he offers the "unbiblical concept of 'meaning'" as "one translation of what the Bible calls 'promise.'"[19] But there is not much substance to these proposals, and we have no others. Elsewhere, Bonhoeffer candidly admits that he is "more able to see what needs to be done than how . . . actually to do it."[20]

MORE THAN HERMENEUTICS

Feil believes Bonhoeffer to be more concerned with the future form and practice of Christianity than with the language used to describe it. The end of religion has more than hermeneutical implications for Christian faith. Bonhoeffer makes this clear in the first of the theological letters from prison when he asks, "What does a church, a congregation, a sermon, a liturgy, a Christian life, mean in a religionless world?"[21] Nonreligious interpretation has an important, but subsidiary, role to play in the process of establishing the religionless form of Christianity. The relation between religionless Christianity and nonreligious interpretation is thus "the relation between life and thought . . . faith and theology, *actus directus* and *actus reflectus*." The challenge posed by a religionless world is essentially a practical one. As Feil submits, "it raises itself, historically, in the praxis of life, and seeks to be solved through action."[22] He believes we misunderstand Bonhoeffer's interest in nonreligious interpretation if we fail to give priority to the ethical dimension and instead see religionless Christianity as primarily a matter of hermeneutics.[23]

Bethge likewise gives precedence to ethics over hermeneutics and takes issue with Ebeling in this regard. Ebeling, he says, warns against making Bonhoeffer "the defender of a new 'form' as against a new language" and thereby neglects Bonhoeffer's larger purpose. While Bonhoeffer is keen to ensure the contemporary relevance of the gospel proclamation and certainly does not underestimate the importance of language and its interpretation, he raises questions—most obviously in the third chapter ("Conclusions") of the

"Outline for a Book"—that are entirely concerned with the future practical shape of Christianity.²⁴

Blessing and Cross: Nonreligious Interpretation in Prison

Nothing like a methodological description of what Bonhoeffer intends by nonreligious interpretation is to be found in his prison writings. Bethge observes that it seems, whenever Bonhoeffer contemplated something of this kind, he was "interrupted by bombing raids."²⁵ Bethge nonetheless believes the prison letters to include several examples of nonreligious interpretation.²⁶

The first is a letter, addressed to Bethge and his wife, Renate, on Christmas Eve 1943, which speaks of absence as a gap kept open by God. Nothing, says Bonhoeffer, "can replace the absence of someone dear to us." We have simply to "endure it." God does not fill the emptiness, but rather, by keeping it empty, helps to "preserve—even if in pain—our authentic communion." Now, "gratitude transforms the torment of memory into peaceful joy. One bears what was beautiful in the past not as a thorn but as a precious gift deep within."²⁷

A few months later, in a letter in which he shares with Bethge his Easter thoughts about dying and death, Bonhoeffer suggests that human beings are generally more concerned about the manner of their dying than they are about vanquishing death. "Socrates mastered the art of dying; Christ overcame death as ἔσχατος ἐχθρός" (1 Cor. 15:26).²⁸ We may, perhaps, aspire to mirror Socrates and yet fail Christ. Death is overcome only by the "new and cleansing wind" of Christ's resurrection. "This is the answer to the δός μοι ποῦ στῶ καὶ κινήσω τῆν γῆν.²⁹ If a few people really believed this and were guided by it in their earthly actions, a great deal would change. To live in the light of the resurrection—that is what Easter means."³⁰

But to live in the light of the resurrection does not mean to live in pious hope of a "better life beyond," a life everlasting, free of all sorrow, hardship, anxiety, and desire. Many Christians do, of course, believe precisely this and, in doing so, miss the essence of both the gospel proclamation and of Paul. "The Christian hope of resurrection," properly understood, says Bonhoeffer, "refers people to their life on earth in a wholly new way." We can no more steal by life's demands "into eternity" than Christ did, and we should not want to do so. Both New and Old Testaments agree that "[t]his-worldliness must not be abolished ahead of its time."³¹

Elsewhere, Bonhoeffer challenges Bethge's view that the Bible does not have much to say "about health, happiness . . . strength . . . and so on." He thinks Bethge mistaken, most obviously in the case of the Old Testament, where "[t]he mediating theological concept . . . between God and the happiness . . . of human beings is that of blessing." In the Old Testament, God's blessing "encompasses all earthly good" and contains all God's promises. Nor are the force and significance of God's Old Testament blessing in any sense lost when we come to the New. To believe the one to have superseded the other is simply to subscribe to "the customary, over-spiritualized [vergeistigt] view of the NT." There is an abundance of joy and suffering in both the Old and the New Testaments, and no suggestion in either that the two states (joy and suffering, blessing and cross) are "mutually exclusive." Indeed, the difference between them "may consist solely in the fact that in the OT the blessing also includes the cross and in the NT the cross also includes the blessing."[32]

Bethge sees evidence of nonreligious interpretation also in the poem "Christians and Heathens" "with its switch from the religious to the nonreligious Christian attitude."[33] Bonhoeffer himself draws attention to this shift in a letter to Bethge which points to the significance of the line, "Christians stand by God in God's own pain."[34] This, he says, is the distinctive mark of the Christian.

> "Could you not stay awake with me one hour?" Jesus asks in Gethsemane [Matt. 26:40b]. That is the opposite of everything a religious person expects from God. The human being is called upon to share in God's suffering at the hands of a godless world. Thus we must really live in that godless world and not try to cover up or transfigure its godlessness somehow with religion.[35]

Finally, says Bethge, we may choose to regard Bonhoeffer's late description of Christ as "the man for others" as an example of nonreligious interpretation.[36]

> God in human form! Not as in oriental religions in animal forms as the monstrous, the chaotic, the remote, the terrifying, but also not in the conceptual forms of the absolute, the metaphysical, the infinite, and so on, either . . . nor again the Greek . . . "God-human form [Gott-Menschgestalt] of the human being in itself." But rather "the human being for others"! therefore the Crucified One. The human being living out of the transcendent.[37]

In all of this, the emphasis is on a full and faithful life, which includes a willingness to share in God's suffering "at the hands of a godless world." There are certainly hints of nonreligious interpretation—for example, when Bonhoeffer speaks of the Christian hope of resurrection as referring people "to their life on earth in a wholly new way," and of Jesus Christ as "the human being for others"—but it is probably more helpful to see these primarily as expressions of Bonhoeffer's prison theology rather than as examples of the kind of language that would be required to make this theology intelligible to a post-religious audience. When, in the prison letters, Bonhoeffer talks about nonreligious interpretation, he does so specifically.

A Turn to the World: Proclamation and Exegesis

Bethge compares sermons and exegeses written in prison with earlier ones and finds in them no evidence of any new system or method of interpretation. He sees this as confirming "how little Bonhoeffer viewed his task as suddenly finding other words."[38]

Bethge nonetheless discerns in the prison sermons and exegeses, as in the letters, unmistakable signs of a nonreligious turn to the world, and of a determination to avoid the kind of religious language—the language of metaphysics, inwardness, and privilege—that Bonhoeffer came increasingly to dislike over the years.[39]

In a meditation written for Eberhard and Renate Bethge at the beginning of June 1944, Bonhoeffer describes how the righteous suffer "from the meaninglessness and perversion of world events." The world insists that this is just the way things are, but where the world sees "business as usual," the righteous see only an affront to God. They share, to some degree at least, "God's own way of perceiving things," and they suffer for it, "just as God suffers at the hands of the world." Like God, too, they respond to the world's cruelty and injustice not with condemnation but with a blessing. And this blessing is the hope of the world, for "[t]he world lives by the blessing of God and of the righteous and thus has a future. Blessing means laying one's hand on something and saying: Despite everything, you belong to God."[40]

In the reflections on the commandments, written at much the same time, Bonhoeffer emphasizes their essential worldliness, and the common-sense role they play in creating and sustaining stable life in community. One doesn't have to be a Christian (or a Jew!) to recognize the importance of these "laws of life," and Christians may rightly "rejoice at the common ground they find with other human beings in such important matters." There is, however, still

> [a] decisive difference between these laws of life and the command of God. There reason speaks; here God speaks. . . . It is not a law but God we are obeying in the Ten Commandments, and our failure when we break them comes not from disobeying a law but from disobeying God.[41]

Bonhoeffer here says of the First Commandment's injunction to "have no other gods besides me" that, whereas it is now customary to describe our gods as "money, sensuality, honor, other people, ourselves," the real situation is rather different—and, perhaps, even more bleak—because, in fact, we have no gods, no idols of any kind. The world has been "stripped" of them, and we are now far too lost "to be capable of having idols and worshiping them." We depend on nothing, deify nothing. If we may still be said to worship anything at all, it can only be "nothingness, extinction, meaninglessness."[42]

The Second Commandment clearly enjoins us not to misuse the name of God,[43] and yet, says Bonhoeffer, we do this constantly. We misuse the name of God when God, or a passage from the Bible, is the answer to every question, as if it were "the most obvious thing in the world" that God responds constantly, and at once, to our entreaties. We misuse the name of God whenever we use God to plug a gap in human knowledge, or in our misguided efforts to stifle genuine scientific inquiry or artistic endeavor. We misuse the name of God whenever we speak as if "we were privy to God's own counsel," and generally by turning the name of God into "an empty human word and insipid chatter." These are offenses worse than blasphemy, because they are the work of religious people who profess a sincere belief in God. The Israelites never spoke the name of God aloud, says Bonhoeffer on more than one occasion,[44] and there is much to be learnt from their example. "It is [he says] certainly better not to speak the name of God than to debase it into a human word." Yet Christians must proclaim "the word of the living, present, righteous, and gracious God" to the world, and they can do this only by praying daily as Christ taught his disciples to pray, "Hallowed be your name."[45]

Turning the World Upside Down: The Early Sermons

We do not have to wait, though, for the years of conspiracy and imprisonment to find evidence of a turn to the world in Bonhoeffer's writings. It is there already, as James Kelley points out, in Bonhoeffer's early sermons.[46] Bonhoeffer, says Kelley, is acutely aware of the problem posed by the need to speak both of God's historical self-revelation in the human being Jesus Christ and of Christ's perpetual presence in the life of the world. Christ is thus to be understood both as "a concrete figure in past history" and as "immediately and objectively present for us here and now."[47]

A good example of Bonhoeffer's concern to make tangible Christ's presence *pro nobis* in the world of everyday experience is to be found in the sermon on Psalm 63:3 ("your steadfast love is better than life") given in Berlin on Thanksgiving Sunday (October 4, 1931).[48] The sermon begins with a vivid description of the psalmist's doomed struggle to hold on to the things he loves in the face of God's determination to wrest everything from him. Religion, says Bonhoeffer, is generally held to make people "happy and harmonious and calm and content," but while this may be true of religion, it is certainly not true of our relationship with "the living God." The psalmist is ripped asunder. A conflict rages within him and becomes more intense by the day as "more and more of that which he had loved is torn away."[49] And God, it seems to the psalmist and to Bonhoeffer, will be satisfied with nothing less than our lives. We must choose between God's loving-kindness and life, between everything we can see, hold, hear, taste, and feel, and something that "we cannot see, cannot hold, cannot understand . . . above and behind everything that happens and yet so close by speaking to us so earnestly."[50]

Bonhoeffer now brings us forward some two and a half thousand years, from the psalmist's own particular experience of faith to the world of the Great Depression. He includes some statistics.

> We have to expect that in the winter seven million people in Germany will be unable to find work; that means hunger will grip fifteen to twenty million people next winter, another twelve million or more in England, twenty or more in America. About sixteen million are starving now in China, and it is not much better in India.[51]

Bonhoeffer encourages the congregation to consider the situation—their situation— carefully. Those who are fit and well fed, with jobs and a roof over their heads, may think of themselves as already happily ensconced in God's grace. The psalmist's struggle with God will seem strange, remote, and largely irrelevant to their experience of life.[52] But shouldn't the abundant signs of God's "steadfast love and kindness," which they assume to be securely theirs, make them at least a little uncomfortable, especially when they remember that "there is nothing, nothing at all" that has made them more deserving of these gifts from God than their "hungry brothers"? Or do they perhaps believe that "God feeds his favorite children and lets the rejected ones go hungry?"[53]

Such a misguided sense of entitlement transforms God's gift of loving-kindness into a curse. "No-one should say: God has blessed me with money and possessions, and then live now as if he and his loving God were alone in the world."[54] God's loving-kindness is not something—a property or asset—that we can simply keep for ourselves. It comes to us rather in the form of a social contract, and places us in a position of "immeasurable responsibility." God says to us in fact: "If you want my loving-kindness to stay with you, serve your neighbor, for in him God himself meets you."[55] And this is how the psalmist's struggle now manifests itself in our lives. We can only hope to continue in God's love if we are ready to risk everything we have for others in their hour of need.

It is good for us at least to understand, says Bonhoeffer, that God's loving-kindness is not something which simply allows us to "go on living, a little happier, a little richer, but essentially unchanged." He is, however, surprised how *little* passion, and how *much* reluctance, we bring to the struggle, and how little we allow it to affect—as it must if we truly value God's love in our lives—"the root of our whole existence."[56] How is it, he asks, that as passionate human beings we are ready to give "so unbelievably much in the battle for the beloved human being" and next to nothing—"a couple of coins in the offering" and a "somewhat pleasant expression"—to God? Do we no longer see God's love for us in Jesus Christ? Have we quite forgotten that it is God alone who sustains us and gives our lives meaning?[57]

We have turned away from God, but God does not give up on us. God's love "follows us and reveals itself to us anew as the eternal promise of God in Jesus Christ."[58] We are never beyond the reach of God's love, just as we are never beyond the reach of God's claim on us. Whatever we may think and do, we remain responsible. God asks us repeatedly, "What is my love worth to you?" And here, the more clearly we perceive the depth of God's love for us, "the more filled with life our answer will be." When, though, Bonhoeffer wonders, "will we get to the point that at least in the Christian community the world of our psalmist breaks in"? When will we have sufficient faith and courage to affirm: "Were they to take our house, goods, honor, child, or spouse, Though life be wrenched away, they cannot win the day. The kingdom's ours forever!"[59]

Kelley believes this sermon to reveal the same basic understanding of God's self-revelation that is to be found in the later lectures on Christology, and in Bonhoeffer's youthful systematics. Here we come face to face with Jesus Christ in the world, and in "the special experience of faith." Faith is brought into relation with "the most specific worldly events" and these become "occasions of encounter with the revelatory reality of God himself."[60]

In a sermon on 2 Cor. 12:9 ("my strength is made perfect in weakness"),[61] which is thought to have been preached in London sometime in 1934, Bonhoeffer sets out to answer a question which confronts "all philosophy of life." This is the question of weakness. What does it mean to be physically or mentally or morally weak in the world?[62]

Bonhoeffer assumes most people do not give this issue—which, for him, is the mystery of dependence on others—much thought, and that they would in any case generally prefer not to dwell on it. But he asks:

> Have you ever thought what outlook on life a cripple, a hopelessly ill man, a socially exploited man, a colored man in a white country, an untouchable—may have? And if so, did you not feel that here life means something totally different from what it means to you and that on the other hand you are inseparably bound together with the unfortunate people, just because you are a man like them . . . and just because in all your strength you will feel their weakness?[63]

Christianity, says Bonhoeffer, is often condemned or dismissed as a "religion of slaves" (Nietzsche) which "owes its success only to the masses of miserable people whose weakness and misery Christianity has glorified," while against it stands an "aristocratic philosophy of life" which assigns ultimate value to strength and power and violence. Bonhoeffer is nonetheless convinced that Christianity's credibility depends unequivocally on "its revolutionary protest against violence, arbitrariness and pride of power" and on "its apologia for the weak." And he is painfully aware that its record, in practice, leaves much to be desired. Christianity, he believes, "has adjusted itself much too easily to the worship of power. It should give much more offence, more shock to the world, than it is doing."[64]

If, then, Christianity is to be true to itself, it must take its stand with the weak. It must not confuse weakness with imperfection, or mistake condescension for humility. Rather, it must strive to establish "a new order of values in the sight of Christ"—an order of values that would transform existing social relations. The strong should serve the weak, and they should do this not out of some misplaced sense of benevolence but with real "care and reverence," because suffering and weakness are holy. "Our God is a suffering God," and all human suffering and weakness partakes in God's own suffering and weakness in the world. Because of this, we can be sure that

> [w]herever a man in physical or social or moral or religious weakness is aware of his existence and likeness with God, there he is sharing God's life, there he feels God being with him, there he is open for God's strength, that is God's grace, God's love, God's comfort, which passeth all understanding and all human values.[65]

Here, too, in this 1934 sermon, is evidence of what Kelley calls the "immediacy and concretion" of Christ's presence in the everyday world of human social interactions. We are taken by stages from a conceptual abstraction, weakness, through a range of lower-level abstractions (e.g., physical, mental, and moral weakness), to specific cases (the cripple, the "hopelessly ill man," the "socially exploited man") which demand a Christian response. Christ is present, concretely, in the neighbor who needs our help. It is here that the encounter with God takes place.[66]

Kelley takes for his final example of "christological concretion" an end of semester sermon given by Bonhoeffer in Berlin in July 1932. The text is John 8:32 ("The truth will make you free"), which Bonhoeffer describes as "perhaps the most revolutionary passage in the whole New Testament." As such, it is "understood only by a very few true revolutionaries." If it became the property of "the crowd," they would only "make a slogan out of it."[67]

In this sermon, Bonhoeffer very deliberately confronts the growing Nazi menace, whose final, successful grab for power is now just months away. We have, he says, made "freedom" and "truth" our own. It is "[o]ur action, our strength, our courage, our race, our morality" that make us free. Our lives are veiled in subterfuge and deceit, and we cannot imagine what the world might look like—and, more importantly, what we might look like—if the veils were stripped away, revealing us "just as we truly are."[68] We have crucified the truth, preferring our own truth to God's truth, our creation to God's creation. We have wrenched ourselves out of communion with God and the neighbor and convinced ourselves that we can live alone. We have "presumed to be God and failed in it," and found a false freedom in the embrace of a lie.[69]

Truth and falsehood are not just words for Bonhoeffer. They are ways of life. And to live a lie means to live the life of a slave, in chains of one's own making. The liar "lives in hatred . . . shackled to himself."[70] But even such a life can be a way to genuine truth and freedom for those who, by the grace of God, come to understand their condition and, in so doing, to realize that only God's truth can set them free. This, says Bonhoeffer, is because "becoming *free* does not mean becoming *great* in the world, free in relation to our brother, free in relation to God." It means rather becoming free "from the lie that I am the only one there . . . free from oneself for others."[71] The truth that sets us free is love, and

> [t]he human being who loves because [he] has been made free by God's truth is the most revolutionary human being on earth. He is the overturning of all values [Umsturz aller Werte][72] . . . he is the most dangerous human being. For he has recognized that human beings are, in their deepest being, untruthful. And he is ready at any time to let the light of truth fall upon them—and that for the sake of love.[73]

But the world has never been inclined to welcome the disturbance caused by the coming of "the knight of truth and love." Such people are always more likely to be scorned and rejected than they are to be celebrated and acclaimed.[74] Bonhoeffer knows God's truth, which is God's love, nonetheless to have concrete, and sometimes revolutionary, implications, and to require of those "few true revolutionaries"[75] who understand it a suitably concrete, and potentially revolutionary, response.

The Bonhoeffer of the prison letters is clearly visible in these early sermons where, already, the encounter with God takes place in the midst of life rather than at its margins. God's love, we are reminded, is not a possession, an entitlement, or a reward. It is God's gift to us and comes with a similarly God-given responsibility to serve others. We must not be ashamed of Christianity's revolutionary apologia for the weak, for "God glorifies himself in the weak as He glorified himself in the cross."[76] God reveals God's love for us in the crucified and risen Christ, and this is the truth that sets us free—free from the lie "that I am the center of the world,"[77] free from ourselves, for others.

FINDING NEW WORDS

The assumption that, whatever else it may be, nonreligious interpretation is not, for Bonhoeffer, a matter of "suddenly finding other words"[78] is common among scholars. A partial exception is Edwin Robertson, who ventures to take the nonreligious interpretation of biblical concepts further than the short distance traveled by Bonhoeffer himself—although, for Robertson, too, this is a matter of finding new ways of understanding existing concepts (creation, fall, faith, repentance, etc.), rather than of "finding other words" for the concepts themselves.[79] Robertson, however, makes little effort to bring his own interpretations into line with Bonhoeffer's broader theology. They are as such of marginal value to the present study.

For example, creation is approached from the perspective of process thought, which seems unlikely to have proved productive for Bonhoeffer, who was not impressed by A. N. Whitehead's "naturalistic anthropology."[80] Robertson seeks to interpret the fall nonreligiously with reference first to Bultmann and demythologization, and then to psychoanalysis; but we know that Bonhoeffer did not support the demythologization project, and that he was deeply skeptical of the merits of psychoanalysis. Robertson's treatment of atonement is more promising, based as it is on Bonhoeffer's own christological understanding of God's weakness in the world. "Can we not," asks Robertson, "see God's persuasive love [Whitehead again!] winning mankind by his weakness, his suffering and his readiness to be for us?"[81] Robertson goes on to describe repentance as a forthright personal assessment of "one's failed condition and a determination to turn round and change."[82] While this is consistent with Bonhoeffer's orthodox understanding of repentance as μετάνοια, it inexplicably fails to engage with what is perhaps the only concrete example we have of nonreligious interpretation by Bonhoeffer himself: the pairing of "repentance" with an "ultimate honesty" that frankly acknowledges the nature of the world in which we now live *etsi deus non daretur*.[83]

In the discussion of faith which follows, Robertson makes no mention of the distinction between faith (wholeness) and religion (partiality) that lies at the heart of Bonhoeffer's critique of religion. Faith, for Robertson, is a changing *human idea* which has become progressively more vulnerable to the challenge of theodicy, although he is encouraged by the "new vision of God which seems to emerge in our day"—a vision which does not distinguish between God's power and God's love because it knows God's power to lie "only and wholly in his love."[84] While there is, perhaps, a brief nod to Bonhoeffer at the end of this last sentence, there is none in Robertson's nonreligious interpretation of "new life," which speaks of conformation to Christ exclusively in terms of "renewal from within, renewal of the mind,"[85] and has nothing at all to say about a worldly "being-there-for-others" through participation in the being of Christ.

Scholars like Bethge and Feil, who prioritize ethics over hermeneutics in their explorations of Bonhoeffer's religionless Christianity, are almost certainly on the right track. Bonhoeffer was looking for ways to shape practical expressions of a new form of Christianity and needed language suitable for this task. But surely Ebeling has a point, too, when he insists on the need to make the gospel intelligible, especially to nonbelievers. A religionless Christianity, if there is to be such a thing, depends both on a particular way of understanding the human encounter with God, and on the development of contemporary forms of expression that are capable of successfully conveying this understanding to a skeptical audience, much of it now largely ignorant of Christian scripture and tradition.

Bonhoeffer did not underestimate the difficulty of this undertaking and, as will be clear from the foregoing discussion, made very little progress with it. He may have left us only one example—in the letter of July 16, 1944, where he equates "repentance" (*Buße*) with "ultimate honesty" (*letzte Redlichkeit*)[86]—although there is at least the hint of another, in almost his last letter to Bethge, where he refers to the "unbiblical concept of 'meaning' [*Sinn*]" as "only one translation of what the Bible calls 'promise' [*Verheißung*]."[87]

Of Repentance and Ultimate Honesty

God, says Bonhoeffer in the letter of July 16, is no longer needed to support humanity's worldly endeavors. God, as a general working hypothesis, has been made obsolete.[88] Even a desperate "*salto mortale* [deadly leap] back to the Middle Ages" will not save the anxious Christian. This *salto mortale* is but a mark of hopelessness, a deception, a pointless longing for a vanished childhood. The only way truly to recapture a lost childlikeness (in the biblical sense of Matthew 18:3)[89] is "through repentance, through *ultimate* honesty!" And this means recognizing that we live in the world *etsi deus non daretur*, which is precisely what God demands that we do![90]

Repentance is still an act of μετάνοια, in the sense of a spiritual conversion or turning to God. The fundamentally honest person will, however, appreciate that this act takes place not in a world that is full of God, but rather in one that is, from the religious point of view, God-forsaken. God has been "pushed out of the world and onto the cross," and helps us now only by virtue of being "weak and powerless in the world."[91] We must follow Christ's example, and this is true μετάνοια—when we think first not of our own needs and fears but allow ourselves instead "to be pulled into walking the path that Jesus walks, into the messianic event, in which Isa. 53 is now being fulfilled!"[92]

Repentance, or "ultimate honesty," is thus best understood as a profound change of perspective. We live *etsi deus non daretur*, with no credible means of escape to some other, better world beyond. And yet, even in this godless place, the hidden God of Jesus Christ gives us strength to turn the spotlight off ourselves and to join freely in Jesus's own "being for others."

Of Promise and Meaning

Bonhoeffer makes the connection between "meaning" and "promise" in the letter to Bethge of August 21, 1944. In this letter, Bonhoeffer stresses the uniqueness of the Christian experience of God. The God of Jesus Christ, he says, bears no relation to the triumphalist God of religion. "What we imagine a God could and should do—the God of Jesus Christ has nothing to do with all that."[93] We can only hope to discern what God promises and fulfills by immersing ourselves "again and again, for a long time and quite calmly, in Jesus's life, his sayings, actions, suffering and dying." In this way, and only in this way, can we "live aware that God is near and present with us." And it is this lived awareness of God's steadfast presence in Jesus Christ that gives real meaning to our lives, for

> [i]f the earth was deemed worthy to bear the human being Jesus Christ, if a human being like Jesus lived, then and only then does our life as human beings have meaning. Had Jesus not lived, then our life would be meaningless, despite all the other people we know, respect, and love.[94]

It is the purpose of the biblical proclamation to make this clear, for "the unbiblical concept of 'meaning'" is after all just "one translation of what the Bible calls 'promise.'"[95]

Heinz Tödt does not think it possible to find a biblical equivalent for the essentially modern concept of "meaning," which he believes to have emerged from the process of secularization in the West, and which he associates, though not exclusively, with existentialist philosophy and nihilism. While "promise," in the biblical sense of the term, speaks of something external to the human being that is "brought from God by the gospel," "meaning" is always a human search for something tangible and, even if vicariously, self-referential in the lives of human beings. Promise, says Tödt, does not depend on us.

> It is a message spoken to and received by the human being, if only they as recipients are capable of hearing and trusting in what they hear. Seeking after meaning, however, the human being hazards all that one's own self is, or hopefully is; for if no meaning is found, one's own life sinks into meaninglessness, haphazardness, bleakness, and nothingness, and is threatened by resignation or fear.[96]

This slide into the abyss of meaninglessness, Tödt believes, is precisely what Bonhoeffer understands to have been the outcome of the secular quest for meaning in Western culture, which reached a nadir in National Socialism. And Tödt, writing some forty years later, prior to the collapse of Soviet-style Communism, and from the perspective then, as now, of a nuclear-armed world, sees no reason to revise Bonhoeffer's assessment. We have at best a fragile confidence in the meaning of our own lives, and good reason to doubt the sustainability of human life on earth. The quest for meaning often seems an "absurdity," swallowed up in "an ocean of meaninglessness." But, Tödt argues, even in the absence of meaning, we still have "a promise in view," in the form of God's self-revelation in Jesus Christ, and the opportunity to participate, through the being of Christ, in "God's loving entry" into an undeserving world.[97]

Tödt thus effectively rejects Bonhoeffer's interpretation (for Bonhoeffer clearly intended the word "meaning" to stand for "promise" in the letter of August 21), having chosen instead to bring "meaning" and "promise" into creative tension as antitheses. But is he right to do so? Must we distinguish between God's action and the human being's existential quest for meaning in this case? Bonhoeffer would certainly have grasped Tödt's intention. The distinction between "meaning" (as something inward and essentially human) and "promise" (as something external and essentially divine) is, after all, highly reminiscent of Barth's, and Bonhoeffer's, understanding of the difference between religion and revelation/faith; but Bonhoeffer would seem to have something else in mind in this passage. "Promise" and "meaning" are not, strictly speaking, equivalent terms, because the one empowers the other, but they are nonetheless closely related. It is God's gift of revelation—the *promise* of new life in Jesus Christ—that makes our lives meaningful, that overcomes meaninglessness, that restores meaning to otherwise meaningless lives. The promise may come from another world, but it operates in this one, which is God's world, too.

NEXT STEPS

I think it reasonable to assume that Bonhoeffer would have persevered with this project if he had had the chance to do so. It was a critical component of his vision for the future of Christianity. He saw this as no straightforward task, and a similar humility is required of anyone who would follow in his footsteps. The question is, of course, which theological/biblical concepts may be thought most likely now to benefit from a nonreligious, or worldly, interpretation?

We have Bonhoeffer's lists,[98] but there is no reason to think of these as somehow fixed or settled. Bonhoeffer's letters certainly do not give this impression. Our aim must be not only to further understanding of what Bonhoeffer seems to have meant by religionless Christianity but also to support and encourage consideration of the possible shape and place of such a Christianity in our context. This means for us, as it did for Bonhoeffer, finding language that allows us to distinguish the real encounter with God in

Jesus Christ from a specious religious experience of God, and that makes the distinction credible to people who may, whether for religious or nonreligious reasons, not be inclined to take it seriously.

For many people, religionless Christianity conjures up images of a strictly human Jesus, a remarkable ethicist and exemplar of right conduct. His divinity falls away. But this was never Bonhoeffer's intention. Thus, among the words needed to make religionless Christianity work are several that present particular challenges to thoroughly "disenchanted" modern minds, including the word God itself, and others with a distinctly arcane ring to them—most obviously perhaps, revelation, incarnation, atonement, and resurrection.

We must, of course, respect Bonhoeffer's overarching objective, which was to find new ways of understanding existing concepts without diminishing the normative value of the concepts themselves. The challenge, as I see it then, is to find language that is compatible not only with Bonhoeffer's nascent sense of a Christ-centered, religionless Christianity but also with the shared understanding of people whose sense of the divine has been greatly attenuated by the dominant assumptions of a world come of age. My own initial response to this challenge is set out in the following pages.

God (Jesus Christ)

There are, of course, other words for God, in the Christian and other religious traditions. Most Christians are familiar, and many are reasonably comfortable, with expressions such as Supreme Being, Ultimate Reality, and even Cosmic Consciousness. But these won't serve our purpose here, because they emphasize God's remoteness rather than God's proximity, and because, in Bonhoeffer's theology, we are compelled to think of God in personal (Trinitarian) and relational terms. God *is*, for human beings, the encounter with Jesus Christ, but Jesus Christ is self-evidently not *the whole* of God and cannot be said to exhaust God's possibilities.

We might then perhaps argue that, in order to come properly to terms with the word God, we must abandon every attempt at a definition. God is not a thing among other things. Indeed, God *as such* is not a viable—in the sense of fixed and bounded—object of thought. The invincibly transcendent God of faith can only ever be "the prerequisite for our thinking, never the proof. For as an object providing proof [God] would no longer be the transcendent."[99] Any word that we may choose to describe this decisive boundary, or limit, to human understanding can only ever be allusive at best, which renders essentially pointless the search for other words to describe an "existing something" that will always remain finally beyond description.

Bonhoeffer is clearly convinced, however, that the only way to make the word God truly meaningful is to bring God into resolute and exclusive relationship with Jesus Christ. Everything that we can expect or hope to know of God is to be found in God's self-revelation in Jesus Christ. We *know* God only in this way, but we know *God* nonetheless. We are otherwise cut off from God by God's timelessness and from the historical Jesus by the passage of time. They touch our lives simultaneously, or not at all. "[I]n the human being Jesus Christ, God is God. Only in Jesus Christ is God present."[100]

Revelation (Otherness)

God speaks, and we listen. Revelation is a gift of grace and love, received in faith. Revelation is neither a product of systematic thinking nor a legacy of the religious imagination. It is always God's initiative; God's way to us. In this encounter, as Eberhard Busch observes (of Karl Barth's theology), it is God who determines "who he is for us, and who we are for him"; and God does this conclusively, "for all times and places."[101] God's self-revelation gives us reliable access to a reality outside ourselves. It is God's thoroughly external claim on us as socially constructed, ethical human beings. If we can accept this, and take it seriously, then the fundamental claim of the *Other*, encountered in revelation, becomes the prototype and basis for all such "outside" claims. It grounds both our experience of reality—our existence—and our humanity.

Incarnation (Mediation)

We may, and do, speak of God's divine transcendence, but we have no real means of thinking this through. God "on the other side of revelation"[102] is not God for us. Christians place their trust in the revealed Word of God—in God's becoming human *for us*—and can thereafter no longer "speak rightly of either God or the world without speaking of Jesus Christ."[103] In Jesus Christ, the "original and essential encounter" with God *and* the human being takes place.[104] He is "the boundary of the being that has been given to me"[105] and the mediator of all my relationships. He stands between me and every other, and before God on my behalf. In his absence, neither God nor human beings could be said truly to exist for me. "There is no human being as such, just as there is no God as such; both are empty abstractions."[106] In Jesus Christ, I recognize my true humanity as something shared, and never solitary.

Atonement (Dying to Self)

The crucifixion is the perfect example of vicarious representative action. A terrible death on the cross is transformed into a gift of love that restores sinful humanity to community with God. Christians are, of course, accustomed to see the cross in the light of the resurrection. If they had failed to recognize the risen Christ, they would almost certainly have forgotten the crucified Jesus. But the converse is also true. Christ's humiliation and exaltation are inseparable. His violent death is every bit as much an irreversible part of Christian experience as is his resurrection from the dead.

Death stands between us and new life with God in Jesus Christ. We must share Jesus's sense of God-forsakenness (Mark 15:34)—of God's absence—on the way to this new life. Matthew 8:17 ("He took our infirmities and bore our diseases") makes it quite clear, says Bonhoeffer, that "Christ helps us not by virtue of his omnipotence but rather by virtue of his weakness and suffering."[107] We may find the image of a God who "is weak and powerless in the world"[108] confronting, but the fact remains that if God knew nothing of weakness and suffering, then God would not know us, and we would have no reason to place our faith in God's saving love.

Once we have established what a theology of atonement, rooted in God's love for the world, means for the Christian understanding of God, then we can also grasp its implications for Christian conduct. Christ's death on the cross—this perfect act of "vicarious representative love"[109]—becomes for his followers a way of liberation, a means of envisaging a positive *dying to self,* and the cornerstone of "a new life in 'being there for others,' through participation in the being of Jesus."[110]

Resurrection (Living for Others)

Our own *being for others in Christ* is an abiding effect of the resurrection. Bonhoeffer does not spare us the need to come to terms with this cryptic phenomenon:

> The body of Jesus comes forth from the tomb, and the tomb is empty. We are unable to grasp how it is possible and thinkable that the mortal and corruptible body is now present as the immortal, incorruptible, transfigured body. The variety of the accounts reporting the encounter of the Risen One with the disciples demonstrates perhaps nothing so clearly as the fact that we are unable to construct an image of the new life in the body of the Risen One.[111]

And because the risen Christ appeared "only to his own"—because "Jesus does not present himself to a neutral authority in order to allow the miracle of his resurrection to be attested before the world"—all certainty of the historicity of the resurrection is finally, and exclusively, a matter of faith.[112]

Bonhoeffer may not share what he calls Barth's "positivism of revelation,"[113] but he cannot accept Bultmann's "typical liberal reductionism" either. There is, for Bonhoeffer, no such thing as demythologized scripture.

"[T]he New Testament is not a mythological dressing up of a universal truth, but this mythology (resurrection and so forth) is the thing itself!"[114]

In an early sermon, Bonhoeffer warns against confusing Christ's death and resurrection with natural symbols of renewal. Good Friday, he says, "is not the darkness that must necessarily yield to light," or the "winter sleep" before the spring. "It is the day on which human beings—human beings who wanted to be like gods—kill the God who became human, the love that became person." The "Holy One of God, that is, God himself" died that day "without any seed of life remaining in him."[115] Christ was killed by human beings and was raised by God from the dead. The resurrection does not change what happened on the cross. It is God's answer to it. Without the resurrection, "the final word" would be ours, and empty. "What [Bonhoeffer asks] is the point of searching for truth if there is no truth, if human beings rather than God represent the ultimate standard for what is true and false?" If Jesus Christ had not been raised on Easter Day, God's "final pronouncement over humankind would be guilt, rebellion . . . a storming of heaven by human beings, godlessness . . . meaninglessness and despair."[116]

To live in the light of the resurrection, though, does not mean to live in pious hope of eternal life. "What matters is not the beyond but this world, how it is created and preserved, is given laws, reconciled, and renewed."[117] Christ's resurrection prepares the way for the Son of God's now exclusively spiritual presence among us. And it is this constant presence—the assurance that "Jesus Christ is the same yesterday and today and forever" (Heb. 13:8)—that is, or should be, most important to us. The resurrection demonstrates that God "has not given up on the earth" but has instead "given it a new future, a new promise."[118] It "refers people to their life on earth in a wholly new way."[119] And we have, like Christ, "to drink the cup of earthly life to the last drop"[120]—to respond faithfully to the ever-changing demands of vulnerable, finite life—for it is precisely here, in the midst of life, that Christ takes hold of us and turns us to face the world.

CONCLUSION

In his prison letters and papers, Bonhoeffer began to consider the implications, for the church and Christian life, of a world without religion. He saw this essentially practical task as requiring a proper hermeneutical foundation. Nonreligious interpretation would have a critical, if subsidiary, role to play in establishing the religionless form of Christianity. It must be able to tell people what Bonhoeffer believed the existing religious language of the church could no longer tell them: "what it means to live in Christ and follow Christ."[121] It must address the christological "who" question—"who is Christ actually for us today?"[122]—and, in the process, take seriously into account the historical and cultural realities of a world come of age.

Sadly, Bonhoeffer had no opportunity to shape, substantively, this interpretive endeavor, but there is no reason to think he would not have labored to do so if he had had the chance. Nonreligious interpretation was an indispensable component of his vision for the future of Christianity. It might thus reasonably be expected to contribute to the ongoing exploration of Bonhoeffer's concept of religionless Christianity, and to our understanding of its relevance for us today.

NOTES

1. *Letters and Papers*, DBWE 8: 364.
2. *Letters and Papers*, DBWE 8: 362.
3. Bonhoeffer does not have a consistent way of describing this task. In the *Letters and Papers from Prison*, he speaks variously of "worldly" reinterpretation (DBWE 8: 373), of "the nonreligious interpretation of theological concepts" (DBWE 8: 429), of "interpreting biblical concepts nonreligiously" (DBWE 8: 455), and of "the worldly interpretation of biblical concepts" (DBWE 8: 457).
4. *Letters and Papers*, DBWE 8: 501–2.
5. *Letters and Papers*, DBWE 8: 373. "And the Word became flesh and lived among us, and we have seen his glory, the glory as of a father's only son, full of grace and truth" (John 1:14).
6. Feil, *The Theology of Dietrich Bonhoeffer*, 46.
7. *Conspiracy and Imprisonment*, DBWE 16: 40–41.
8. *Letters and Papers*, DBWE 8: 390.
9. *Letters and Papers*, DBWE 8: 389. It is hard to associate these sentiments with the author of *Discipleship* (1935–1936) and *Life Together* (1938)—books which confidently affirm the possibility of vibrant, contemporary life with Christ, in already challenging times. That we must do so is testimony to Bonhoeffer's ever keener sense of the depravity which surrounds him, and to the increasingly perilous, and ethically equivocal, personal circumstances in which he finds himself.
10. *Letters and Papers*, DBWE 8: 389.
11. Wüstenberg, *A Theology of Life*, 123.
12. *Letters and Papers*, DBWE 8: 501.
13. The problem of non-religious interpretation [says Ebeling] arises for Bonhoeffer not from any doubt of Jesus Christ, but precisely from faith in Jesus Christ. It is not Jesus Christ, but the word God, indeed all religious concepts as such, that he finds problematical. The question of non-religious interpretation derives directly from the foundation and heart of his theology, from his Christology. Non-religious interpretation is for Bonhoeffer nothing other than Christological interpretation.

Ebeling, *Word and Faith*, 107.

14. Ebeling, *Word and Faith*, 109.
15. Ebeling, *Word and Faith*, 112–13.
16. Ebeling, *Word and Faith*, 125.
17. Ebeling, *Word and Faith*, 125–26.
18. *Letters and Papers*, DBWE 8: 478.
19. *Letters and Papers*, DBWE 8: 515.
20. *Letters and Papers*, DBWE 8: 475.
21. *Letters and Papers*, DBWE 8: 364.
22. Feil, *The Theology of Dietrich Bonhoeffer*, 193.
23. Feil, *The Theology of Dietrich Bonhoeffer*, 46.
24. Bethge, *Dietrich Bonhoeffer*, 879–80. The questions raised in the third chapter of the "Outline" concern the future of the church and the clergy. *Letters and Papers*, DBWE 8: 503–4.
25. Bethge, *Dietrich Bonhoeffer*, 885. It wasn't just Allied bombers that prevented Bonhoeffer from devoting more time to the task of nonreligious interpretation. He simply wasn't ready to do so. In addition to the frank admission that he was "more able to see what needs to be done than how . . . actually to do it" (*Letters and Papers*, DBWE 8: 475), there are signs of procrastination as, for example, in the letter to Bethge of July 8, where he writes, "So, now would be the time to speak concretely about the worldly interpretation of biblical concepts. But it's just *too* hot today!" *Letters and Papers*, DBWE 8: 457.
26. Bethge, *Dietrich Bonhoeffer*, 885.
27. *Letters and Papers*, DBWE 8: 238.
28. ἔσχατος ἐχθρὸς καταργεῖται ὁ θάνατος. "The last enemy to be destroyed is death."
29. "Give me [the point, the place outside the earth] where I can stand and I will move the earth [from its hinges]" (Archimedes, cited in Pappus, *Collectio* 8.11).
30. *Letters and Papers*, DBWE 8: 333.
31. *Letters and Papers*, DBWE 8: 447–48.
32. *Letters and Papers*, DBWE 8: 491–93. Schwöbel believes the Old Testament to serve as the hermeneutical key for an understanding of the New Testament which permits Bonhoeffer to reject "all tendencies towards spiritualisation." The Old Testament does not distinguish between internal and external, between the individual and the social, between the body and the spirit. From this perspective, nonreligious interpretation means to interpret the Bible "holistically" with respect both to God's ubiquitous embrace of all reality and to human life as "a multi-dimensional whole." Schwöbel, "'Religion' and 'Religionlessness,'" in Nielsen, Nissen, and Tietz, 162.
33. Bethge, *Dietrich Bonhoeffer*, 885; *Letters and Papers*, DBWE 8: 460–61.
34. *Letters and Papers*, DBWE 8: 461.
35. *Letters and Papers*, DBWE 8: 480.
36. Bethge, *Dietrich Bonhoeffer*, 885.
37. *Letters and Papers*, DBWE 8: 501.
38. Bethge, *Dietrich Bonhoeffer*, 885.
39. Bethge, *Dietrich Bonhoeffer*, 886.

40. Dietrich Bonhoeffer, "*Daily Text* Meditation for June 7 and 8, 1944," in *Conspiracy and Imprisonment*, DBWE 16: 632.

41. Dietrich Bonhoeffer, "Exposition on the First Table of the Ten Words of God," in *Conspiracy and Imprisonment*, DBWE 16: 634.

42. "Exposition on the First Table of the Ten Words of God," DBWE 16: 638. Bonhoeffer refers acidly to this anti-God nothingness in the *Ethics* fragment "Heritage and Decay," where he describes the West as deprived of its former unity in Christ and now plunged into nothingness [Nichts].

> This nothingness into which the West is sliding is not the natural end, the dying, the sinking of a flourishing community of peoples. Instead, it is . . . a specifically Western nothingness: a nothingness that is rebellious, violent, anti-God, and antihuman. . . . It is nothingness as God . . . a creative nothingness that blows its anti-God breath into all that exists, creates the illusion of waking it to new life, and at the same time sucks out its true essence until it soon disintegrates into an empty husk and is discarded.
>
> *Ethics*, DBWE 6: 127–28.

43. "You shall not make wrongful use of the name of the LORD your God, for the LORD will not acquit anyone who misuses his name" (Exod. 20:7).

44. "That the Israelites never say the name of God aloud is something I often ponder." *Letters and Papers*, DBWE 8: 189. "The Israelites dealt with the danger of such misuse of God's name through the prohibition against speaking this name aloud at all." "Exposition on the First Table of the Ten Words of God," DBWE 16: 641. I am simply following Bonhoeffer's train of thought here. The claim that the Israelites never spoke the name of God aloud is not true of Old Testament times, and greatly oversimplifies a lengthy and complex traditioning process.

45. "Exposition on the First Table of the Ten Words of God," DBWE 16: 641–42.

46. James Patrick Kelley, "Christological Concretion and Everyday Events in Three of Bonhoeffer's Sermons," in Kelly and Weborg, 100–13.

47. Kelley, "Christological Concretion and Everyday Events in Three of Bonhoeffer's Sermons," in Kelly and Weborg, 100–1.

48. Dietrich Bonhoeffer, "Sermon on Psalm 63:3, Berlin, Thanksgiving Sunday, October 4, 1931 (?)," in *Ecumenical, Academic, and Pastoral Work*, DBWE 11: 402. The date is uncertain. Bethge annotated Bonhoeffer's original handwritten draft: "Thanksgiving, October 4, 1931? Evening Service."

49. "Sermon on Psalm 63:3," DBWE 11: 402.

50. "Sermon on Psalm 63:3," DBWE 11: 403.

51. "Sermon on Psalm 63:3," DBWE 11: 404.

52. "Sermon on Psalm 63:3," DBWE 11: 403.

53. "Sermon on Psalm 63:3," DBWE 11: 404.

54. "Sermon on Psalm 63:3," DBWE 11: 405.

55. "Sermon on Psalm 63:3," DBWE 11: 405.

56. "Sermon on Psalm 63:3," DBWE 11: 405–6.

57. "Sermon on Psalm 63:3," DBWE 11: 406–7.

58. "Sermon on Psalm 63:3," DBWE 11: 407.

59. "Sermon on Psalm 63:3," DBWE 11: 407–8. Bonhoeffer here quotes the fourth verse of Martin Luther's hymn, "A Mighty Fortress Is Our God."

60. Kelley, "Christological Concretion and Everyday Events in Three of Bonhoeffer's Sermons," in Kelly and Weborg, 104.

61. Bonhoeffer wrote the sermon in English and cites the King James Version of the Bible.

62. Dietrich Bonhoeffer, "Sermon for Evening Worship Service on 2 Corinthians 12:9, London, 1934 (?)," in *London, 1933–1935*, ed. Keith Clements (Minneapolis: Fortress Press, 2007), DBWE 13: 401. The date is uncertain.

63. "Sermon on 2 Corinthians 12:9," DBWE 13: 401–2.

64. "Sermon on 2 Corinthians 12:9," DBWE 13: 402. Bonhoeffer had little confidence overall in the church's capacity for serious, and sustained, opposition to state-sanctioned injustice. "Must it be that Christianity, which began in such a tremendously revolutionary way long ago, is now conservative for all time? That each new movement must forge a path for itself without the church, that time after time the church does not see what has actually happened until twenty years after the fact?" Dietrich Bonhoeffer, "Sermon on Colossians 3:1–4, Berlin, June 19, 1932," in *Ecumenical, Academic, and Pastoral Work*, DBWE 11: 459. Pugh, in his study of Bonhoeffer's religionless Christianity, identifies religious interpretation with theologies of power that "rest comfortably with the suffering of others in the name of some larger cause." Nonreligious interpretation, on the other hand, serves the need of those who understand such theologies to have been "overturned by the God who suffers." Jeffrey C. Pugh, *Religionless Christianity: Dietrich Bonhoeffer in Troubled Times* (London: T&T Clark, 2008), 101. Whereas the religious impulse would have us search for God in some quite separate and sacred realm outside the world of our experience, religionless Christianity inspires an entirely different relationship with God, grounded in the encounter with Jesus Christ as the human being for others. God is thus always close at hand, in the thick of life. Faith, says Pugh, for Bonhoeffer, "in the end is a lived moment." Pugh, *Religionless Christianity*, 103. Bonhoeffer makes this abundantly clear in the letter to Bethge of July 21, 1944, when he says that "one only learns to have faith by living in the full this-worldliness of life . . . [by] living fully in the midst of life's tasks, questions, successes and failures, experiences, and perplexities." *Letters and Papers*, DBWE 8: 486. For Pugh, religionless Christianity is "profoundly subversive" because it encourages a compassion, grounded firmly in Christ's suffering, that makes no allowance for "historical contingencies." Pugh, *Religionless Christianity*, 112. Instead, it "relativises all social orders." This leads Pugh to believe that the church is perhaps "best . . . shaped in the contemporary setting by commitments that place it in a position of exile." Pugh, *Religionless Christianity*, 161.

65. "Sermon on 2 Corinthians 12:9," DBWE 13: 403–4.

66. Kelley, "Christological Concretion and Everyday Events in Three of Bonhoeffer's Sermons," in Kelly and Weborg, 105–6.

67. Dietrich Bonhoeffer, "Sermon on John 8:32, Berlin, Ninth Sunday after Trinity (Worship Service at the End of the Semester), July 24, 1932," in *Ecumenical, Academic, and Pastoral Work*, DBWE 11: 465.

68. "Sermon on John 8:32," DBWE 11: 469.

138   *Chapter 4*

69. "Sermon on John 8:32," DBWE 11: 469–70.
70. "Sermon on John 8:32," DBWE 11: 470.
71. "Sermon on John 8:32," DBWE 11: 471.
72. Bonhoeffer takes inspiration from an expression used by Nietzsche to describe the coming *Übermensch*. But, where Nietzsche refers to a "revaluation" or "transvaluation" of all values (*Umwertung aller Werte*), Bonhoeffer employs a variation "popular at the time and add[s] a more forceful meaning to the original." "Sermon on John 8:32," DBWE 11: 471, ed. fn. 38. The verb *umstürzen* means "to overturn." *Ein Umsturz* is a "coup (d'état)."
73. "Sermon on John 8:32," DBWE 11: 471–72.
74. "Sermon on John 8:32," DBWE 11: 472.
75. "Sermon on John 8:32," DBWE 11: 465.
76. "Sermon on 2 Corinthians 12:9," DBWE 13: 404.
77. "Sermon on John 8:32," DBWE 11: 471.
78. Bethge, *Dietrich Bonhoeffer*, 885.
79. Edwin Robertson, *Bonhoeffer's Heritage: The Christian Way in a World without Religion* (London: Hodder & Stoughton, 1989).
80. *Barcelona, Berlin, New York*, DBWE 10: 310; *Theological Education Underground*, DBWE 15: 460.
81. Robertson, *Bonhoeffer's Heritage*, 119.
82. Robertson, *Bonhoeffer's Heritage*, 120.
83. *Letters and Papers*, DBWE 8: 478.
84. Robertson, *Bonhoeffer's Heritage*, 123.
85. Robertson, *Bonhoeffer's Heritage*, 126.
86. *Letters and Papers*, DBWE 8: 478.
87. *Letters and Papers*, DBWE 8: 515.
88. *Letters and Papers*, DBWE 8: 425–26.
89. "Truly I tell you, unless you change and become like children, you will never enter the kingdom of heaven" (Matt. 18:3).
90. *Letters and Papers*, DBWE 8: 478.
91. *Letters and Papers*, DBWE 8: 479.
92. *Letters and Papers*, DBWE 8: 480. "Surely he has borne our infirmities and carried our diseases; yet we accounted him stricken, struck down by God, and afflicted. But he was wounded for our transgressions, crushed for our iniquities; upon him was the punishment that made us whole, and by his bruises we are healed" (Isa. 53:4–5). The German editors note the significance of the word "now" (inserted afterward by Bonhoeffer) in this context. "This *present* aspect, the 'now' in which Isa. 53 is fulfilled in the present moment, is noteworthy because until then Bonhoeffer had *always* seen the suffering of God's servant as accomplished on the cross of Golgotha." *Letters and Papers*, DBWE 8: 481, ed. fn. 50.
93. *Letters and Papers*, DBWE 8: 514–15.
94. *Letters and Papers*, DBWE 8: 515.
95. *Letters and Papers*, DBWE 8: 515.
96. Heinz Eduard Tödt, *Authentic Faith: Bonhoeffer's Theological Ethics in Context*, trans. David Stassen and Ilse Tödt (Grand Rapids: Eerdmans, 2007), 16–17.

97. Tödt, *Authentic Faith*, 27.
98. *Letters and Papers*, DBWE 8: 373, 502.
99. "Lectures on Christology," DBWE 12: 301.
100. "Lectures on Christology," DBWE 12: 313.
101. Eberhard Busch, *The Great Passion: An Introduction to Karl Barth's Theology*, trans. Geoffrey W. Bromiley (Grand Rapids: Eerdmans, 2004), 88.
102. *Act and Being*, DBWE 2: 90.
103. *Ethics*, DBWE 6: 54.
104. *Ethics*, DBWE 6: 253.
105. "Lectures on Christology," DBWE 12: 305.
106. *Ethics*, DBWE 6: 253.
107. *Letters and Papers*, DBWE 8: 479.
108. *Letters and Papers*, DBWE 8: 479.
109. *Sanctorum Communio*, DBWE 1: 156.
110. *Letters and Papers*, DBWE 8: 501.
111. Dietrich Bonhoeffer, "Reflection on Easter: Resurrection," in *Conspiracy and Imprisonment*, DBWE 16: 474.
112. "Reflection on Easter," DBWE 16: 475–76.
113. *Letters and Papers*, DBWE 8: 373.
114. *Letters and Papers*, DBWE 8: 430.
115. Dietrich Bonhoeffer, "Sermon on 1 Corinthians 15:17, Barcelona, Easter Sunday, April 8, 1928," in *Barcelona, Berlin, New York*, DBWE 10: 487.
116. "Sermon on 1 Corinthians 15:17," DBWE 10: 488. The mature Bonhoeffer finds no cause to reconsider this argument, but repeats it, in his March 1940 reflection on Easter, writing: "The cross was the end, the death of the Son of God, curse and judgment on all flesh. If the cross had been the last word about Jesus, then the world would be lost in death and damnation without hope; then the world would have triumphed over God." But God raised the God-human Jesus Christ from the dead, "not, like spring, according to a fixed law, but out of the incomparable freedom and power of God, which shatters death." "Reflection on Easter," DBWE 16: 471.
117. *Letters and Papers*, DBWE 8: 373. Baillie insists that

> the only knowledge we can have of eternal life is that it comes to us through our present foretasting of its joys. All that we can know of the other life *there* is what we know of it *here*. For even here there is *another* life that may be lived, a life wholly other than that which commonly bears the name and yet one which may be lived out in this very place where I now am ... this other life is the life everlasting.
>
> John Baillie, *And the Life Everlasting* (Oxford: OUP, 1956), 251.

118. "Reflection on Easter," DBWE 16: 474.
119. *Letters and Papers*, DBWE 8: 447.
120. *Letters and Papers*, DBWE 8: 448.
121. *Letters and Papers*, DBWE 8: 389.
122. *Letters and Papers*, DBWE 8: 362.

Chapter 5

Mystery, Faith, and Wholeness

So far, I have explored the Christology which serves both to establish and to expand the boundaries of Bonhoeffer's inescapably truncated sketch of a religionless form of Christianity, and the hermeneutical approach with which this form might most profitably be associated. I have also examined the sociohistorical presupposition which Bonhoeffer thought made such a religionless Christianity necessary, and the critique of religion which tells us what kind of Christianity he believed to be coming to an end.

It is time now to consider other aspects of Bonhoeffer's thought which seem to me to enable a further consolidation and enrichment of his christological vision for a religionless age. These include the place of mystery and paradox in Bonhoeffer's thinking, his determination to preserve a sense of life's wholeness in face of the growing ascendancy of historically conditioned forces of disintegration, and the critical significance of the "Christ reality" for bringing us into the presence of God.

A HOLY MYSTERY

There is, in all expressions of faith, a necessary tension between language and silence: the sense, on the one hand, of a shared understanding of God mediated through language, in the absence of which God either disappears or is rendered unintelligible, and, on the other, of a final ineffability that lies entirely beyond the reach of human thought, words, and images, and which mocks our efforts to impose on others our exclusive ideas of God.

In his December 1939 "Meditation on Christmas," Bonhoeffer describes the incarnation as a "holy mystery, which theology was instituted to preserve and protect." All Christian theology, he says, has its origin in this unique and miraculous event, in the event of God's becoming human.

> What foolishness, as if it were the task of theology to decode God's mystery, pulling it down to the commonplace, miracle-less words of wisdom based on human experience and reason! Whereas this alone is its charge—to keep the miracle of God a miracle, to comprehend, defend, and exalt the mystery of God, precisely as mystery.[1]

Bonhoeffer freely acknowledged the limits of human understanding. As we saw in chapter 3, he began the lectures on Christology in the summer of 1933 by emphasizing the mystery of transcendence. We have simply to accept the fact, he told his students, that the Word of God became a real human being. We cannot prove this, because it is in the very nature of transcendence to condition thought rather than to substantiate it.[2] Thus, it is in wordless affirmation of God's revelation that the church comes first to "speak" of Christ. "In proclaiming Christ, the church falls on its knees in silence before the inexpressible."[3]

The Silent Soul

Bonhoeffer's youthful sermon on Psalm 62:2 is a sublime meditation on the healing power of silence. He begins with the image of a pious man who, many years ago, "knelt down before God in the solitude and silence of the holy Jewish temple and spoke these words: 'My soul is silent before God, who helps me.'"[4] The image has a gentle, distant, dreamlike quality. It inspires in us a certain imprecise longing but, or so Bonhoeffer believes, no real desire for understanding. Is there, he asks, "still something like the soul in an age such as ours?" There is, but it speaks so quietly as to be barely audible amid the turmoil within us. We risk losing it entirely and may awaken one day to find ourselves empty and soulless, "a leaf before the wind."[5]

We have a responsibility to take the soul seriously and will be held accountable for it. The soul is God's gift of life to us. "It is the love within us and the longing and the sacred restlessness and the responsibility and joy and pain. It is the divine breath breathed into a transitory being."[6] If we are truly to understand this, we must learn to be silent in God's presence, and thus to give the soul respite from the chaotic din of life. In this silence, we lose the capacity for speech. It is as if "an alien but beneficent hand is laid upon our lips." In this silence is a blissful beholding, an act of capitulation to the superior power of "the wholly other." In this silence, God has "the first and last word concerning us," and we make no attempt to justify ourselves. The soul becomes silent before God, ready to hear, and to obey, God's will for it.[7]

We are, however, often strangely reluctant to expose ourselves to the "fire of God's love."[8] We hold back because we fear the silence that could reveal the specious and desultory nature of our lives, just as we fear the lonely encounter with God, "lest he suddenly get too close to us."[9] We must have the courage daily to submit to the judgment of God's Word.

> None of us is so rushed that we cannot find ten minutes a day during the morning or evening to be silent, to focus on eternity alone ... and in the process look deeply into ourselves and far beyond ourselves, either by reading a couple of biblical passages or, even better, by becoming completely free and allowing our soul to travel to the house of the Father, to the home in which it finds peace.[10]

At the center of Bonhoeffer's thought, says Ernst Feil, is a mystery of faith which reason does not comprehend, and to that center it seeks always to return.[11] Theology, for Bonhoeffer, is constrained by its subject matter. It must not overreach itself with its truth claims, for its leitmotif is a mystery which brings us eventually to a place simply of silent affirmation. It depends on paradox for its formulations because "that is how structures of thought are broken down and space is created for the mystery."[12]

Godless Mysticism

While theological reflections on mystery and silence commonly invite association with the traditions of Christian mysticism, they do so much less readily in Bonhoeffer's case. Bonhoeffer believed mysticism to be a religious outcome of the essentially anti-Christian "Greek spirit" of humanism, which invests every human being with a measure of divinity, and history with a sense of purpose which draws it steadily closer to God.[13] Mysticism, for Bonhoeffer, is the religious endeavor to achieve some form of unity—whether intellectual, voluntaristic, or emotional—with God "on one's own initiative and based on one's own divine potential." But the gulf between God and human beings simply cannot be bridged in this way. It is "precisely the Christian idea itself" which must reject, as hubris and an affront to the honor which belongs to God alone, these[14] "seemingly most beautiful blossoms" of the Christian religion.[15]

Bonhoeffer believes mysticism (understood in this thoroughly anthropocentric, religious sense) to be fundamentally incompatible with the gospel of Jesus Christ. This is because mysticism, along with liberal, pietistic, and ethical theology, encourages an anthropocentric (and therefore false) understanding of transcendence, which the Bible, with its profound sense of God's grace at work in the creation, and in the incarnation, crucifixion, and resurrection of Jesus Christ, does not know.[16] Indeed, mysticism may be regarded as symptomatic of the phenomenon of "Western godlessness," whose god is "the new human being," and which, in what Bonhoeffer describes as "every possible Christianity"—nationalist, socialist, rationalist, and mystical—"turns against the living God of the Bible, against Christ."[17]

As a young doctoral student, Bonhoeffer was especially wary of the potential for a mystical sense of community with God to transgress "the boundary of the I-You-relation" by promoting the idea of "unification" or "mystical fusion."[18] For Bonhoeffer, there can be no "final assimilation," no "fusion of our supposedly divine nature" with God. Human beings are never lost in God, or in one another.[19] They exist always in ethical responsibility,[20] and are thus "real only in sociality," but they remain ultimately, primally, that which God willed and created individually.[21] If this were not so, then Bonhoeffer's basic social category—the I-You relation—would be fatally undermined. And because it is the divine You that creates the human You "from whom my I arises,"[22] we can see that Bonhoeffer's aversion to what he calls "mystical fusion" stems in part from its incompatibility with a concept of personhood which is grounded fundamentally in our relation to God as archetypal Other. These critically important, existence-defining dualisms—Creator/creature, I/You—must not be obscured.

Mysticism, for Bonhoeffer, stands irremediably on the wrong side of the divide between religion and revelation. It is caught up in the primary fallacy of idealism, where the mind mistakes its own imaginings for observed, genuinely external phenomena. In mysticism, as in idealism, the I is self-enclosed. "It relates itself to itself, and consequently to God, in unmediated reflection." God is "completely locked into consciousness."[23]

Despite these firmly expressed misgivings, Bonhoeffer is clearly familiar with contemplative practice, and especially with the perils of solitary meditation. His description of its hazards closely echoes those of teachers in the Christian mystical and other great contemplative traditions, as, for example, when he says of silence that it

> can be a dreadful wasteland with all its isolated stretches and terrors. It can also be a paradise of self-deception. One is not better than the other. . . . [L]et none expect from silence anything but a simple encounter with the Word of God. . . . This encounter . . . is given to [Christians] as a gift. Their silence will be richly rewarded if they do not set any conditions on . . . it, but simply accept it as it comes.[24]

And he could strike something very close to a mystical note himself on occasion. For example, in a biblical reflection on the break of day, thought to have been written at Finkenwalde in the summer of 1935, he describes the morning, every morning, as "a new beginning for our lives." As such,

[i]t is not our own plans and worries . . . that should fill the first moments of each new day, but rather God's liberating grace, God's blessed nearness. . . . Before the heart opens itself up to the world, God wishes to open it up to God's gaze; before the ear perceives the innumerable voices of the day, it should hear the voice of the Creator and Redeemer in the early morning. God prepared the quietness of the first morning for God alone. And thus should it belong to God.[25]

It may be nonetheless safely assumed that this passage is not intended to convey what Bonhoeffer would have called a mystical, inwardly focused yearning for God but rather a very deliberate openness to the Word of God which comes always from outside. There is, for Bonhoeffer, no religious a priori, no "mold in human beings into which the divine content of revelation, too, may pour,"[26] but it would seem there is still a depth (rather than a space) in us where the wordless encounter with God takes place. The practice of silent meditation has, particularly for the young Bonhoeffer, the potential to take us beyond human words, thoughts, and forms to a place where we can simply *be* with God.

The Language of Paradox

Bonhoeffer, James Kelley argues, understood the need for Christians confidently to embrace paradoxical language. Christians speak both of God's historical self-revelation in Jesus Christ and of the unbroken presence of Jesus Christ among them still. They will always be misunderstood if their assertions are taken literally, and yet they can do no other than affirm the "both/and" quality of the truth they confess. Paradox is by nature Delphic and arcane. It is also inescapable, Kelley says, because it "roots in the fundamental understanding of God to which Christians testify."[27]

This is especially true of Christology—of what Bonhoeffer refers to as that "peculiar area of scholarship" which rests on the assumption that "Christ is the very Word of God."[28] Christology is concerned with just one question, the question "who are you?" And in this question lies a mystery that is, finally, too deep for words. It is a question that can really only be asked "after the self-revelation of the other to whom one puts the question has already taken place." People do not set out on some blind quest for God. Those who truly search for God "already know who God is." Bonhoeffer quotes Pascal: "You would not seek me if you had not already found me."[29]

In God's self-revelation, we reach "the boundary of the being that has been given to [us]"[30] and find the transcendent embodied in the Otherness of the God-human Jesus Christ. The exemplary formulation of this thesis is to be found in the Chalcedonian Definition of the Faith of 451. While Monophysites insist on the unity of the divine and human natures, and Nestorians make "a plain distinction between them,"³¹ the Definition of Chalcedon affirms ἕνα καὶ τὸν αὐτὸν Χριστόν . . . ἐν δύο φύσεσιν, without confusion, without change, without distinction, without separation.³²

As Bonhoeffer points out, no attempt is made here to combine these contrasting qualities into a positive affirmation of faith in Christ. In fact, it is no longer possible to make "any positive assertion . . . about what happens in Jesus Christ," because in him we have now simultaneously to consider all possibilities relating to God and the human being. After Chalcedon, one can no longer "talk about the human and divine natures of Jesus Christ as about things or facts." One can no longer simply "think of a concept of God and draw a line there."³³ Bonhoeffer is very comfortable with this outcome. In Chalcedon he celebrates "an objective, living assertion about Christ that goes beyond all conceptual forms," encompassing everything "in its very clear yet paradoxical agility."³⁴ Here, "[m]aterial thinking reaches its limit at the point where it has to acknowledge that the opposite, contradictory assertion is just as necessary as its own assertion" and the "how" question is overcome by forcing us to recognize that "this 'how' of relationship is impossible to think through."³⁵ Indeed, after Chalcedon, "we can no longer say, how shall we think about the difference of the two natures and the unity of the person but rather: who is this human being who is said to be God?"³⁶ Ernst-Albert Scharffenorth sees in Bonhoeffer a modern champion of the Chalcedonian formula, whose paradoxes he (Bonhoeffer) regards as indispensable for Christology.³⁷

The Hidden Wisdom of God

We are impoverished by the lack of mystery in modern life. Bonhoeffer goes so far as to tell his German-speaking congregation in London in May 1934 that life is worth living only "to the extent that it keeps its respect for mystery.³⁸ By honoring mystery, we keep within us some of the child we used to be."³⁹

But it is more often the case that we find mystery offensive. We are inclined to avoid, or to dismiss, what we cannot explain, and to disregard what is evidently not at our disposal.

> *That the roots of all that is clear and obvious and understandable lie in mystery*, that is what we do not want to hear. If we do hear it, then we want to get to the bottom of this mystery, to calculate and explain it. We want to dissect it, and we thereby only succeed in killing the life in it and still do not find the mystery.⁴⁰

There is, though, no getting behind the mystery of God. God's wisdom is hidden from us. God's thoughts are not our thoughts, and we must not claim to know the mind of God. God's being is mystery "because it speaks of a home in which we cannot—not yet—be at home."[41] There is thus no point in struggling to bring God into plain sight, or in trying to adapt God to a thoroughly human understanding of what we assume to be God's ways.

> Instead, all our thinking about God must serve only to make us see how completely beyond us and how *mysterious* God is, to make us glimpse the mysterious and hidden wisdom of God in all its mystery and hiddenness, rather than making it any less so—and thus perhaps give us a glimpse of the mystery of that home from which it comes.[42]

Should proof be required of the world's blindness to the mystery of God, we need think only of Christ's crucifixion for, as Paul said, if the rulers of the age had known the wisdom of God, "they would not have crucified the Lord of glory" (1 Cor. 2:8). Jesus Christ is the "unrecognized mystery of God in the world." In him, the glory of God is revealed, paradoxically, in "lowliness and poverty. . . . That God did not remain far above human beings but rather comes *close* to us and loves us, *God's love and closeness—that is the mystery of God, the holy mystery prepared for those who love God*."[43]

Feil finds here, in "the directness of preaching," a clear statement of Bonhoeffer's conviction that "mystery is the root of everything comprehensible."[44] But mystery is not, principally, for Bonhoeffer a rhetorical device. It is rather a theological description of the incarnation—that "holy mystery, which theology was instituted to preserve and protect."[45] And Bonhoeffer leans heavily on this "holy mystery," including in his later writings where God's acceptance of *all* humanity in Jesus Christ,[46] Christ's role as sole mediator between God and the world,[47] his sinless bearing of guilt,[48] the largely hidden conformation of some to the crucified and risen Christ[49] (while so many others still fail to recognize him),[50] and the good that comes from "surrendering to God the deed that has become necessary and is nevertheless . . . free,"[51] are all shrouded in mystery.

Faith

Faith, too, is essentially mysterious. In *Act and Being*, Bonhoeffer describes faith as turned always toward Christ, "towards that which comes from outside." It is only in faith that "I know that I believe," while "in reflection on faith in Christ I know nothing."[52]

Faith is to theology as the *actus directus* is to the *actus reflexus*.[53] In the *actus directus*, consciousness is wholly outwardly directed, whereas in the *actus reflexus*, consciousness is both self-aware and, not unusually, self-preoccupied. It is not, says Bonhoeffer, that the *actus directus* provides no material for reflection, but that, because it is here focused exclusively on Christ, it simply does not enter into such reflection.[54] As the act of faith, it "rests on the objectivity of the event of revelation in Word and sacrament."[55]

Faith demands no special qualifications. We have only to be open to God's Word, and ready to admit it, unconditionally, into our hearts. In God's self-revelation, we come face-to-face with Jesus Christ. As Bonhoeffer says, simply but memorably, of Peter, in a sermon on Matthew 16:13–18, "Peter is nobody really, nobody but a person who confesses, a person who has met Christ standing in his path and has recognized him, and who now confesses his faith in Christ."[56]

Bonhoeffer characteristically believes the life of faith to rest ultimately on an external foundation, quite outside ourselves. This foundation is "the living, dying, and rising of the Lord Jesus Christ,"[57] without whom "the world is enclosed in the I."[58] The life of faith means "to be captivated by the gaze" of Jesus Christ, to see only him.[59] Faith is thus, as John de Gruchy suggests, "not a certainty that we possess, but a certainty that comes to possess us, the mystery of grace that makes believing possible in the first place."[60]

The Arcanum

What, Bonhoeffer asks in the first of the theological letters from prison, "does a church, a congregation, a sermon, a liturgy, a Christian life, mean in a religionless world?" Is this, perhaps, where the "arcane discipline" (*Arkandisziplin*),[61] which serves to protect and preserve the mysteries of the Christian faith, comes into its own?[62] As Eberhard Bethge observes, we misunderstand Bonhoeffer's intentions completely if we assume religionless Christianity to mean the absence of a worshiping, sacramental church, and its replacement simply "by *caritas*."[63] The church remains the place where "the mysteries of the Christian faith are sheltered against profanation."[64] It is most certainly not, however, a place of escape for, says Bethge, in "the *arcanum* Christ takes everyone who really encounters him by the shoulder, turning them around to face their fellow human beings and the world."[65] Worldliness and an arcane discipline together serve to balance and correct one another. "In isolation, arcane discipline becomes liturgical monasticism and non-religious interpretation an intellectual game."[66]

In his introduction to the *Letters and Papers from Prison*, de Gruchy reflects on Bonhoeffer's insistence on the need for the church to strike a balance between its worldly and sacred functions. An outward-looking, service-oriented church must surrender neither its distinctively Christian identity nor the mystery of its faith in Christ. Hence, Bonhoeffer's appeal to the "arcane discipline" (*disciplina arcani*) of the ancient church, which provides a discreet space for the mysteries of the faith (prayer, worship, sacraments, creed) to play their indispensable part in sustaining the church's own "life of faith, hope, and love."[67]

Gerhard Müller and Albrecht Schönherr similarly draw attention to the tensions that inevitably characterize a church which is at once "the place of God's presence in the world" and God's instrument of activity "on behalf of the world." Bonhoeffer's theology, they argue, is never free of such tensions, but this gives us no reason to neglect the profound shift in his thinking that transformed the world from "the place to which God's attention turns" into one of rich, pluriform encounter with God.[68] In an emerging "post-Christian" society, a *disciplina arcani* gives the increasingly isolated Christian strength both to witness to Christ and to join actively in the life of a world come of age.[69]

Andreas Pangritz notes that Bonhoeffer first employs the term "arcane discipline" in a seminary setting, at Finkenwalde, where, on several occasions, he uses it "to recall a certain practice of the early church in her relation to the outsiders."[70] At Finkenwalde, the phrase is deployed exclusively in defensive mode, as Bonhoeffer seeks out a spiritual sanctuary for a beleaguered church in a "wicked" world.[71] Pangritz, though, believes the primary function of an "arcane discipline" to have changed by the time we come to the *Letters and Papers from Prison*. There is still something to protect, but now the mysteries of faith are no longer so much at risk of worldly profanation as they are in danger of profanation by a "positivism of revelation" which is rooted in the church itself. This positivism of revelation threatens to make a law out of faith, and to turn mysteries into "religious propaganda."[72] The gift of the gospel becomes a demand, and grace is obscured.

But while it is certainly true that Bonhoeffer juxtaposes Karl Barth's alleged "positivism of revelation" with an "arcane discipline" in the letter of May 5, 1944, this is not his central concern. In a lecture on catechesis, given at Finkenwalde in February 1936, Bonhoeffer remarks that the efforts of the early church to preserve, through the catechumenate, the mystery entrusted to it, had spared neither the church nor its mysteries "the derision and incomprehension of the world."[73] And it is clearly this that most concerns him when, at much the same time, he writes in *Discipleship* of the "costly grace" of the gospel "which must be sought again and again": costly, "because it calls to discipleship"; grace, "because it calls us to follow *Jesus Christ*." Costly grace is the "living word" of God," a "holy treasure" to be kept safe from sacrilege.[74] And it is its antithesis, "cheap grace," that has led to the collapse of the church in Nazi Germany:

> We gave away preaching and sacraments cheaply . . . we absolved an entire people, unquestioned and unconditionally; out of human love we handed over what was holy to the scornful and unbelievers. We poured out rivers of grace

without end, but the call to rigorously follow Christ was seldom heard. What happened to the insights of the ancient church, which in the baptismal teaching watched so carefully over the boundary between the church and the world, over costly grace? What happened to Luther's warning against a proclamation of the gospel which made people secure in their godless lives?[75]

Bonhoeffer never really changed his mind on this issue. The view from prison is essentially the same as it was from the seminary. Within a week or two of the letter of May 5, 1944, in the baptismal address for his nephew and godson, Dietrich Bethge, we find Bonhoeffer lamenting the state of a church that has so lost its way as to "become incapable of bringing the word of reconciliation and redemption to humankind and the world."[76] A new dawn will one day usher in a new language of righteousness and truth but, until that day comes, "the Christian cause will be a quiet and hidden one," supported by "people who pray and do justice and wait for God's own time."[77]

If Pangritz is right—that an "arcane discipline" is now required more to protect the church from itself (from a positivism of revelation) than from the depredations of outsiders—we should be able to detect different motives at work over time here; but there is really only one. Bonhoeffer has not come to fear a bold, propagandistic misuse of the mysteries of faith. If this were in fact the case, it would suggest a strength and confidence on the part of the church in its dealings with the world of which Bonhoeffer saw very little evidence during his relatively brief career as a theologian and anti-Nazi conspirator. No, Bonhoeffer feared in 1944 exactly what he had feared in 1936: a cheapening of God's grace associated with the scornful exploitation of the profound mystery of Christ by a skeptical world, aided and abetted by a self-serving, sometimes cynical and sometimes blind, church.

WHOLENESS

There is, Bonhoeffer tells his Barcelona congregation in that early sermon on Psalm 62:2, no lasting satisfaction, no genuine fulfillment, in worldly endeavors. This is because there is nothing whole in the world, "so that every success, be it ever so great, is still only a partial success." We are driven inexorably to repeat or to improve on it, and to satisfy other existing or emerging desires. True peace is to be found only in wholeness, and wholeness only in God. "All human activity and searching is ultimately directed toward God and finds its ultimate fulfillment only in him."[78]

Much later, in prison, Bonhoeffer is frequently moved to reflect on the fragmentary nature of life, as he fights to preserve the sense of wholeness and continuity that was so important to him. In December 1943, he tells Bethge that he has constantly in mind a line from a hymn by the seventeenth-century

German theologian, Paul Gerhardt: "Calm your hearts, dear friends; / whatever plagues you, / whatever fails you, / I will restore it all." But just how is he to understand this act of restoration? Bonhoeffer assumes Gerhardt to mean that nothing is lost, because

> in Christ all things are taken up, preserved . . . transparent, clear, liberated from the torment of self-serving demands. . . . The doctrine originating in Eph. 1:10 of the restoration of all things . . . is a magnificent and consummately consoling thought. The verse "God seeks out what has gone by" [Eccl. 3:15] is here fulfilled.[79]

A month later, he remarks that it used to be the case that "just one of the problems we now have to deal with was enough to occupy us fully." The world has since become much more challenging, and more dangerous, but Christians must not allow themselves to be divided or torn asunder, for those who cannot discern—in their thinking and acting—a way of integration have failed the test of the present, and the future.[80]

Bonhoeffer struggles to console fellow prisoners who have been terrified by frequent air raids, because he can "almost never say anything." Rather than offer a false or disingenuous kind of comfort, he prefers to leave "the distress *without interpretation.*"[81] He is also puzzled by the "forgetfulness" which seems to be an effect of the precarious lives he and his unhappy companions now lead. It is not just the passing thought, the fleeting impression, that fails to take hold. So much else, of profound importance (ties of love, friendship, loyalty), is also either lost or abandoned.

> Nothing holds fast. . . . Everything is short term. . . . But the good things like justice, truth, beauty, all great achievements, need time and steadfastness, "memory," or else they degenerate. Anyone who doesn't have the sense of a past to answer for and a future to plan for is "forgetful," and I don't know where to take hold of such persons . . . and bring them to their senses. Everything one can say, even if it makes an impression at the moment, is lost to forgetfulness.[82]

Nazism, war, and imprisonment naturally contributed much to Bonhoeffer's sense of life's increasing tendency to fragmentation, but there is a longer perspective in play here, too, which has to do with the gradual ascendancy of analytic and reductionist ways of thinking over previously dominant integrative-hierarchical ones. For Bonhoeffer, the nineteenth century marked a change in the mode of scholarship, from extensive learning to intensive study, as a precursor to the recent appearance of the "specialist." Now there are only "technicians." Intellectual existence has become "a torso." Where, he asks, "do you see an intellectual 'life's work' these days?

Where is anyone gathering, working through, and developing what it takes to accomplish such?"[83]

Bonhoeffer thinks it nonetheless plausible to get a sense of the whole from a suitably qualified part, even though the whole may never come to full expression. In the fragment of a life, it is still possible to see "what the whole was intended and designed to be, and of what material it is made." This is not true of all fragments, of course. Some will never serve this purpose and must be discarded. But others—Bach's *Art of the Fugue*, for example—"remain meaningful for hundreds of years, because only God could perfect them."

> If [says Bonhoeffer] our life is only the most remote reflection of such a fragment, in which, even for a short time, the various themes gradually accumulate and harmonize with one another and in which the great counterpoint is sustained from beginning to end . . . then it is not for us . . . to complain about this fragmentary life of ours, but rather even to be glad of it.[84]

Experience has taught Bonhoeffer that the center of gravity of the mature human being is always wherever that person happens to be, at any moment of life. "A man is always a whole person and wholly present."[85] The alternative is to remain a captive, a plaything, of one's desires. Desirelessness is true poverty, and "we are the richer for it." In prison, Bonhoeffer is "surrounded almost entirely by people clinging to their desires, so that they're not there for anyone else." But even in such a place, it is best "to live fully in the present . . . as if there were no wishes and no future." This allows us to be both true to ourselves and a source of strength and comfort to many who are unable to realize this condition.[86]

Bonhoeffer believes Christians to be particularly well-placed to cultivate this very necessary sense of presence and wholeness, because their faith allows, and indeed encourages, them to accommodate "many different dimensions of life at the same time." It seemed to him that most of his fellow prisoners simply could not do this. When, for example, "the bombers come, they are nothing but fear itself; when there's something good to eat, nothing but greed itself." Christians, on the other hand, are at least potentially able to hold God and the world together. They weep with those who weep and rejoice with those who rejoice. They fear for their lives but not to the exclusion of other, and finally more important, considerations. "What a liberation it is to be able to *think* and to hold on to these many dimensions of life in our thoughts."[87]

Bonhoeffer's unfailing sense of God's providence allows him to incorporate life's unlooked-for twists and disappointments into a seamless and still meaningful whole. In April 1944, he assures Bethge that he has never regretted the decision he took in the summer of 1939 to return to Germany from the United States. Instead, he says, "I am wholly under the impression that my life . . . has gone in a straight line, uninterrupted, at least with regard to how I've led it." If he died in prison, this "would have a meaning that I believe I could understand"—as also, of course, would the restoration of his personal freedom and a return to theological work.[88]

These thoughts are most poignantly expressed in a poem composed in December 1944 some weeks after he was transferred from Tegel military prison to the SS prison in Berlin's Prinz-Albrecht-Straße. Here, "By faithful, quiet powers of good surrounded" (*Von guten Mächten treu und still umgeben*), Bonhoeffer writes:

And should you offer us the cup of suffering,
though heavy, brimming full and bitter brand,
we'll thankfully accept it, never flinching,
from your good heart and your beloved hand.
But should you wish now once again to give us
the joys of this world and its glorious sun,
then we'll recall anew what past times brought us
and then our life belongs to you alone.[89]

God alone knows whether he will survive the period of his imprisonment, but Bonhoeffer will accept the outcome with equanimity, whether it brings suffering or joy. His confidence in God's unfailing presence and goodness is unassailable:

By powers of good so wondrously protected,
we wait with confidence, befall what may.
God is with us at night and in the morning
and oh, most certainly on each new day.[90]

Some months earlier, in one of the Tegel letters, he tells Bethge

> how little, in contrast to almost all the others here, I wallow in past mistakes . . . thinking . . . that if I had done this or that differently, how much would have turned out otherwise today. That does not torment me at all. Everything seems to have taken its inevitable, necessary, and straightforward course, determined by a higher providence.[91]

Bonhoeffer's confidence in life's providential direction also has a more explicitly worldly side, stemming in large part from a strong sense of himself as a well-credentialed member of Germany's intellectual upper middle class, or *Bildungsbürgertum*. This comes through very clearly in his "Thoughts" on the baptism of the infant Bethge where he writes of the approaching end of "the old village parsonage" (the world of the Bethges) and of "the old middle-class" (the world of the Bonhoeffers) but goes on to assure his audience that "the old spirit" will survive the present crisis, for which it shares responsibility, and eventually "create new forms for itself."

> To be deeply rooted in the soil of the past makes life harder, but also richer and more vigorous. There are fundamental truths in human life to which it always returns sooner or later. We can't hurry it; we have to be able to wait. "God seeks out what has gone by," the Bible says (Eccl. 3:15).[92]

Bonhoeffer hopes his godson will have the opportunity "to plan and build up and give shape to a new and better life," but knows that, for his own generation, the world will never again be what he had earlier had reason to expect it to be. He had expected to be able to plan and to pursue, with characteristic energy and determination, a life's work of his own choosing. But while it is still possible for him to think of life as lived always in the loving presence of God, the mundane sense of orderliness and predictability that he believed to have been the world of his parents' and grandparents' experience is now gone. "[W]e cannot even plan for the next day. . . . Our lives . . . have become formless or even fragmentary."[93]

The personal and theological dimensions of the concept of wholeness, and the tension between it and fragmentation, were always important to Bonhoeffer and did not command attention only in prison. We can see this, for example, in the Barcelona sermon on Psalm 62:2. Bethge sees it, too, in the young postgraduate's desire for the direct experience of Indian spirituality, which he describes as Bonhoeffer's "natural drive toward action and rational analysis" seeking out "its passive counterpoint of contemplation and the intuition of synthesis."[94]

In the biblical reflection on morning, written for the brethren at Finkenwalde, Bonhoeffer brings the ideas of wholeness and presence together in a beautiful meditation.

> Each new morning is a new beginning for our lives. Each day is a self-contained whole. The present day is the boundary of our cares and toils (Matt. 6:34; James 4:14). It is long enough to find or to lose God, to keep faith or to fall into sin and disgrace. God created day and night that we might not wander around without limits but rather might already see our goal, namely, evening, lying before us in the morning. Just as the ancient sun rises daily anew, so also is God's eternal mercy new every morning (Lam. 3:23). Being able to grasp God's ancient faithfulness anew each morning, being able to begin a new life with God daily in the midst of one's present life with God, that is the gift God gives us with each new morning.[95]

The idea of human wholeness is, for Bonhoeffer, fundamentally biblical. As far as he can see, the Bible does not distinguish between the outward and the inward life. "It is always concerned with the ἄνθρωπος τέλειος, the whole human being, even in the Sermon on the Mount, where the Decalogue is extended into the 'innermost' interior."[96] The heart, in the biblical sense, is not some separated, hidden place but "rather the whole person before God." And God knows that we are as sensitive, and as susceptible, to the proddings of the external world as we are to the promptings of the inner self.[97] Bonhoeffer wants to preserve the "polyphony of life" and understands this to be God's will, too. "God, the Eternal, wants to be loved with our whole heart, not to the detriment of earthly love or to diminish it, but as a sort of cantus firmus to which the other voices of life resound in counterpoint."[98]

The church, too, which is "nothing but that piece of humanity where Christ really has taken form," is, or should be, concerned only with human wholeness. Indeed, the church is the epitome of such wholeness—the apotheosis of the God-reconciled human being roused to new life in Christ. As such, its principal concern must be "with the existence in the world of human beings in all their relationships," rather than with life's fragmentary religious functions and expressions.[99]

CONCLUSION

There is no reason to think that anything in this chapter would not have survived the transition to a religionless Christianity. Indeed, a significant proportion of the material in it is drawn from Bonhoeffer's drafts for the *Ethics*, and from his prison letters, and may thus properly be associated with the early stages of that transition.

Bonhoeffer believes that the principal task of theology is to respect and to preserve God's mystery. Perhaps nowhere is the significance of this task more evident, and more challenging, than in Christology, which rests on the assumption that God became human. This cannot be proved objectively. We have simply to accept the reality that is given with God's self-revelation in Jesus Christ. Transcendence can neither be explained nor explained away. Revelation is a gift of God which can only be received and acknowledged in faith. The soul is silent before God, "tensely listening" and ready to obey God's will.[100]

As soon as we pass from silence to words, from a state of unconditional acceptance to one of active interpretation, we are forced into antinomies. Bonhoeffer believes paradox to be of the very essence of Christian theology, and is drawn strongly to the language of Chalcedon, which affirms the one person of Christ in two natures, "without confusion, without change, without division, without separation."[101] This, he says, was never intended to be a plain statement of fact. It has always been an affirmation of faith. Neither God nor God's relation to the world is capable of fixed definition. God's freedom is not constrained by human speculation.

The encounter with God is, for Bonhoeffer, neither intuitive nor emotive (as it was, for example, for Friedrich Schleiermacher and liberal Protestant theology) but is instead based exclusively on the Word of God which comes always from outside. In Christ, Christians see neither themselves nor their own faith. "They see only Christ . . . their Lord and God."[102] There is, of course, no compelling reason to accept this distinction—between religious inwardness and revelation—nor any rational means of proving its validity. It is quite possible to argue, and generally more plausible to the modern mind, that the brain is not only the means of understanding revelation but also its source. Bonhoeffer's distinction is made in faith. It reflects a particular orientation to life and its possibilities.

In all of this, the basic human disposition can only be one of openness and humility: openness to a reality beyond the closed circle of the self—to a genuinely transcendent Other—and the humility to support both such an expansive view, and such a limited understanding, of the cosmos in which human life is embedded. We do not have the measure of God because, if we did, God would no longer be God. We know as much about God as God chooses to tell us, and even this much will be ours only if we listen closely to God's Word. Those who crucified Jesus Christ were not listening, and quite failed to recognize the mystery of "God's love and closeness" to the world.[103]

Clifford Green, in his introduction to the *Ethics*, remarks how often Bonhoeffer invokes the wholeness and simplicity of an ethic based on God's act of reconciliation in Jesus Christ.[104] As Bonhoeffer says,

> Whoever confesses the reality of Jesus Christ as the revelation of God confesses in the same breath the reality of God and the reality of the world, for they find God and the world reconciled in Christ. Just for this reason the Christian is no longer the person of eternal conflict.[105]

We may safely leave all two-realms thinking behind, for as "reality is one in Christ, so the person who belongs to this Christ-reality is also a whole." The world does not keep us from Christ, nor does Christ keep us from the world. It is entirely possible to belong completely to Christ and to stand "at the same time completely in the world."[106] But for those who fail to recognize the reality of humanity's reconciliation with God in Jesus Christ, and for whom self-knowledge is the ground of all knowing,

> everything splits apart—is and ought, life and law . . . idea and reality, reason and instinct, duty and inclination . . . necessity and freedom . . . the universal and

the concrete, the individual and the collective; and even truth, justice, beauty, and love conflict with one another just as do desire and aversion, happiness and sorrow.[107]

The reality of God and the reality of the world come together in the one realm of the Christ-reality. In Jesus Christ, God's promise is fulfilled because, in and through him, all humanity is reconciled and awakened to new life with God. It is Jesus Christ, and only him, who gives our lives meaning and purpose. If he had not lived, then our lives would be meaningless, "despite all the other people we know, respect, and love."[108] Jesus Christ, we may remember, calls us "not to a new religion but to life."[109]

NOTES

1. "Meditation on Christmas," DBWE 15: 528–29.
2. "Lectures on Christology," DBWE 12: 301.
3. "Lectures on Christology," DBWE 12: 300.
4. Dietrich Bonhoeffer, "Sermon on Psalm 62:2, Barcelona, Sixth Sunday after Trinity, July 15, 1928," *Barcelona, Berlin, New York*, DBWE 10: 500. Verse 62:1 in the English enumeration. The translation has been altered to conform to Bonhoeffer's German.
5. "Sermon on Psalm 62:2," DBWE 10: 500.
6. "Sermon on Psalm 62:2," DBWE 10: 501.
7. "Sermon on Psalm 62:2," DBWE 10: 502.
8. "Sermon on Psalm 62:2," DBWE 10: 502.
9. "Sermon on Psalm 62:2," DBWE 10: 503.
10. "Sermon on Psalm 62:2," DBWE 10: 504. Some years later, Bonhoeffer prepared for the seminarians at Finkenwalde a "Guide to Scriptural Meditation" in which he advocates a minimum of thirty minutes daily meditation before work. There is, Bonhoeffer again says here, "meditation that is free and meditation that is bound to Scripture," but he now clearly recommends meditation bound to scripture in order properly to guide prayer and to discipline thinking. We must not neglect "this daily encounter with Scripture, and if we have not already done so, we must begin immediately. For in it we have eternal life." Dietrich Bonhoeffer, "Guide to Scriptural Meditation, Finkenwalde, 22 May 1936," in *Theological Education at Finkenwalde*, DBWE 14: 931–36.
11. Feil, *The Theology of Dietrich Bonhoeffer*, 5.
12. Feil, *The Theology of Dietrich Bonhoeffer*, 46–47.
13. "Jesus Christ and the Essence of Christianity," DBWE 10: 355.
14. viz. humanism and mysticism.
15. "Jesus Christ and the Essence of Christianity," DBWE 10: 356.
16. *Letters and Papers*, DBWE 8: 373.
17. *Ethics*, DBWE 6: 122.
18. *Sanctorum Communio*, DBWE 1: 84.

19. *Sanctorum Communio*, DBWE 1: 287.
20. *Sanctorum Communio*, DBWE 1: 48.
21. *Sanctorum Communio*, DBWE 1: 84.
22. *Sanctorum Communio*, DBWE 1: 55.
23. *Act and Being*, DBWE 2: 53.
24. *Life Together*, DBWE 5: 86. The Benedictine monk, John Main, a late twentieth-century champion of the contemplative spiritual path, likewise insists that meditation "must take place in an entirely ordinary, natural way." John Main, *Silence and Stillness in Every Season: Daily Readings with John Main*, ed. Paul T. Harris (Singapore: Medio Media, 2010), 34. In the silence and stillness of meditation, one should neither rest in any passing joy nor fly from the experience of sterility. Main, *Silence and Stillness in Every Season*, 268, 281. Meditation requires courage and perseverance. It is "the prayer of faith, because we have to leave ourselves behind before the Other appears and with no pre-packaged guarantee that He will appear. The essence of poverty consists in this risk of annihilation. This is the leap of faith from ourselves to the Other. This is the risk involved in all loving." Main, *Silence and Stillness in Every Season*, 39.
25. "Biblical Reflection: Morning," DBWE 14: 865.
26. *Act and Being*, DBWE 2: 57.
27. Kelley, "Christological Concretion and Everyday Events in Three of Bonhoeffer's Sermons," in Kelly and Weborg, 100.
28. "Lectures on Christology," DBWE 12: 301.
29. "Lectures on Christology," DBWE 12: 303.
30. "Lectures on Christology," DBWE 12: 305.
31. "Lectures on Christology," DBWE 12: 341.
32. One and the same Christ . . . in two natures. "Lectures on Christology," DBWE 12: 342. The text of the Definition may be consulted in J. Stevenson, ed., *Creeds, Councils and Controversies: Documents Illustrating the History of the Church, AD 337–461* (New Edition) (London: SPCK, 1989), 350–54.
33. "Lectures on Christology," DBWE 12: 342.
34. "Lectures on Christology," DBWE 12: 343.
35. "Lectures on Christology," DBWE 12: 353.
36. "Lectures on Christology," DBWE 12: 350.
37. Ernst-Albert Scharffenorth, Afterword, *Berlin*, DBWE 12: 490. We may recall, too, Feil's comment on the role of paradox in breaking down structures of thought and creating space for the mystery. Feil, *The Theology of Dietrich Bonhoeffer*, 46–47.
38. And real mystery, says de Gruchy, is not just a secret waiting to be shared, or a conundrum which has, so far, escaped resolution. Mystery is certainly "hidden like a secret; but unlike a secret, mystery never ceases to invite enquiry and exploration, for there is always more to be discovered. . . . Mystery . . . leads us beyond the boundaries of the ordinary into the deep things of life." de Gruchy, *Led into Mystery*, 36–37.
39. Dietrich Bonhoeffer, "Sermon on 1 Corinthians 2:7–10, London, Trinity Sunday, May 27, 1934," in *London*, DBWE 13: 360. De Gruchy reminds us of the importance Jesus attached to the childlike capacity "to see things as they are and

intuitively [to] grasp their significance." While it is not, of course, possible for us, as adults, fully to recapture the guilelessness of childhood, we can still benefit from what the French philosopher Paul Ricoeur calls a "second naïveté,"

> that is a fresh, chastened ability to see and hear the truth in the tale, the fact in the fiction, the mystery beneath the real, and to recognize that a great deal else in which we place our confidence as sophisticated adults is ephemeral at best and dangerous at worst. . . . We need loop-holes in ordinary life through which we can catch glimpses of something sublime amid the mundane.

de Gruchy, Led into Mystery, 44.

40. "Sermon on 1 Corinthians 2:7–10," DBWE 13: 361.
41. "Sermon on 1 Corinthians 2:7–10," DBWE 13: 362.
42. "Sermon on 1 Corinthians 2:7–10," DBWE 13: 362.
43. "Sermon on 1 Corinthians 2:7–10," DBWE 13: 362.
44. Feil, *The Theology of Dietrich Bonhoeffer*, 6.
45. "Meditation on Christmas," DBWE 15: 529.
46. It is the mandate of the church to proclaim God's revelation in Jesus Christ. However, it is the mystery of this name that it denotes not merely an individual human being, but at the same time comprises all of human nature within itself. Jesus Christ can always only be proclaimed and witnessed to as the one in whom God has bodily taken on humanity.

Ethics, DBWE 6: 403.

47. "The figure . . . of the reconciler, of the God-man Jesus Christ, steps into the middle between God and the world, into the center of all that happens. In this figure is disclosed the mystery of the world, just as the mystery of God is revealed in it." *Ethics*, DBWE 6: 83.

48. The fact that Jesus, in his innocence, willingly "took the guilt of all human beings upon himself" means that all truly responsible action now has something of that quality. It includes a measure of culpability. "Those who, in acting responsibly, seek to avoid becoming guilty, divorce themselves from the ultimate reality of history, that is, from the redeeming mystery of the sinless bearing of guilt by Jesus Christ, and have no part in the divine justification that attends this event." *Ethics*, DBWE 6: 234.

49. To be conformed to the risen one . . . means to be a new human being before God. We live in the midst of death; we are righteous in the midst of sin; we are new in the midst of the old. Our mystery remains hidden from the world. . . . As long as the glory of Christ is hidden, so the glory of the new life also is "hidden with Christ in God" (Col. 3:2).

Ethics, DBWE 6: 95.

50. "There is no explaining the mystery that only a part of humanity recognizes the form of its savior." *Ethics*, DBWE 6: 96.

51. As responsible action, the good takes place without knowing, by surrendering to God the deed that has become necessary and is nevertheless . . . free, surrendering it to God, who looks upon the heart, weighs the deeds, and guides history. Thus a

profound mystery of history . . . is disclosed to us. Precisely those who act in the freedom of their very own responsibility see their activity as flowing into God's guidance. Free action recognizes itself ultimately as being God's action, decision as God's guidance, the venture as divine necessity. In freely surrendering the knowledge of our own goodness, the good of God occurs. Only in this ultimate perspective can we speak about good in historical action.

Ethics, DBWE 6: 284–85.

52. *Act and Being*, DBWE 2: 94.
53. This is the psychological equivalent of early Protestantism's theological distinction between *fides directa* (direct faith) and *fides reflexa* (reflexive faith). *Act and Being*, DBWE 2: 28, ed. fn. 17.
54. *Act and Being*, DBWE 2: 100.
55. *Act and Being*, DBWE 2: 158. By the time we come to the *Ethics*, however, we find that the *actus reflexus*, too, is finally an act of faith, when it is done "responsibly." The ideologically driven act of reflection carries its justification along with it. It is essentially self-sufficient, and self-regarding. The historically responsible action, on the other hand, has, and seeks, no such understanding of itself. Here, "after responsibly weighing all circumstances" in the light of Christ, the deed is surrendered to God at the very moment of execution. *Ethics*, DBWE 6: 225.
56. Dietrich Bonhoeffer, "Sermon on Matthew 16:13–18, Berlin, Sixth Sunday after Trinity, July 23, 1933," in *Berlin*, DBWE 12: 478–79.
57. *Ethics*, DBWE 6: 147.
58. *Act and Being*, DBWE 2: 157.
59. *Ethics*, DBWE 6: 147.
60. de Gruchy, *Led into Mystery*, 120.
61. Bonhoeffer translates the Latin phrase *disciplina arcani* as *Arkandisziplin*. In previous editions of *Letters and Papers from Prison*, this phrase has been rendered in English as "secret discipline," and in *Discipleship* as "discipline of the secret." Here, though, the editors and translators have followed Bonhoeffer's example, translating it simply as "arcane discipline," on the understanding that

> Bonhoeffer is referring not to something done in secret but to the mysteries of the Christian faith, which have been revealed in Christ and are made known and preserved in the life of the church. These are "hidden" (the literal meaning of "arcane") . . . in the church's liturgical life (sacraments, prayer, and creed), rather than thrust upon the world in a "take it or leave it" way that profanes them.

de Gruchy, Introduction, *Letters and Papers*, DBWE 8: 32.

62. *Letters and Papers*, DBWE 8: 364–65.
63. Bethge, *Dietrich Bonhoeffer*, 881–82.
64. *Letters and Papers*, DBWE 8: 373.
65. Bethge, *Dietrich Bonhoeffer*, 883.
66. Bethge, *Dietrich Bonhoeffer*, 884.
67. de Gruchy, Introduction, *Letters and Papers*, DBWE 8: 29.

68. Gerhard L. Müller and Albrecht Schönherr, Afterword, *Life Together*, DBWE 5: 136.
69. Müller and Schönherr, Afterword, *Life Together*, DBWE 5: 139–40.
70. Andreas Pangritz, "The Understanding of Mystery in the Theology of Dietrich Bonhoeffer," in Nielsen, Nissen, and Tietz, 15.
71. Pangritz, "Understanding Mystery," in Nielsen, Nissen, and Tietz, 15–16.
72. Pangritz, "Understanding Mystery," in Nielsen, Nissen, and Tietz, 17–18.
73. Dietrich Bonhoeffer, "Lecture on Catechesis (1935–1936 Student Notes)," in *Theological Education at Finkenwalde*, DBWE 14: 555.
74. *Discipleship*, DBWE 4: 45.
75. *Discipleship*, DBWE 4: 53–54. Kelly speculates that Bonhoeffer may have borrowed the expression "cheap grace" from Kierkegaard. While Bonhoeffer was critical of what Kelly describes as Kierkegaard's "radical subjectivism," he saw in him nonetheless "a kindred soul who . . . could lament the ways in which Christianity could be seduced so easily into patterns of comfort and pusillanimity that . . . denied the gospel call to follow Christ to the cross." Geffrey B. Kelly, "Kierkegaard and Bonhoeffer," in Frick, 159, 164.
76. *Letters and Papers*, DBWE 8: 389.
77. *Letters and Papers*, DBWE 8: 390.
78. "Sermon on Psalm 62:2," DBWE 10: 504.
79. *Letters and Papers*, DBWE 8: 229–30. "Blessed be the God and Father of our Lord Jesus Christ, who . . . has made known to us the mystery of his will, according to his good pleasure that he set forth in Christ, as a plan for the fullness of time, to gather up all things in him, things in heaven and things on earth" (Eph. 1:9–10). "I know that whatever God does endures forever; nothing can be added to it, nor anything taken from it; God has done this, so that all should stand in awe before him. That which is already has been; that which is to be, already is; and God seeks out what has gone by" (Eccl. 3:14–15).
80. *Letters and Papers*, DBWE 8: 278.
81. *Letters and Papers*, DBWE 8: 284.
82. *Letters and Papers*, DBWE 8: 284.
83. *Letters and Papers*, DBWE 8: 305–6.
84. *Letters and Papers*, DBWE 8: 306.
85. *Letters and Papers*, DBWE 8: 324.
86. *Letters and Papers*, DBWE 8: 325.
87. *Letters and Papers*, DBWE 8: 404–5.
88. *Letters and Papers*, DBWE 8: 352–53.
89. *Letters and Papers*, DBWE 8: 550.
90. *Letters and Papers*, DBWE 8: 550.
91. *Letters and Papers*, DBWE 8: 358.
92. *Letters and Papers*, DBWE 8: 385.
93. *Letters and Papers*, DBWE 8: 387.
94. Bethge, *Dietrich Bonhoeffer*, 148.
95. "Biblical Reflection: Morning," DBWE 14: 864. "So do not worry about tomorrow, for tomorrow will bring worries of its own. Today's trouble is enough for

today" (Matt. 6:34). "Yet you do not even know what tomorrow will bring. What is your life? For you are a mist that appears for a little while and then vanishes" (James 4:14). "The steadfast love of the LORD never ceases, his mercies never come to an end; they are new every morning; great is your faithfulness" (Lam. 3:22–23).

96. *Letters and Papers*, DBWE 8: 456. Matt. 5:17–48. V. 48: "Be perfect [τέλειοι: 'whole,' 'complete,' 'fulfilled'], therefore, as your heavenly Father is perfect [τέλειος]."

97. *Letters and Papers*, DBWE 8: 457.

98. *Letters and Papers*, DBWE 8: 394.

99. *Ethics*, DBWE 6: 97.

100. "Sermon on Psalm 62:2," DBWE 10: 502.

101. "Lectures on Christology," DBWE 12: 342; Stevenson, *Creeds, Councils and Controversies*, 352–53.

102. *Act and Being*, DBWE 2: 158.

103. "Sermon on 1 Corinthians 2:7–10," DBWE 12: 362.

104. Green, Introduction, *Ethics*, DBWE 6: 9.

105. *Ethics*, DBWE 6: 62.

106. *Ethics*, DBWE 6: 62.

107. *Ethics*, DBWE 6: 308–9.

108. *Letters and Papers*, DBWE 8: 515.

109. *Letters and Papers*, DBWE 8: 482.

Chapter 6

Christ without Religion

There can be no Christianity, of any description, without Christ. But is it really possible to conceive of Jesus Christ—or, more properly, of God's self-revelation in Jesus Christ—as theologically compelling in the absence of a religious framework which draws meaning and vigor from sweeping assumptions of God's manifest and reliable, preserving, rescuing, and retributive power? What good can it do us to place our faith in a God who "is weak and powerless in the world"?[1] Do the critique of religion, the concept of religionless Christianity, and the nonreligious interpretation of theological/biblical terms collectively open up new and helpful ways of knowing and understanding God in Jesus Christ? I would argue, on the strength of the evidence presented so far in this book, that the answer to this question must be yes. My objective in this final chapter is to give this affirmation a coherent contemporary shape, and to explore its implications for theology.

BONHOEFFER'S PRISON THEOLOGY

Bonhoeffer's prison theology presupposes the approach of "a completely religionless age"[2] and seeks to craft an appropriately radical Christian (and thoroughly christocentric) response to life in a (Western) world that has come progressively to trust, more and more exclusively, in its autonomous human capacities.

Bonhoeffer begins with a restatement of the question that has consistently informed his theology. What, he asks, is Christianity, "or who is Christ actually for us today?"[3] But he does so now under very different personal circumstances. The theologian and pastor has joined the German resistance. He has been arrested, imprisoned, and faces possible execution. Life and theology have together conspired to convince him that God expects people to manage their lives "without God."[4] The "God of the Bible" has not abandoned us, but the powerful God of religion is gone. God has consented "to be pushed out of the world and onto the cross," and helps us now *only* by virtue of being "weak and powerless" in the world.[5]

Christ's death and resurrection have thus to be regarded not, principally, as intimations of another life in some quite different, and better, place, but of new life in this one. We are called "to share in God's suffering at the hands of a godless world"[6] and can do this only by living intentionally worldly lives. Those who have a real desire for God must, like Christ, "drink the cup of earthly life to the last drop."[7] God *is* the encounter with the crucified and risen Christ, and we are restored to new life with God by the act of faithful participation in the being of Jesus, "the human being for others."[8]

The church, too, is only the church when it is there for others. It has a responsibility not only to *tell* people "what a life with Christ is" but also to *show* them;[9] and this, Bonhoeffer believed, the German Protestant churches, in particular, had largely failed to do in his lifetime.[10] The church, he said, in a message to those gathered at the baptism of his godson, Dietrich Bethge, in May 1944, was concerned only with its self-preservation. It had become so completely self-absorbed as to be "incapable of bringing the word of reconciliation and redemption to humankind and to the world."[11]

Bonhoeffer knew that if Christianity was to transition successfully to a religionless age, it would have to change not only its ways of thinking but also its ways of speaking. He hoped to shape practical expressions of a new, religionless form of Christianity, and understood this work to demand a proper hermeneutical foundation, including language suitable for people who knew little of Christian scripture and tradition. By finding new ways of explaining existing theological and biblical concepts, nonreligious language must convey what Bonhoeffer believed religious language to be no longer capable of communicating convincingly. It must tell people "what it means to live in Christ and follow Christ."[12] It must address the question of Christ's contemporary identity and bear exemplary witness to the relevance of Jesus Christ in a world come of age.

THE AGE OF RELIGION IS PAST

I have considered Bonhoeffer's bold foundational claim—the claim that "[w]e are approaching a completely religionless age"[13]—in light of both positive and critical readings of secularization theory, and judged each to support, in its own way, a broadly sympathetic analysis of his hypothesis.

This analysis cannot be sustained, however, without qualification. We clearly do not live in a religionless age. Large parts of the world are very religious indeed, and even that Western form of Christianity, which Bonhoeffer so confidently believed to be passing away, has not done so. A substantial majority of Westerners still profess a religious affiliation of some (generally Christian) kind. Contrary to the assumptions of mainstream secularization theory, modernity, it would seem, does not produce inevitably secular outcomes.

Modernity is more persuasively associated with exponential growth in human knowledge of the material universe, and with the attendant acquisition of sophisticated new technologies. It has facilitated a multiplication of worldviews (both religious and secular), encouraged contestability, and led people to believe they have a much larger say in their personal and shared destinies than a smaller, God-centered, less intelligible world previously allowed them. God is no longer the answer to every troubling question, and belief in God is no longer axiomatic. Indeed, in many Western social contexts, the governing presumption is now one of unbelief. As Gerhard Ebeling says so well, even "the religious are now so to speak only partially religious—to be precise, in the religious province of their being, whereas for the rest over broad stretches of their life their existence is in fact as non-religious as any."[14]

While ours is not the world Bonhoeffer envisioned, it is sufficiently like it to justify a conditional, but nonetheless essentially positive, assessment of his historical premise.

THE CRITIQUE OF RELIGION

In the letter of July 16, 1944, Bonhoeffer draws Eberhard Bethge's attention to what he believes to be "the crucial distinction" between Christianity and religion—all religion. This he finds in Matthew 8:17 ("He took our infirmities and bore our diseases") which "makes it quite clear that Christ helps us not by virtue of his omnipotence but rather by virtue of his weakness and suffering!"[15]

This distinction, between power and weakness—between the powerful, but ultimately illusory, God of religion and the compassionate, vulnerable God of the gospel—lies at the heart of both Bonhoeffer's critique of religion and his concept of a religionless Christianity. Other elements of the critique—the religious preoccupation with personal salvation and a better world beyond; the failure to recognize that Jesus Christ "makes crucial claims on our entire lives"[16]; God as the solution only to problems we cannot yet solve; and the subordination of an ethic of service to privileged assertions of entitlement—all are honed by this distinction, and come together as a collectively convincing whole.

But religion is also, and most fundamentally, hubris. For this insight, which was his starting point, Bonhoeffer is indebted to the early theology of

Karl Barth. It was Barth who first convinced Bonhoeffer of the vanity of all human efforts to establish communion with God. Faith is not to be confused with religion. Faith is from God, a gift of grace, while religion is always an exclusively human invention. Barth understood "[a]ll human possibilities, including the possibility of religion, [to] have been . . . surrendered to God on Golgotha." We have died with Christ to religion and its laws, and "been removed from that life under the dominion of law, which is death."[17] In the resurrection, "religion and grace confront one another as death and life," and we stand before God as God's obedient servants "under grace . . . as men who have passed from death to life."[18]

Bonhoeffer already knew this very well when, in 1928, as a young pastor in Barcelona, he spoke of the soul's desire "to acquire power over the eternal," and described religion, not unsympathetically, as "the most grandiose and most gentle of all human attempts to attain the eternal from out of the anxiety and restlessness of the heart."[19] Barth's significance for Bonhoeffer declines as Bonhoeffer is drawn more and more deeply into practical ecclesiastical and political activities. But it reemerges (with an acknowledged, though qualified, authority) in the prison letters which, despite their repeated criticism of Barth's failure to embrace the consequences of his own pioneering critique of religion, are still grounded in the conviction that religion simply cannot make good its claim to bring us into the presence of God. Only the grace of God, which has nothing to do with religion, can do this. There is, finally, no way from below to above. There is no human path to God.

In the prison letters, Barth's critique of religion's immanent, structural failure to bridge the gap between God and human beings shares the spotlight with Wilhelm Dilthey's historicism and philosophy of life. Life and faith are brought into positive relationship, and both are accorded christological significance. It is faith, rather than religion, that ushers us into new life in Christ. And it is this compelling vision of "new life in 'being there for others,' through participation in the being of Jesus"[20] that pervades Bonhoeffer's reflections on a new, religionless form of Christianity, befitting life with Christ in a post-religious age.

CONSISTENCY AND CONTINUITY IN BONHOEFFER'S THEOLOGY

The key elements of Bonhoeffer's prison theology—its affirmation of the life of faith lived wholly in the world, its subordination of power to weakness, the call to share in God's suffering in, and for, the world, and the promise of new life in Christ's "being there for others"—draw on a rich mix of theological ideas rooted firmly in his earlier work. Of these ideas, I understand the experience of transcendence, the mystery of God's becoming human in Jesus Christ, the notion of Christ *pro me* and for others, vicarious representative action, freedom for others, and the vision of one reality in Christ, to have particular significance for Bonhoeffer's religionless Christianity project. They are revisited briefly below.

The Mystery of Transcendence

Only by transcending the limits of reflection—the limits of a world "enclosed in the I"[21]—can we be sure of the existence of anything outside ourselves. Authentic self-understanding demands an object of knowledge—a genuine Other—that "challenges and limits" the I. The "being of God in revelation" is just such an object of knowledge. It does not depend on the I whose being and existing it precedes in every respect. It is the bedrock of all otherness. The I cannot contain it. It is not at the disposal of human beings. Human existence is always already a "being in" and, in the "being of revelation," human knowledge is suspended in "a being-already-known."[22] This is the mystery of God's becoming human in Jesus Christ, and it is the sole task of theology "to comprehend, defend, and exalt [this mystery] precisely as mystery."[23]

The God-Human Jesus Christ

In God's self-revelation, we are brought to "the boundary of the being that has been given to [us]."[24] There we find the transcendent uniquely embodied in the Otherness of the God-human Jesus Christ. Jesus, says Bonhoeffer, is "the God who became human as we became human." Jesus Christ is no more or less human than any other human being, and yet this human being is the very Word of God. These are not "two isolated existing realities." God's *"vertical Word from above"* neither adds nor subtracts "but rather qualifies this entire human being as God." We may accept this claim, or we may reject it, but there is effectively nothing more to be said. Jesus Christ is "God in our faith alone."[25]

Bonhoeffer finds, in the Chalcedonian Definition of the Faith, the consummate expression of this understanding. Its famous affirmation—"one and the same Christ . . . in two natures, without confusion, without change, without division, without separation"[26]—embraces every possibility relating to God and the human being. It does not seek to reconcile them but rather proclaims God's sovereignty and God's mystery with a "clear yet paradoxical agility."[27]

Only in the one whole person of the God-human is it possible to speak of Jesus Christ's ongoing presence among us. The risen Christ is still the human Jesus, who can be present to us only because he is human, and "eternally with us in the now" only because he is God.[28] We can explain Christ's ever-unfolding presence in no other way, for we are denied access to the historical Jesus by the passage of time, and to God by eternity. The "human Christ" and the "God-Christ" must be thought "simultaneously" if they are really to be thought at all. Neither may truly be said to exist for us in isolation. "Only in Jesus Christ is God present."[29]

Christ Pro me

Having established Jesus Christ as "the God who became human," Bonhoeffer then brings us into direct and personal relationship with him. He makes the point with extraordinary vigor in the Christology lectures when he says, "I can never think of Jesus Christ in his being-in-himself, but only in his relatedness to me."[30] Christ is thus both my limit—the boundary of my being[31]—and my true center—the one who "stands in my place . . . before God, *pro me*."[32] Indeed, as the one "through whom are all things and through whom we exist" (1 Cor. 8:6), he is the mediator of every creaturely relationship with the Creator. To think otherwise is to deceive ourselves. It is to fall prey to the illusion of immediacy, for there is in truth "no way from us to others than the path through Christ, his word, and our following him."[33]

Mark's gospel describes Levi's paradigmatic response to Jesus's call. Jesus "said to him, 'Follow me,' And he got up and followed him" (Mark 2:14). The true disciple looks only to Christ and follows him in love. On this path of faithful obedience, we are conformed by Christ to the God who has become human. This, however, is no superhuman path of perfection or excess. "Pretension, hypocrisy, compulsion, forcing oneself to be something different, better, more ideal than one is—all are abolished." Christ wants us only to become "the human beings that we really are."[34] He wants us to know ourselves to be truly a part of the whole of humanity, which is borne by him.[35] God did not become human in order that we might become divine but rather that we might become truly "human before God."[36]

Already in *Discipleship*, and certainly by the time we come to the prison letters, the place of Bonhoeffer's christological emphasis has changed. Christ is no longer "there" quite so obviously for me personally (*pro me*) as he is *for others* generally. I would suggest, however, that Bonhoeffer is most unlikely to have reached this essentially ethical conclusion if he had not first established its essentially theological foundation. The faith that I have in a personal, ontological bond with Christ must be extended to other people. To the extent that I have come to share Bonhoeffer's characteristically relational view of Christ, I will understand this to apply, at least potentially, to every human being. Indeed, it is this (inescapably shared) bond with the "being of revelation," with "a being-already-known,"[37] a genuine Other, that convinces me of the real "otherness of the other"[38]—that carries with it the assurance of a real outside.

Bonhoeffer's Concept of Person

There is, Bonhoeffer maintains, no such thing as the truly isolated, thoroughly autonomous individual. There are separation and plurality, certainly, but the sense of self, of I-ness, is grounded exclusively in relationship, with God first, and then with other people. A person is not a fixed or static entity but rather a relentlessly dynamic one, existing "always and only in ethical responsibility." Our very being depends on our recognizing, and acknowledging, the claim of the other. Only by accepting, or rejecting, the claim of a You—and by doing so "again and again in the perpetual flux of life"—can we be said to assume responsibility, and thereby to demonstrate our understanding of what is, for Bonhoeffer, most characteristic of human existence. No other concept of personhood preserves "the *fullness of life* of the concrete person."[39]

Freedom for Others

Human beings, says Bonhoeffer, are unique among God's creatures, because they are made in the very image of God. In them, "the free Creator looks upon the Creator's own self."[40] This means that human beings, too, are free, because it is unthinkable that anything other than a free creature could bear the image of God.[41] Bonhoeffer, though, does not have in mind here the popular Western notion of freedom as essentially the absence of constraint. Freedom, for Bonhoeffer, is grounded in what he calls God's own free decision "to be bound to historical human beings." In Jesus Christ, the unconditioned freedom of the self-subsistent God assumes a very different form, the covenantal form of "God's *given* Word."[42] And just as God has chosen to be free for, rather than from, human beings, so is their freedom now a freedom only *for* the other. Thus, freedom, too, can only truly be conceived as a relation. "Being free means 'being-free-for-the-other,' because I am bound to the other."[43]

The immeasurable variety of God's creation must not be compromised by "a false uniformity, by forcing people to submit to an ideal, a type, or a particular image of the human." Every human being is a singular expression of God's love and must be "allowed to be in freedom the creature of the Creator."[44] We may not presume to constrain "God's free and sovereign act of creation" by allowing our prejudices to dictate the appearance of God in others. Here, as always and everywhere, it is Christ the mediator who stands between me and every other, checking thereby the persistent and deadly urge to transform the other into a figure of my own design.[45]

Vicarious Representative Action

We first meet "the life-principle" of vicarious representative action (*Stellvertretung*) in Bonhoeffer's earliest published work, as the embodiment, in Jesus Christ, of God's love for human beings.[46] Jesus assumes the whole burden of human sin and takes it with him to the cross. Sin is overcome by an act of love, which restores us to community with God, and makes human community also "a reality in love once again."[47] Only in Christ's own church-community is this act of love fully understood, and emulated.

Vicarious representative action comes over time, though, to acquire a broader significance in Bonhoeffer's theology. In Christ, humanity is always something shared and never solitary. Ontology and ethics are inseparable. Human beings live naturally in the ethical situation of encounter. They may, of course, seek to avoid this, by notionally reducing the ethical task to the selective application of certain fixed principles—and then "withdrawing from responsibility for the whole, to a purely private bourgeois existence, or even into the monastery"—but this simply betrays a false understanding of ethics, and a shallow appreciation of life. The isolationist approach, says Bonhoeffer, will always fail "due to the *historicity [Geschichtlichkeit] of human existence.*"[48]

In Bonhoeffer's *Ethics*, vicarious representative action is worldly, responsible action, freely undertaken by human beings out of love for other "real" human beings.[49] And because all such action takes place necessarily within history, it will always entail risk, and a degree of moral ambiguity. Those who act responsibly "in their own freedom" must themselves weigh the merits of their actions and be responsible for their decisions. There are no formal, saving rules of the game to which they can appeal—for in this case "they would no longer be truly free"[50]—just as there is no "ultimately dependable [human] knowledge of good and evil"[51] in this God-reconciled, but still fallen, *sicut deus* world. The responsible actor must, therefore, surrender to God, at the very moment of execution, "[t]he deed that is done, after responsibly weighing all circumstances in light of God's becoming human in Christ."[52]

One Realm

Bonhoeffer rejects the traditional Christian notion of a divided reality. As long, he says, as Christ and the world are conceived as opposing (sacred and profane) realms, we are left with two equally false choices. We must either give up on reality "as a whole" by placing ourselves in just one of the two realms, or we must try to stand in both simultaneously, which simply leaves us hopelessly conflicted.[53] Bonhoeffer aspires to replace two-realms thinking with "*the one realm of the Christ-reality [Christuswirklichkeit]*, in which the reality of God and the reality of the world are united."[54] In Jesus Christ, God's ultimate reality reveals itself "in the middle of the real world."[55]

The Christ-reality is symbolic both of Christ's inclusiveness and of human wholeness. Of Christ's inclusiveness, because Christ's work of redemption leaves no one out. In Jesus Christ, all human beings, without exception, are reconciled with God.[56] And of human wholeness, because "[a]s reality is *one* in Christ, so the person who belongs to this Christ-reality is also a whole."[57] There is no need to choose between Christ and the world. Christians are no longer conflicted but stand rather as whole persons "before the whole earthly and eternal reality that God in Jesus Christ has prepared for them."[58]

The concept of human wholeness has, for Bonhoeffer, a solid biblical foundation. The Bible, he says, is concerned solely with "the whole person before God."[59] God wants us to preserve—by fully embracing life's challenges and opportunities, tasks and trials, successes and failures—the splendid "polyphony" that God has made possible for us.[60] This divinely sanctioned "polyphony of life" is implicitly rich in risk and reward. We may rely on God's love (the *cantus firmus*) to shield us from "disaster" (*Unheilvolles*) but it is "polyphony" that makes us whole.[61]

RELIGIONLESS CHRISTIANITY REDESCRIBED

I believe the essence of Bonhoeffer's theology is to be found in these ideas. Meanwhile, in the letters and papers from prison lie the seeds of something new, of which we would appear to have neither the flower nor the fruit until we examine them afresh in light of Bonhoeffer's earlier work. In that light, the concept of religionless Christianity—of Jesus Christ without religion—emerges with surprising clarity. A significant number of Bonhoeffer's enduring theological convictions seem quite naturally to belong to it.

For example, in Bonhoeffer's religionless Christianity, the God who consents to be pushed out of the world and onto the cross—the God who became human in Jesus Christ—is still the One who created us and whose love sustains us. The absence of religion does not alter the fact that the freedom which belongs to us as human beings made in God's image is a freedom only for others—a freedom to be risked, time and again, in uncertain deeds of love for which we must take responsibility. In Bonhoeffer's religionless Christianity, there is still just one reality—one *Christuswirklichkeit*—which is symbolic both of Christ's inclusiveness and of human wholeness.

By reaching back and drawing selectively on the whole of his theology, I wish to venture a more comprehensive description of religionless Christianity than has survived Bonhoeffer's final months in prison. In doing so, I make no claim to have anticipated Bonhoeffer's intentions. Nor, though, have I done deliberate violence to his ideas, or otherwise knowingly attributed to him ways of thinking and feeling which are easily dismissed as inconsistent with what we know of his life and work.

Religionless Christianity in Its Christological Context

Bonhoeffer's religionless Christianity is intended to facilitate a Christian response to life in a world where God is no longer commonly regarded as an essential element of human self-understanding. Its confronting sense of God's withdrawal from public life—the conviction that God is "weak and powerless in the world"[62]—sets it apart from everything Bonhoeffer believes to be characteristic of the religious understanding. We find that "only the suffering God can help."[63] As such, religionless Christianity distinguishes between the powerful, but chimerical, God of religion (with whom it has no affinity) and the compassionate, vulnerable God of the gospel (in whom it places an unswerving trust). We know God only through God's self-revelation in Jesus Christ, and this event—which is the event of God's becoming human—is decisive for ontology and for ethics.

It follows that there is no such thing as the "religious a priori"—that specious "mold in human beings into which the divine content of revelation, too, may pour."[64] God is not a legacy of the religious imagination. Rather, God reveals God's self to us in the life, death, and resurrection of Jesus Christ. The divine Logos appears to us in the shape of a human being whose transcendence is grounded firmly in presupposition and not subject to proof.[65]

God is the encounter with Jesus Christ and, in this encounter, we reach the boundary, or limit, of our existence. We come face to face with the eternally transcendent Other, and it is this that gives us confidence that we are not alone in a world of our own imagining. But Jesus Christ is not only "the boundary of the being that has been given to me."[66] He is also the one who stands where I should stand, but cannot, before God, *pro me*.[67] The crucified and risen Christ is both archetypal Other and the true center of every human being. He is, as such, quintessentially "the human being for others"[68] and can be understood in no other way. There is no such person as "Christ-in-himself."[69]

This absence of independent existence, which is to be discerned, foundationally, in Christ, is determinative for religionless Christianity. In Christ, we recognize our true humanity as something shared and never solitary. There is no such thing as the truly isolated, thoroughly autonomous individual. The sense of I-ness is grounded exclusively in relationship—with God, and with other people. Life is innately social and necessarily involves accepting responsibility for others. Human freedom, too, is comprehensible only as a relation, rooted in God's own free decision "to be bound to historical human beings."[70] Just as God has chosen to be free for human beings, rather than from them, so is our freedom now a freedom only for the other. As responsible human beings, we are at once bound to other people and free for them.

Religionless Christianity does not recognize the traditional division of reality into antonymous (sacred and profane) realms. It concedes just *"the one realm of the Christ-reality . . . in which the reality of God and the reality of the world are united."*[71] Jesus Christ is the very presence of God in the world. In the *Christuswirklichkeit*, we can no longer speak truly either of God or the world unless we speak also of him.[72] Bonhoeffer's concept of the Christ-reality signals Christ's inclusiveness. In Jesus Christ, all humanity is reconciled with God. There are no exceptions. No one is excluded from Christ's work of redemption. The Christ-reality is also representative of human wholeness. Those who see themselves as belonging to this one reality do not have to choose between Christ and the world. It is quite possible to belong entirely to Christ and, at the same time, to stand completely in the world.[73]

In religionless Christianity, faith and life sit comfortably together. The God-human Jesus Christ is not the gateway to some other world, but the essence of life in this one. Christians live not in the shadow of the imagined God of religion, but wholly in the presence of the veridical God of the gospel, whose violent death on the cross attests, as nothing else could, to God's selfless love for human beings. They now ask not what *more* God can do for them, but what they can do for God, because they take seriously "the suffering of God in the world."[74] They know that they have, like Christ, "to drink the cup of earthly life to the last drop."[75] For them, life in the Christ-reality is a fully responsible, compassionate, exceptionless sharing in the pains—as well as the delights—of finite creaturely existence.

RELIGIONLESS CHRISTIANITY IN COMMUNITY

Before I conclude this exploration of Bonhoeffer's religionless Christianity with a final look at the question which impels the whole of his theology—the question "Who is Jesus Christ?"—I have first to address several matters arising from the discussion so far, whose careful exposition I believe to be of particular significance for the sense of Bonhoeffer's theology which this book seeks to convey. One of them is the place of the church in his thinking.

On April 8, 1945, Bonhoeffer conducted a Sunday service at the request of other prisoners, the majority of whom were Catholic, in a school classroom in the Bavarian town of Schönberg. Shortly thereafter, two men arrived to escort him onwards to execution at Flossenbürg. A British prisoner, Payne Best, remembers Bonhoeffer saying to him, "This is the end—for me the beginning of life," before hurrying downstairs to meet his executioners.[76] He was hanged the next morning. Bonhoeffer is variously remembered—as a theologian, a Christian martyr, a symbol of resistance, a prophet of the oppressed—but he died, as he lived, a pastor and faithful servant of Christ.

Just as we can be sure then that, from Bonhoeffer's perspective, there is no such thing as religionless Christianity without the God-human Jesus Christ, so, too, can we be sure that there is no such thing as religionless Christianity without Christ's church. "Religionless" Christians, no less than "religious" ones, are firmly associated, in Bonhoeffer's mind, with a community of believers.

Bonhoeffer had a strong aesthetic sense of the church and its rituals which, if not awakened, was certainly reinforced by a youthful visit to Rome in the spring of 1924. He was impressed by the splendor and magnificence of the Catholic Church's Holy Week services, as he was also by the church's universality,[77] and by the vitality of its religious life.[78] Indeed, it was a Vesper service at the Trinità dei Monti on Palm Sunday that first prompted him to think he was "beginning to understand the concept of 'church.'"[79] He found the service "almost indescribable."[80] Evensong was sung by young novices

> with unbelievable simplicity [and] grace. . . . The impression left by these novices was even greater than would have been left by real nuns, because every trace of routine was missing. The ritual was truly no longer merely ritual. Instead, it was worship in the true sense. The whole thing gave one an unparalleled impression of profound, guileless piety.[81]

Bonhoeffer's aesthetic sensibilities are here enriched and intensified by an authenticity—an unfeigned sense of the glory of God—which greatly appealed to him. It will be evident that such effects are produced only in a community gathered for worship, and Bonhoeffer was never simply a casual observer of such occasions. He writes of the Palm Sunday morning Mass in St. Peter's: "I was fortunate to stand next to a Catholic woman who had a Missal, so that I could follow everything."[82]

In a sermon given some years later in Barcelona, Bonhoeffer compares the Protestant experience of "church" unfavorably with its Catholic counterpart. There is, he says,

> a word that evokes tremendous feelings of love and bliss among Catholics who hear it, a word that stirs in them the most profound depths of religious feeling ranging from the awe and dread of judgment to the bliss of God's presence, but a word that assuredly also evokes feelings of home for them, feelings of the sort only a child feels in gratitude, reverence, and self-surrendering love towards its mother, the feelings that come over us when after a long time away we once again enter our parents' home, our own childhood home.[83]

Protestants, on the other hand, according to Bonhoeffer, are largely indifferent to the word "church," which they associate with banality, superfluity, and boredom. But this, he says, will be their undoing if they are "unable to find in this word a new, or rather the original meaning."[84]

Bonhoeffer makes another revealing comparison in the report of his year of study (1930–1931) at Union Theological Seminary in New York. There he contrasts the uninspiring lecture-like quality of sermons in the "white" churches he visited with his experience of African American churches, where "the 'black Christ' is preached with captivating passion and vividness." Only among African Americans, he writes, could one really "hear someone talk in a Christian sense about sin and grace and the love of God and ultimate hope."[85]

While these observations tell us more about Bonhoeffer's early ecclesiology than they do about today's multifarious expressions of the word "church," they are important because they help us to understand what Bonhoeffer believes the church, to be truly church, must be. The church, for Bonhoeffer, is not a *building* that one enters from time to time but rather a *place* that one inhabits constantly, the place where the heart belongs, to Christ and to Christ's church-community. It is that place where, in the language of his doctoral thesis, the structural "being-with-each-other" and responsible "acting-for-each-other" of the members of the church-community together constitute "the specific sociological nature of the community of love."[86] Belonging to the community of God is not just a matter of joining a congregation. It means to participate in "the pilgrimage of God's chosen people through the world under the banner of Christ," to live "from within Christ . . . with all those who love Christ."[87] Christians may live, like Christ, in the midst of enemies, or "remain alone in distant lands," but they are subsumed nonetheless into a community of faith.[88] Members of this community sacrifice themselves for others "with a joyous heart." They pray for one another and forgive one another's sins. These three great strengths of the Christian church-community—sacrifice, intercession, and the forgiveness of sins—are "the blood of Christ's body holding everything together."[89]

All Christian community has just one foundation—Jesus Christ. It is as such a spiritual rather than a psychic, or emotional, reality. It is the community of those who are called by Christ to Christian service, not the domain of those who seek to "bind others to themselves."[90] Bonhoeffer warns against the danger of getting caught up in the *experience* of Christian community, of confusing some false human ideal with "a reality created by God in Christ in which we may participate."[91] Those who seek to create, or to recover, in Christian community, some fanciful image of the perfect life will always be disappointed. "We hold fast in faith [says Bonhoeffer] to God's greatest gift, that God has acted for us all and wants to act for us all. This makes us joyful and happy, but it also makes us ready to forgo all such experiences if at times God does not grant them."[92] It is faith rather than experience that holds the community together.

Whereas, for the young Bonhoeffer, Christ is not only the sole foundation of church-community but also present *only* in this community,[93] he is compelled, by the logic of his own Christology, progressively to moderate this understanding. Because Jesus bears the whole of human nature,[94] because, in him, the form of humanity is created anew,[95] and because, through him, all human beings, without exception, are reconciled with God,[96] it necessarily follows that Jesus Christ is present in every human being. While it is certainly remarkable that "only a part of humanity recognizes the form of its savior,"[97] Jesus Christ can nonetheless only be proclaimed "as the one in whom God has bodily taken on [all] humanity,"[98] and the church is obliged to reflect this understanding.

But what, Bonhoeffer asks in the first of the theological letters from prison, "does a church, a congregation, a sermon, a liturgy, a Christian life, mean in a religionless world?"[99] He leaves us only a very preliminary sketch of the church in a religionless age, but there is material enough to warrant a certain amount of practical exegesis. The church, he says, has a responsibility not only to proclaim Christ but also to show people what it really means to live with, and in, him.[100] And it can do this only by giving up its wealth, its power, and its pride. The church must lead by example, not by decree. Indeed, the church is only truly church when it—like Christ—is there for others.[101] At the same time, an outward-looking, service-oriented church will take steps to safeguard its distinctively Christian identity. In this context, an arcane discipline, which allows the mysteries of the faith (prayer, worship, sacraments, creed) to play their crucial part in the life of the church, may give increasingly isolated Christians strength and confidence to live, before and with God, in a world without God.[102]

I think we may reasonably assume Bonhoeffer's experience of the relationship between church and state in Nazi Germany—the experience of the church "fighting during these years only for its self-preservation"[103]—to have been the principal motivation for the call which so perplexed Bethge and others: the call for the church to "give away all its property to those in need," and for the clergy to "live solely on the freewill offerings of the congregations and perhaps be engaged in some secular vocation."[104] Whether or not we are inclined to accept these particular challenges to the prevailing order, Bonhoeffer's aim here is surely to reduce the church's vulnerability to external manipulation, by limiting the opportunities available to those outside the church materially to obscure the revelation of God in Christ.

Much the same can be said of Bonhoeffer's appeal to the church to eschew "the vices of hubris . . . power, envy, and illusionism" in favor of the virtues of "authenticity, trust, faithfulness, steadfastness, patience, discipline, [and] humility."[105] The church has no right to seek to create a privileged place for itself. God gives the church its "characteristic place" in the world as "the place of God himself."[106] Here, as always, Bonhoeffer seeks to focus our attention exclusively on "the one Word of God whom we have to hear, and whom we have to trust and obey in life and death."[107] In this context, the vices may be seen as consonant with Bonhoeffer's critique of religion, while the virtues are those of a community which has set its mind on Christ.

Bonhoeffer is, I think, most unlikely to have lost faith in the expressions of worship which moved him so profoundly as a young man in Rome and New York, or indeed in the form of Christian life in community that inspired the book *Life Together*. But the church is always, for Bonhoeffer, more than simply "this or that building with the bell tower."[108] We may, perhaps, think of Bonhoeffer's "religionless" Christians as a worldly, agapeic community of faith whose members have no desire to "control, coerce, and dominate" others with their love,[109] and who, whether alone or in company, but always in the presence of Jesus Christ, strive only to hear and serve the Word. They underestimate neither "the significance of the human 'example'" inspired by Jesus's own humanity[110] nor the importance of deciding for themselves what they "really believe."[111] Leaving matters of faith to a church, of any kind, is not acceptable to them. It will not do to say that "it depends not on me but on the church," or that "I do not have my faith at my disposal." Nothing absolves them of the requirement to be honest with themselves.[112] They may, and should, expect to find, in community with one another, abundant sources of inspiration, strength, and common purpose, but they will not find there a place of escape from the world, or from their worldly responsibilities as followers of Christ.

Bonhoeffer always believed a sound ecclesiology to depend on a profound Christology—on an assured sense of Christ's steadfast presence, and of God's church-community as "a reality of revelation"[113] in the form of *Christus als Gemeinde existierend*.[114] Bonhoeffer's vision of a socially responsible church turned firmly toward the world, on the other hand, took longer to consolidate, although its origins almost certainly lie in his youthful experience of the Social Gospel movement in the United States which, as Bethge says, made an "ineradicable impression" on him.[115] Christ is in no way diminished, though, by Bonhoeffer's progressive change in orientation. The power of Christ's love is not compromised by the universality of his embrace, which now reaches into the most hidden, godless corners of the world.[116] But the nature of Christian life has changed for him. Christians still enjoy the benefits of church-community, but there is a very real sense in which the whole world is now their church, because it is there, and not just in fellowship with other Christians, that the encounter with Jesus Christ takes place. The true measure of faith is thus not fidelity to a religious institution, but rather a genuine willingness to share, wholeheartedly, the burden of Christ's love for all humanity.

The Place of Metaphysics in Bonhoeffer's Theology

It may also be helpful to clarify Bonhoeffer's attitude to metaphysics which, in the critique of religion, is generally associated with what he believed to be essentially erroneous religious notions of divine power, rather than with philosophical reflection on the nature of being, modality, causation, space and time, and so on.

It would be wrong to assume, though, from the critique of metaphysics and inwardness in the prison letters, that Bonhoeffer had come to regard metaphysics per se—including its precious sense of the transcendent—as inimical to a modern, post-religious understanding of the reality of Jesus Christ. For one thing, the event of God's becoming human must always have, by virtue of its extraordinary and essentially unprovable character, a metaphysical quality, and this is manifestly true also of the Chalcedonian Definition of the Faith, which Bonhoeffer finds so compelling.

Bonhoeffer's problems with metaphysics stem principally from its religious associations with the "God of the gaps," with the *deus ex machina* who is wheeled in "to solve insoluble problems or to provide strength when human powers fail"—the God who preys on human weakness.[117] Bonhoeffer is critical, too, of the pious religious person's metaphysical preoccupation with a future state of being or grace, which he thinks more conducive to the superfluous cultivation of otherworldly hopes, fears, and fantasies than to practical expressions of faith and obedience.

Metaphysical propositions may generally be said to serve a useful theological purpose for Bonhoeffer when they help to express the mystery that is Jesus Christ but are of no real value when employed as false means of avoiding the need to come to terms with the finally unavoidable limits of human existence.

Weak and Powerless in the World

There is, too, the cognate matter of God's perfections, especially God's omnipotence. Bonhoeffer does not generally question this. For example, in a sermon given in February 1933, shortly after Hitler's appointment as chancellor of Germany, Bonhoeffer reminds his audience of God's exclusive claim "to honor and praise," and speaks of "the living Lord . . . who has all power in his hands."[118] And as late as the *Ethics*, he makes the entirely orthodox claim that, in Christ's resurrection, God, "in love and omnipotence," overcomes death and "calls a new creation into life."[119]

There is, though, always and inevitably a certain tension between any simple view of God's omnipotence and the ambiguity of the cross of Jesus Christ,

> which is the sign of powerlessness, dishonor, defenselessness, hopelessness, meaninglessness, and yet is also where we find divine power, honor, defense, hope, meaning, glory, life, victory . . . God's lordship over all the world.[120]

In the *Letters and Papers from Prison* the emphasis is on God's powerlessness. Bonhoeffer describes God as "weak and powerless in the world," and Christ as our help "not by virtue of his omnipotence but rather by virtue of his weakness and suffering!" This, he says, is what distinguishes Christianity from "all religions." Whereas religion is always about power, about the *deus ex machina*, the Bible reveals the powerlessness and the suffering of God. It shows us that "only the suffering God can help."[121]

And he goes further. In the "Outline for a Book," Bonhoeffer seems genuinely ready to question the practical value of the word "omnipotence" itself. The answer to the question "Who is God?" he says, is "[n]ot primarily a general belief in God's omnipotence, and so on." This is no "genuine experience of God but just a prolongation of a piece of the world."[122] Abstract, metaphysical assertions of God's omnipotence, omniscience, and omnipresence reduce these words to essentially empty symbols of that nonexistent human way to God which seeks to construct for itself the God it imagines God must be.

But God can only truly be known in the "being of revelation," in Jesus Christ, and in Jesus Christ, God has consented "to be pushed out of the world and onto the cross." Now, all faith and hope are vested in a God who is "weak and powerless in the world," and who "in precisely this way, and only so, is at our side and helps us."[123] Only the suffering God can help because only the suffering God truly knows what God has made. Only the suffering God can bring God's creatures into compassionate relation with the divine life.

It is Bonhoeffer's invincible confidence in God's constant love and unfailing goodness that sustains him, rather than the promise of relief from life's uncertainties. It is this, too, that allows him to trust in God's providence, and to grant life a discernible, because intelligible, continuity, irrespective of its outcomes. The all-powerful God of religion is not the God who is revealed in Christ. Omnipotence will always appear strained, arbitrary, inconsistent, and sometimes cruel, but the crucified and humiliated one, who sustains and makes us whole by assuming the burdens of a godless and sinful world, will never disappoint us.[124] God is not, of course, exhausted in God's self-revelation, but we can at least be sure, as Eberhard Busch says, that "in it God gives *himself* and not something else to be known, and that he is not someone other than whom he gives himself to know."[125]

Violence and Nonresistance

And, finally, there is the matter of vicarious representative action (*Stellvertretung*) as the expression of an ethic which enables an appropriately Christian response to the vagaries of historical existence, and which cannot, as such, be reduced to a set of fixed principles. Bonhoeffer's increasingly religionless understanding of *Stellvertretung* as worldly, responsible action, freely risked, in faith, for the benefit of other human beings, is perhaps nowhere more thoroughly embodied than in his complex attitude to violence and nonresistance.

In a lecture on Christian ethics given in Barcelona in February 1929, the twenty-three-year-old Bonhoeffer told his small German audience that love for one's enemy must be condemned as ethically perverse if it meant surrendering one's real neighbor "to destruction, in the most concrete sense."

> God gave me my mother, my people [Volk]. For what I have, I thank my people; what I am, I am through my people, and so what I have should also belong to my people; that is in the divine order [Ordnung] of things, for God created the peoples. . . . [L]ove for my people will sanctify murder, will sanctify war.[126]

Bonhoeffer soon abandoned such *völkisch*, Protestant formulations, and was never truly comfortable with the thought of war.[127] His eldest brother, Walter, died at just eighteen years of age of shrapnel wounds received late in the First World War, when Dietrich was twelve. His mother gave him Walter's confirmation Bible at his own confirmation three years later. According to Bethge, "Bonhoeffer used it throughout his life for his personal meditations and in worship."[128] At Union Theological Seminary in 1930–1931, Bonhoeffer was much influenced by the staunch pacifism of a fellow student, the Frenchman Jean Lasserre, who deepened his understanding of the Christian's obligation to eschew violence. For Bonhoeffer, too, a large part of Gandhi's appeal lay in the Mahatma's resolute pursuit of practical measures of nonviolent resistance. Bonhoeffer mentions his hopes of visiting Gandhi in a July 1934 letter from London to Reinhold Niebuhr, under whom he had studied in New York. It is time, he tells Niebuhr, to bring the focus of church opposition to the National Socialist state back to the Sermon on the Mount. "For my part, I am planning to go to India quite soon to see what Gandhi knows about such things and what there is to learn there."[129]

Bonhoeffer devoted the bulk of his ecumenical energies, in the first half of the 1930s, to the avoidance of war in Europe. Nowhere is this more vividly expressed than in his famous call for peace at an ecumenical gathering of Christian churches in Fanø, Denmark, in the summer of 1934.

> Why [he asks] do we fear the fury of the world powers? Why don't we take the power from them and give it back to Christ? . . . The hour is late. The world is choked with weapons, and dreadful is the distrust which looks out of all men's

eyes. The trumpets of war may blow tomorrow. For what are we waiting? Do we want to become involved in this guilt as never before?¹³⁰

Peace cannot be guaranteed by treaties, or by money, or by "universal peaceful rearmament." All of these, he says, confuse peace with safety, whereas, in fact, peace "can never be made safe." It can only be risked. Peace cannot bring security because the guarantees that security requires are built on mistrust and mistrust is one of the principal architects of war.¹³¹

In a document distributed to participants in a youth peace conference in Czechoslovakia in July 1932, Bonhoeffer distinguishes between the right to struggle for truth and justice, and the right to wage war.

> In the fallen world [he says] there is a right to struggle. This does not mean there is a right to war. Just as the use of torture cannot be justified by the necessity of legal process, so too one cannot derive the right to war out of the necessity of struggle. War as a *means* of struggle is an action forbidden us today by God, because it represents the external and internal destruction of human beings and thus robs us of the gaze toward Christ.¹³²

Michael DeJonge divides Bonhoeffer's statements on peace into four classes:

> 1) those that leave open the question of Christian participation in violence, 2) those that affirm peace or nonviolence but make clear their provisional character, 3) those that affirm peace or nonviolence without making explicit their provisional character, and 4) those that explicitly consider violence.¹³³

He includes the Czechoslovakian lecture in the second, explicitly provisional, category, because Bonhoeffer there describes international peace as "God's commandment for us today," and as "God's will for our time."¹³⁴ But, and in addition to the very clear antiwar sentiments expressed in this passage, Bonhoeffer also says in this lecture that whoever knows something of the history of war will know also how much the nature of war has changed. War is no longer "battle." It is

> absolutely destructive.... Today's war destroys soul and body. Because there is no way for us to understand war as God's order of preservation and therefore as God's commandment ... today's war, the next war, must be *condemned* by the church.... We should not balk here at using the word "pacifism.".... [W]e are concerned here with a very specific means of struggle forbidden today by God.¹³⁵

DeJonge similarly classifies (as explicitly provisional) Bonhoeffer's August 1932 address at an International Youth Conference in Gland, where he says, seemingly without reservation:

> Today there should be no war—the cross does not want it. One must make a distinction: in the world that has fallen away from God, struggle is inevitable, but there should be no war. War in its present-day form lays waste to God's creation and obscures the view of revelation. . . . The church forsakes obedience whenever it sanctions war. The church of Christ stands against war in favor of peace among the peoples, between nations, classes, and races.[136]

While it is certainly possible to argue, consistent with DeJonge's claim, that Bonhoeffer here, too, clearly envisages other possible times and situations that would justify war, and the church's support for war, it is equally plausible, particularly in the wake of Europe's recent experience of total war, that Bonhoeffer finds it hard to imagine a future war that would be other than "absolutely destructive," and bound as such to lay waste God's creation and to rob all human beings of "the gaze towards Christ."

DeJonge's typology is a helpful antidote to the overreaching of "anabaptist" claims to find in Bonhoeffer a thoroughly kindred spirit of Christian pacifism. (Indeed, so keen is Stanley Hauerwas to claim Bonhoeffer for the cause that he chooses quixotically to leave open the question whether Bonhoeffer knew that the anti-Nazi conspiracy of which he eventually became a part necessarily involved tyrannicide.[137]) Bonhoeffer's "concrete" historical circumstances, and rational, liberal Protestant foundations, will not allow him to rest entirely comfortably in the pacifist space. But by deploying, as a counterweight to the "anabaptists," what he calls Bonhoeffer's "non-commitment to nonviolence," DeJonge may, if perhaps unwittingly, *understate* Bonhoeffer's consistently strong attachment to Christ's commandment of peace.

By the end of the decade, with war now inevitable, Bonhoeffer became increasingly concerned to evade military service. His second, brief visit to the United States, in the summer of 1939, was at least partly motivated by this concern, as, subsequently, was his work for the *Abwehr* (Military Intelligence) at the initiative of his brother-in-law, Hans von Dohnanyi. Bonhoeffer knew that, if he was in fact ever summoned to serve in the German armed forces,[138] he would almost certainly refuse, and pay for his conscientious objection with his life. But war was one thing; the struggle for truth and justice quite another. And, by October 1940, when Bonhoeffer formally joined the staff of the *Abwehr* as a confidential agent, he was fully convinced of the need for Hitler's forced removal from power. In this case, at least, tyrannicide was justified.

Bonhoeffer's struggle to reconcile the language of the Sermon on the Mount with the historically attested depths of human depravity is most clearly expressed in what is otherwise almost certainly his least worldly book, *Discipleship*, which takes Matthew chapters 5–7 as its inspiration.[139] Here, in an exegesis of Matthew 5:38–42,[140] Bonhoeffer describes Jesus as affirming the Old Testament "power of retribution to convict and overcome evil" by turning it on its head. For Jesus, "just retribution" lies in not resisting injustice.[141]

> With this statement [says Bonhoeffer] Jesus releases his community from the political and legal order, from the national form of the people of Israel, and makes it into what it truly is, namely, the community of the faithful that is not bound by political or national ties. God's chosen people of Israel did exist in a political form in which, according to the divine will, retribution consisted of returning a blow for a blow. For the community of disciples, which makes no national or legal claims for itself, retribution means patiently bearing the blow, so that evil is not added to evil.[142]

Evil is suffered to "run its course" but, because it encounters no resistance, cannot sustain itself. "Assault is condemned by not being met with violence. The unjust claim on my coat is answered by my giving up my cloak as well. The exploitation of my service becomes obvious as exploitation when I set no limit to it."[143] The voluntary renunciation of violence requires both absolute fidelity to Jesus and absolute selflessness. There is no other way that "evil can be overcome."[144]

Bonhoeffer notes that the Reformation distinction between private and public persons is "foreign to Jesus."[145] I am not released from the obligation to obey Christ by virtue of my responsibilities in life's "official" sphere. How can such a distinction be truly helpful?

> Wherever I am attacked, am I not simultaneously the father of my children, the pastor of my congregation, the statesman of my people? For this reason, am I not required to fight back against any attack, just because of my responsibility for my office? Am I not always myself in my office, too, who stands alone before Jesus?[146]

It is this sense of "aloneness" (which is really the most profound sense of personal responsibility before God) that is critical to understanding here. Jesus's followers, says Bonhoeffer, "are always completely alone, single individuals who can act and make decisions finally only by themselves."[147]

Bonhoeffer again conjures this powerful image—of standing alone before God—and takes it further, in the *Ethics*, where he makes it clear that "[t]hose who are responsible act in their own freedom, without the support of people, conditions, or principles." They must "judge, weigh, decide, and act on their own," before "surrendering to God the deed that has become necessary and is nevertheless . . . free, surrendering it to God, who looks upon the heart, weighs the deeds, and guides history."[148] Bonhoeffer has, however, already carried this sense of aloneness, this deeply personal sense of responsibility, with him for a long time. As early as February 1929, he told his audience in Barcelona:

> Christians act according to how God's will seems to direct them. . . . Ethical decisions lead us into the most profound solitude, the solitude in which a person stands before the living God. Here no one can help us . . . here God imposes a burden on us that we must bear alone. Only in the realization that we have been addressed by God, that God is making a claim on us, does our self [Ich] awaken. Only through God's call do I become this "self," isolated from all other people, called to account by God, confronted, alone, by eternity.[149]

This leads him to conclude—inconsistently with the later exegesis of Matthew 5:38–42 in *Discipleship*, and long before, as a member of the Resistance, he had special need of such a conclusion—that

> [t]here are no acts that are bad in and of themselves; even murder can be sanctified. There is only faithfulness to or deviation from God's will. There is no law with a specific content, but only the law of freedom, that is, bearing responsibility alone before God and oneself.[150]

Although Bonhoeffer elsewhere dismisses the idea of the ethical isolation of the individual as a "fictitious notion,"[151] he does not in fact contradict himself. We are driven, and indeed defined, by the ethical situation of encounter, but finally, and solely, responsible—before God—for our actions.

Bonhoeffer is nonetheless ready to accept—even as he wrestles with the Sermon on the Mount in *Discipleship*—that evil, in its historical manifestations, commonly "rampages most wildly" among the weak and the defenseless.[152] In light of this, it is wrong to interpret the assertion that "evil will only be conquered by good"[153] as wisdom for everyday life. Indeed, the idea that nonresistance should serve as a principle for secular life jeopardizes "the order of the world which God graciously preserves."[154]

But while this may seem reassuringly obvious to most of us, Bonhoeffer reminds us that, in Jesus Christ, we are not in the presence of what he calls a "programmatic thinker." We may indeed long for someone to provide us with general (and appropriately flexible) ethical guidance for life in a complex and ambivalent world, but it won't be him.

> Rather, the one speaking here about overcoming evil with suffering is he who himself was overcome by evil on the cross and who emerged from that defeat as the conqueror and victor. There is no other justification for this commandment of Jesus than his own cross. Only those who there, in the cross of Jesus, find faith in the victory over evil can obey his command.[155]

Jesus calls his disciples "into communion with his passion." Only by their willingness to participate in the cross of Christ can Jesus's disciples hope to make his passion "visible and credible to the world."[156]

The life of the disciple is an "extraordinary" life and *must* be extraordinary if it is to be called Christian. It is the way of "perfect purity, perfect truthfulness, perfect nonviolence . . . [and] undivided love for one's enemies."[157] These, for Jesus, are baseline, not ideal or exceptional, requirements. They are deeds to be done "[n]ot in ethical rigor, not in the eccentricity of Christian ways of life, but in the simplicity of Christian obedience to the will of Jesus."[158] How, though, are we to reconcile this injunction with Bonhoeffer's earlier dismissal of the idea that the principle of nonresistance might serve "as general secular wisdom for life in the world"?[159] It is, of course, possible that the word "extraordinary" is intended to apply only to Jesus's closest followers, including Bonhoeffer's fellow seminarians at Finkenwalde, but this does not appear to be the case when he speaks of a "specialness," an "extraordinariness," in the absence of which "what is Christian is absent."[160]

There is thus evidently tension between what Bonhoeffer clearly understands to be Christ's expectations of those who follow him and Bonhoeffer's assessment of his own, and others', real world options—as, for example, in the tension between the ideal of "perfect nonviolence" and the reality of perfect impotence, short of martyrdom, in the face of shameless Nazi brutality.

In the essay "After Ten Years," written primarily for fellow conspirators at the turn of the year 1942–1943, a few months before his arrest, Bonhoeffer reminds us that "we are not Christ" and must not "burden ourselves with impossible things." But he goes on:

> We are not Christ, but if we want to be Christians it means that we are to take part in Christ's greatness of heart, in the responsible action that in freedom lays hold of the hour and faces the danger, and in the true sympathy that springs forth not from fear but from Christ's freeing and redeeming love for all who suffer. Inactive waiting and dully looking on are not Christian responses.[161]

We are not Christ, but it is still Christ who sets the standard. As the source and perfect expression of our humanity, he is our example and guide to life.

Bonhoeffer thus takes a selective view of Jesus's admonition to offer no resistance to the aggressor, finding in Christ's passion alone confirmation that "suffering love is the retribution for and the overcoming of evil."[162] Those who truly understand in faith the nature of Jesus's "victory over evil" may find the strength to follow him all the way to the cross, but martyrdom will not serve as a general model for life in the world. There are other options.

Bonhoeffer's involvement in the plot to kill Hitler compelled him to consider very carefully what was required of the free and responsible Christian in the face of a ruthless, absolutizing despotism. Germans, he wrote, at the end of 1942, are only "beginning to discover what free responsibility means. It is founded in a God who calls for the free venture of faith to responsible action and who promises forgiveness and consolation to the one who on account of such action becomes a sinner."[163]

Bonhoeffer's judicious use of traditional Lutheran approaches to social order (kingdoms, orders, and estates) led him to attribute to each of church and state a qualified autonomy under God's sovereignty, and a conditional legitimacy, based on mutually reinforcing commitments to live by the cross of Christ. Bonhoeffer early rejected "'pseudo-Lutheran' orders of creation thinking" (which he saw as too easily, and too often, used to claim a divine warrant for tyranny) in favor of what he called "orders of preservation," which lent conditional support to various ways of structuring human life in society, as long as they were turned toward Christ.[164] But he subsequently abandoned all talk of "orders," and spoke instead of four mandates: family, work, government, and church.[165]

The mandates were of divine rather than human origin, and the bearer of the mandate was to be understood as acting solely "as a vicarious representative, as a stand-in for the one who issued the commission."[166] The word "mandates" was preferred to "orders" because "thereby their character as divinely imposed tasks [Auftrag], as opposed to determinate forms of being, becomes clearer."[167] The mandates were not autonomous domains, following their own rules, but rather interdependent instruments of God's self-revelation in Jesus Christ. "Only in their being with-one-another [Miteinander], for-one-another [Füreinander], and over-against-one-another [Gegeneinander] do the divine mandates . . . communicate the commandment of God as it is revealed in Jesus Christ."[168] They were divine "in the midst of the world," and they were divine "only because of their original and final relation to Christ." Nor were they to be identified with any particular historical form of institution. Indeed, "[i]n the concrete case, persistent, arbitrary violation of this task through concrete forms of work, marriage, government, and church extinguishes the divine mandate."[169]

By the end of 1942, when he wrote his New Year reflections, "After Ten Years," for fellow conspirators, Bonhoeffer had already long believed the Nazis to have forfeited any claim they may once conceivably have had to embody a legitimate expression of the divine mandate to govern. In Nazi Germany, the state's bond with Christ and the cross had been shattered; its God-given legitimacy as an instrument of law and order annulled. Nothing, says Bonhoeffer, can deprive us of our "co-responsibility for the course of history."[170] Evil must be exposed "and, if need be, prevented by use of force."[171]

"Who stands firm?" Bonhoeffer asks, when the ethical concepts on which we depend—reason, principle, conscience, freedom, duty, and virtue—prove no match for evil in its numerous seemingly noble and beguiling disguises. "[O]nly the one who is prepared to sacrifice all of these when, in faith and in relationship to God alone, he is called to obedient and responsible action."[172] Christians must "act according to how God's will seems to direct them,"[173] and are fully accountable to God for their actions. Bonhoeffer thus leaves room for maneuver with respect to the proper Christian response to tyranny, oppression, and injustice but rather less with regard to the idea that we are finally responsible, before God, for our actions.[174] It is equally clear, though, that, for Bonhoeffer, the integrity of this approach depends entirely on our willingness to grant Christ—the compassionate, suffering God of the gospel—the conclusive part in every act of discernment. The moment we lose sight of Christ as the one who stands in our place before God, *pro nobis*, a "conversation" with "God" can easily become something else altogether and take us just about anywhere we may choose to go.

STILL AN IMPORTANT VOICE

Bonhoeffer's theological legacy is rich and diverse. He has been received and read differently at different times, in different places, and by different churches. John de Gruchy attributes this to the "piecemeal way in which his writings have become known," to their "varied and often fragmentary nature," to problems of translation, and to the popular, and often political, appropriation of elements of Bonhoeffer's work by and for various causes.[175] Now, though, following the publication of excellent critical German and English editions of Bonhoeffer's complete works, there is no longer any good reason why anyone who wishes to get a reliable sense of the whole should not be able to do so.

De Gruchy observes that Bonhoeffer's theology is so closely related to his life and historical context as to make them virtually inseparable. While it is certainly true to say that "all thought is embedded in social location," there is, in Bonhoeffer's case, evidence of a more deliberate intention to bring theology, history, and life into close and direct relation.[176] Bonhoeffer's strongly felt need to situate himself within, and increasingly over against, a national historical situation of consuming wickedness transformed him into a controversial political figure. It is, therefore, perhaps hardly surprising that others have since chosen to appropriate Bonhoeffer's theology for a range of political purposes. As de Gruchy points out, Bonhoeffer does not fit easily into any recognized ideological framework, whether of the right or of the left, but that is different from finding in his work, as Christians most certainly have, paths and approaches which help them "to engage in the struggle for justice and liberation more faithfully in terms of the gospel."[177]

Wayne Floyd believes Bonhoeffer's thought to be "most fertile when it is allowed to act as a catalyst for the theological work of others." There is always, of course, the possibility of a "creative misuse" of Bonhoeffer's theology, but this is less to be feared than a lobotomizing of "the 'radicality' of his vision."[178] Nowhere is the radical open-endedness of Bonhoeffer's theology more evident than in his letters from prison, which challenge us to keep faith with Christ in a world that no longer takes him seriously. In those letters, Bonhoeffer is clearly seeking a way of helping his fellow Christians to grasp the situation in which they now find themselves—to accept and, indeed, to embody this autonomous world come of age—without abandoning Christ. Seen in this light, and regarded holistically as part of a life's work, Bonhoeffer's religionless Christianity is best understood as a natural outcome of his ongoing theological endeavor.

But just who, today, is likely to find Bonhoeffer's arguments for a new, religionless form of Christianity compelling? What remaining theological significance is to be attributed to Jesus Christ in the absence of the comprehensively almighty, but illusory, God of religion? How does a God "who is weak and powerless in the world" help us? Bonhoeffer's religionless Christianity is naturally of some continuing historical interest, but might it reasonably be expected positively to influence the way people see the world today?

We can safely assume that many of a secular disposition would happily affirm Bonhoeffer's religionless premise without, however, generally feeling the need to save Christ from the wreck of religion. Uncritically religious people, on the other hand, are unlikely to see any need for a religionless form of Christianity and may take some comfort in contemporary sociology's qualified retreat from its own "end of religion" paradigm. If religionless Christianity may, perhaps, be thought likely to have a special appeal for any particular group, it could be for those who stand, self-consciously, in what Charles Taylor calls the Jamesian open space—those who take their stand deliberately "at the mid-point of the cross-pressures that define our culture,"[179] where they can feel the winds pushing them "now to belief, now to unbelief"[180]—as well as for the many others, both religious and nonreligious, who simply find themselves in this space from time to time and may welcome the chance to rest more comfortably in it.

Bonhoeffer is especially helpful here because he spares us the choice of two unsatisfactory alternatives: a choice between earth and heaven; the choice between a self-enclosed, entirely secular humanism and an ultimately unconvincing otherworldly transcendentalism. In Bonhoeffer's religionless Christianity, a genuine existentialism (by which I mean a thoroughly worldly life of constant decision, risk, responsibility, and uncertainty) is held in dialectical tension with a genuine Other (a real outside), while the power of

Christ's freeing and redeeming love unlocks a larger life of constant and profound fellowship with Jesus Christ. His death and resurrection do not point to new life in some other place but rather to a new way of living—of "being for others"—in this, now post-religious, one. The alternative is to live and die in our small selves.

Christians might thus reasonably be expected to place their trust in a God "who is weak and powerless in the world" simply because they know God, so understood, to be loving and faithful. They will be content to "live as those who manage their lives without God" because they know that God is there nonetheless; that the God whose absence is so keenly felt by once religious people is not, and never was, the God "before whom [they] stand continually."[181] They depend on the power of love that comes to them by virtue of Christ's passion. They know that "only the suffering God can help,"[182] because only in the presence of the crucified and risen Christ, only in the presence of the one who is both fully human and wholly God, does the human encounter with God take place.

Bonhoeffer's religionless Christianity, read in the context of his broader theology, draws ideas that are not easily held together—ideas of otherness and interdependence—into complementary relationship. Together they provide a strong foundation for a radical theological anthropology. In Jesus Christ, God assumes "the whole of human nature."[183] Our sense of I-ness rests on the awareness of the active presence of God (the divine You) in *other* people. We have our being only in relation to a You, and thus *ex*-ist "always and only in ethical responsibility," by accepting, or rejecting, an external claim.[184] In Bonhoeffer's theology, it is not the *idea* of "being for others" that is new. Notions of selflessness have frequently been advanced as a Christian ideal. These, however, are generally presented as the antithesis of a more natural human inclination to prioritize an independent sense of self—an ethical autonomy—which does not depend on the claims made on us by others. Bonhoeffer, though, would have us understand that to assume human beings are somehow wired to live this way—in ethical isolation, individualistically, "atomistic[ally]"[185]—is to misunderstand, fundamentally, the nature of life. The idea of "being for others" is not a new way of being human. It is, rather, the way of being truly human and is as such characteristic of Christ's inclusiveness; of life lived, theologically speaking, in the *Christuswirklichkeit* shared by God and human beings, whence springs the sense of human wholeness, and confidence in God's unfailing goodness and compassion. We may, and frequently do, of course, repudiate this, and cling instead to that illusory notion of the isolated individual which religion, as Bonhoeffer conceives it, shares with some expressions of secularity; but, for Bonhoeffer, the reality is that our "being for others" is synonymous with the life with God which is our life and thus with our humanity.

WHO THEN IS JESUS CHRIST ACTUALLY FOR US TODAY?

I conclude this exploration of Bonhoeffer's religionless Christianity with a final look at the question which impels his theological journey from its largely academic beginnings to its very deliberately lived end—the question that, in Bonhoeffer's incipient prison theology, takes the form, "what is Christianity, or who is Christ actually for us today?"[186]

The answer to this question is, of course, readily available to us, in its most concise form. It is subsumed in the answer to another question—the question: Who is God?—in the "Outline for a Book," which effectively brings the theological letters from prison to a close. The two questions are essentially the same for Bonhoeffer; and the answer, too, is the same in each case: Jesus Christ is God; God is the encounter with Jesus Christ. And Jesus is there *only* for others. Those who follow him in faith enter into new life with God, in "'being there for others,' through participation in the being of Jesus."[187]

In Jesus Christ, God became human as we are human. Christ's weakness and powerlessness belong inescapably to finite biological life, just as his love and compassion—the Spirit of Christ in every human being—belong inescapably to God. Life and love together are God's gift to us. And we must have faith that God enters fully into human joy and suffering because, if this were not so, then creation would surely be as much a mystery to God as God is, finally, to God's creation.

Bonhoeffer, says Gaylon Barker, did not want to impose God on the world. Rather, he wanted Christians to be clear about their own beliefs. "He was concerned about the church's confession and the integrity of its witness."[188] As Bonhoeffer says in a note from July 1944, "A confession of faith expresses not what someone else '*must*' believe, but what one *believes* oneself."[189] In the Christian confession of faith, Jesus Christ is not imposed on others, but rather presses the claim of the other on us. We meet Christ in other people who may spare him no thought at all, and find in this an unfailing source of wonder, strength, and joy. In this fallen world, we are empowered, by a "sweeping, uncompromising christocentrism,"[190] to see the grace of God in Christ at work in every act of love and human kindness, and to reach a new understanding of the abiding presence of Christ in every human being.

For Bonhoeffer, Christ is everywhere, and in everyone, notwithstanding the fact that "only a part of humanity recognizes the form of its savior."[191] Jesus Christ, says Bonhoeffer, "is not only with us in lonely hours." He confronts us "in every step we take, in every person we meet." It is "God himself [who] speaks to us from every human being."[192] Christians must learn to recognize, and to acknowledge, Christ in every human being because, in the God-reconciled world of the incarnation, every human being bears the image of God. And this must serve to inform and guide Christian conduct in pluralistic societies, where Jesus Christ is but one of many expressions of belief in the transcendent.

But might this vision of Jesus Christ not also, perhaps, serve to facilitate a particular kind of interfaith encounter, one grounded in the explicit recognition of God's claim on us, as faithful and ethically responsible human beings, to be there always and only *for* others, irrespective of the otherwise largely incidental specifics of a person's identity? This "human being for others" is not, of course, to be found in Zionism, or Muslim fundamentalism, or Hindu nationalism, or ethnocentric varieties of Buddhism, any more than it is to be discerned in militant expressions of Christianity. Indeed, the "human being for others" is most unlikely to be found in any expression of faith which has not subjected itself to something very like Bonhoeffer's critique of religion—the critique of metaphysics, inwardness, and privilege—because it is precisely this that clears the way for God, the way from above to below. Unless, in Barth's phrase, religion is "taken out of the way,"[193] the radical significance of God's self-emptying love for God's creation must remain hidden from us. The real encounter with God will always be an incontrovertible, because faithful, experience of O/otherness. No religious idea of God can truly escape the closed circle of the self. Unless and until we rid ourselves of the gods of our own devising, and open our hearts to the presence of God in every human being, we will continue to inhabit a fallen, dead *Ichwelt*[194] of our choosing, and will not have the experience of transcendence—that sure sense of the beyond, in the midst of life—which Bonhoeffer calls "encounter with Jesus Christ."

NOTES

1. *Letters and Papers*, DBWE 8: 479.
2. *Letters and Papers*, DBWE 8: 362.
3. *Letters and Papers*, DBWE 8: 362.
4. *Letters and Papers*, DBWE 8: 478.
5. *Letters and Papers*, DBWE 8: 479–80.
6. *Letters and Papers*, DBWE 8: 480.
7. *Letters and Papers*, DBWE 8: 448.
8. *Letters and Papers*, DBWE 8: 501.
9. *Letters and Papers*, DBWE 8: 503–4.
10. *Letters and Papers*, DBWE 8: 500.
11. *Letters and Papers*, DBWE 8: 389.
12. *Letters and Papers*, DBWE 8: 389.
13. *Letters and Papers*, DBWE 8: 362.
14. Ebeling, *Word and Faith*, 132.

15. *Letters and Papers*, DBWE 8: 479.
16. "Jesus Christ and the Essence of Christianity," DBWE 10: 342.
17. Barth, *Romans*, 233.
18. Barth, *Romans*, 234.
19. "Sermon on Romans 11:6," DBWE 10: 481–82.
20. *Letters and Papers*, DBWE 8: 501.
21. *Act and Being*, DBWE 2: 157.
22. *Act and Being*, DBWE 2: 107–8.
23. "Meditation on Christmas," DBWE 15: 528–29.
24. "Lectures on Christology," DBWE 12: 305.
25. "Lectures on Christology," DBWE 12: 353.
26. "Lectures on Christology," DBWE 12: 342; Stevenson, *Creeds, Councils and Controversies*, 352–53.
27. "Lectures on Christology," DBWE 12: 343.
28. "Lectures on Christology," DBWE 12: 312.
29. "Lectures on Christology," DBWE 12: 313.
30. "Lectures on Christology," DBWE 12: 314.
31. "Lectures on Christology," DBWE 12: 305.
32. "Lectures on Christology," DBWE 12: 327.
33. *Discipleship*, DBWE 4: 95.
34. *Ethics*, DBWE 6: 94.
35. *Discipleship*, DBWE 4: 285.
36. *Ethics*, DBWE 6: 96.
37. *Act and Being*, DBWE 2: 107–8.
38. "Lectures on Christology," DBWE 12: 303.
39. Bonhoeffer's argument is here directed principally against idealism which, he believes, fails to appreciate the importance of the "value-related" moment. Idealism, he says, "has no understanding of the moment in which the person feels the threat of absolute demand. The idealist ethicist knows what he ought to do, and, what is more, he can always do it precisely because he ought. Where is there room, then, for distress of conscience, for infinite anxiety [Angst] in the face of decisions?" *Sanctorum Communio*, DBWE 1: 48–49.
40. *Creation and Fall*, DBWE 3: 63–64.
41. *Creation and Fall*, DBWE 3: 61.
42. *Act and Being*, DBWE 2: 90–91.
43. *Creation and Fall*, DBWE 3: 63.
44. *Ethics*, DBWE 6: 94.
45. *Life Together*, DBWE 5: 44.
46. *Sanctorum Communio*, DBWE 1: 147.
47. *Sanctorum Communio*, DBWE 1: 157.
48. *Ethics*, DBWE 6: 220.
49. *Ethics*, DBWE 6: 238.
50. *Ethics*, DBWE 6: 283.
51. *Ethics*, DBWE 6: 284.
52. *Ethics*, DBWE 6: 225.

53. *Ethics*, DBWE 6: 57–58.
54. *Ethics*, DBWE 6: 58.
55. *Ethics*, DBWE 6: 54.
56. *Ethics*, DBWE 6: 67.
57. *Ethics*, DBWE 6: 62.
58. *Ethics*, DBWE 6: 73.
59. *Letters and Papers*, DBWE 8: 457.
60. *Letters and Papers*, DBWE 8: 486.
61. *Letters and Papers*, DBWE 8: 394.
62. *Letters and Papers*, DBWE 8: 479.
63. *Letters and Papers*, DBWE 8: 479.
64. *Act and Being*, DBWE 2: 57.
65. "Lectures on Christology," DBWE 12: 301.
66. "Lectures on Christology," DBWE 12: 305.
67. "Lectures on Christology," DBWE 12: 324, 327.
68. *Letters and Papers*, DBWE 8: 501.
69. "Lectures on Christology," DBWE 12: 314.
70. *Act and Being*, DBWE 2: 90.
71. *Ethics*, DBWE 6: 58.
72. *Ethics*, DBWE 6: 54.
73. *Ethics*, DBWE 6: 62.
74. *Letters and Papers*, DBWE 8: 486.
75. *Letters and Papers*, DBWE 8: 448.

76. Bethge, *Dietrich Bonhoeffer*, 926–27. Bonhoeffer's last words to Best, as recorded in Best's letter to George Bell of October 13, 1953, are much less enigmatic: "Will you give this message from me to the Bishop of Chichester, 'tell him that this is for me the end, but also the beginning—with him I believe in the principle of our Universal Christian brotherhood which rises above all national hatreds and that our victory is certain.'" *Conspiracy and Imprisonment*, DBWE 16: 468–69. While Bonhoeffer's words here have a distinctly ecumenical ring to them, they signal nonetheless clearly that he knew he was about to die.

77. "The universality of the church was illustrated in a marvelously effective manner. White, black, yellow members of religious orders—everyone was in clerical robes united under the church. It truly seems ideal." Extract from diary entry for Palm Sunday. Dietrich Bonhoeffer, *The Young Bonhoeffer: 1918–1927*, ed. Paul Duane Matheny, Clifford J. Green, and Marshall D. Johnson (Minneapolis: Fortress Press, 2003), DBWE 9: 88.

78. Although Bonhoeffer believed the Roman Catholic church to be showing signs of calcification, there were "many religious establishments where a vital religious life still plays a part." The Protestant church, he observes in a letter to his parents, "often seems like a small sect when compared to the enormous range of the local festivals." *Young Bonhoeffer*, DBWE 9: 111.

79. *Young Bonhoeffer*, DBWE 9: 89.
80. *Young Bonhoeffer*, DBWE 9: 88.
81. *Young Bonhoeffer*, DBWE 9: 89.

82. *Young Bonhoeffer*, DBWE 9: 88.
83. Dietrich Bonhoeffer, "Sermon on 1 Corinthians 12:27, 26, Barcelona, 29 July 1928," in *Barcelona, Berlin, New York*, DBWE 10: 505.
84. "Sermon on 1 Corinthians 12:27, 26," DBWE 10: 505.
85. "Report on Year of Study in New York", DBWE 10: 315.
86. *Sanctorum Communio*, DBWE 1: 191.
87. "Sermon on 1 Corinthians 12:27, 26," DBWE 10: 506–7.
88. *Life Together*, DBWE 5: 27–28.
89. "Sermon on 1 Corinthians 12:27, 26," DBWE 10: 508–9.
90. *Life Together*, DBWE 5: 38–40.
91. *Life Together*, DBWE 5: 38.
92. *Life Together*, DBWE 5: 47.
93. *Sanctorum Communio*, DBWE 1: 158.
94. *Discipleship*, DBWE 4: 217.
95. *Ethics*, DBWE 6: 96.
96. *Ethics*, DBWE 6: 66–67.
97. *Ethics*, DBWE 6: 96.
98. *Ethics*, DBWE 6: 403.
99. *Letters and Papers*, DBWE 8: 364.
100. *Letters and Papers*, DBWE 8: 500.
101. *Letters and Papers*, DBWE 8: 503–4.
102. *Letters and Papers*, DBWE 8: 365, 479.
103. *Letters and Papers*, DBWE 8: 389.
104. *Letters and Papers*, DBWE 8: 503.
105. *Letters and Papers*, DBWE 8: 503.
106. "Nature of the Church," DBWE 11: 279.
107. Article 1 of the Barmen Theological Declaration of May 1934, drafted by Karl Barth. Cited in Werpehowski, "Karl Barth and Politics," *Cambridge Companion to Karl Barth*, 229–30.
108. "Sermon on 1 Corinthians 12:27, 26," DBWE 10: 506.
109. *Life Together*, DBWE 5: 44.
110. *Letters and Papers*, DBWE 8: 503–4.
111. *Letters and Papers*, DBWE 8: 502.
112. *Letters and Papers*, DBWE 8: 502–3.
113. *Sanctorum Communio*, DBWE 1: 127.
114. "Christ existing as church-community." *Sanctorum Communio*, DBWE 1: 141.
115. Bethge, *Dietrich Bonhoeffer*, 165.
116. *Ethics*, DBWE 6: 67.
117. *Letters and Papers*, DBWE 8: 366.
118. Dietrich Bonhoeffer, "Sermon on Judges 6:15–16; 7:2; 8:23, Berlin, February 26, 1933," in *Berlin*, DBWE 12: 462.
119. *Ethics*, DBWE 6: 158.
120. "Sermon on Judges 6:15–16," DBWE 12: 467.

121. *Letters and Papers*, DBWE 8: 479. This idea is by no means new to Bonhoeffer. In May 1942, he tells the Leibholz family, "for me the idea that God himself is suffering has always been one of the most convincing teachings of Christianity. I think God is nearer to suffering than to happiness and to find God in this way gives peace and rest and a strong and courageous heart." *Conspiracy and Imprisonment*, DBWE 16: 284.

122. *Letters and Papers*, DBWE 8: 501.

123. *Letters and Papers*, DBWE 8: 479.

124. In her study of Bonhoeffer's impact on the theology of Jürgen Moltmann, Schliesser follows Moltmann in describing God's suffering as indistinguishable from God's being. God's suffering, she says, "is as encompassing as God's love." Christine Schliesser, "'Love of Life'—The Impact and Influence of Dietrich Bonhoeffer's Life and Thought on Jürgen Moltmann," in *Engaging Bonhoeffer*, ed. Matthew D. Kirkpatrick (Fortress Press, 2016), 198. She then quotes from Müller-Fahrenholz's *Theology of Moltmann*: "That is the only way in which the question of theodicy can be endured, as it cannot be answered." Geiko Müller-Fahrenholz, *The Kingdom and the Power: The Theology of Jürgen Moltmann* (London: SCM, 2000), 144.

125. Busch, *The Great Passion*, 64.

126. Dietrich Bonhoeffer, "Basic Questions of a Christian Ethic," in *Barcelona, Berlin, New York*, DBWE 10: 370–72.

127. Even in this early lecture on Christian ethics, Bonhoeffer makes it clear that, if he were to take up arms for the sake of the German people, it would be "with the terrible knowledge of doing something horrible.... As a Christian, I will suffer from the entire dreadfulness of war. My soul will bear the entire burden of responsibility in its full gravity." Bonhoeffer, "Basic Questions of a Christian Ethic," DBWE 10: 372. There is evidence already in this passage of the profound sense of personal responsibility for one's actions that characterizes Bonhoeffer's later work.

128. Bethge, *Dietrich Bonhoeffer*, 28.

129. *London*, DBWE 13: 183–84. Bonhoeffer hoped to find in India new sources of inspiration for a Western Christianity in decline. Bonhoeffer's grandmother first suggested the idea of visiting India to him in 1928, while he was in Barcelona. But it was in London, in 1934, that the most explicit plans were made. On May 22, Bonhoeffer told his grandmother that he was again thinking of going to India, where he believed there was much to be learned. Christianity, he observed, had "come from the East originally, but it has become so westernized and so permeated by civilized thought that, as we can now see, it is almost lost to us." *London*, DBWE 13: 152. By November, Bonhoeffer had secured an invitation from Gandhi to visit him. Bethge, *Dietrich Bonhoeffer*, 408. He hoped to benefit from Gandhi's experience of nonviolent resistance and faithful life in community. Indeed, Rasmussen speculates that, in the Hindu Gandhi, Bonhoeffer may even have caught a glimpse of Christ himself, "a vision that perhaps here in Gandhi and his India was the gospel in other words and deeds." Larry Rasmussen, "Bonhoeffer, Gandhi, and Resistance," in *Reflections on Bonhoeffer: Essays in Honor of F. Burton Nelson*, ed. Geffrey B. Kelly and C. John Weborg (Chicago: Covenant Publications, 1999), 52. But it wasn't to be. Bonhoeffer was delayed in London, and eventually forced to choose between India and the

Berlin-Brandenburg Preachers' Seminary of the Confessing Church of the Old Prussian Union, which opened under his direction at Zingsthof in April 1935.

130. Dietrich Bonhoeffer, "The Church and the Peoples of the World," in *London*, DBWE 13: 309.

131. "The Church and the Peoples of the World," DBWE 13: 308–9.

132. Dietrich Bonhoeffer, "Framework for a Lecture in Czechoslovakia: Toward a Theological Foundation for the Work of the World Alliance, July 26, 1932," in *Ecumenical, Academic, and Pastoral Work*, DBWE 11: 371.

133. DeJonge, *Luther*, 177.

134. Dietrich Bonhoeffer, "Lecture in Ciernohorské Kúpele: On the Theological Foundation of the Work of the World Alliance," in *Ecumenical, Academic, and Pastoral Work*, DBWE 11: 364.

135. "Lecture in Ciernohorské Kúpele," DBWE 11: 366–67.

136. Dietrich Bonhoeffer, "Address at the International Youth Conference in Gland," in *Ecumenical, Academic, and Pastoral Work*, DBWE 11: 380.

137. Stanley Hauerwas, *Performing the Faith* (Eugene, OR: Wipf and Stock, 2015), 35–36.

138. Bonhoeffer would have been happy to serve as a military chaplain, but this path was effectively closed to him. Only pastors who had served in the armed forces were eligible for such appointments. Bethge, *Dietrich Bonhoeffer*, 666.

139. In the letter to Bethge of July 21, 1944, Bonhoeffer writes, "For a long time . . . I thought I . . . could learn to have faith by trying to live something like a saintly life. I suppose," he says, "I wrote *Discipleship* at the end of this path. Today I clearly see the dangers of that book, though I still stand by it. Later on I discovered, and am still discovering to this day, that one only learns to have faith by living in the full this-worldliness of life." *Letters and Papers*, DBWE 8: 486.

140. "'You have heard that it was said, "An eye for an eye and a tooth for a tooth." But I say to you, Do not resist an evildoer. But if anyone strikes you on the right cheek, turn the other also; and if anyone wants to sue you and take your coat, give your cloak as well; and if anyone forces you to go one mile, go also the second mile. Give to everyone who begs from you, and do not refuse anyone who wants to borrow from you'" (Matt. 5:38–42).

141. *Discipleship*, DBWE 4: 132.

142. *Discipleship*, DBWE 4: 132–33.

143. *Discipleship*, DBWE 4: 133. Marcus Borg draws on the work of Walter Wink to provide a sociopolitical context for these actions. He writes, "There is a . . . conventional way of reading this cluster of sayings as commending passive acceptance of wrongdoing: don't resist somebody who beats you; go the extra mile; don't insist on your own rights." Most Christians think of this passage as referring to the personal, rather than to the political, domain. There is no reason to object to war, or capital punishment, for example. "Official violence is okay." But this, Borg argues, is in fact to misunderstand the text. For one thing, the Greek verb, which is commonly translated "resist" ("Do not resist an evildoer" Matt. 5:39), most often means "resist with violence," while each of the three statements which follows this admonition exemplifies a means of nonviolent resistance. For example, and whereas a slap on

the right cheek with the back of the hand "presupposes a situation of domination," the person who turns the other cheek forces an aggressor to deliver an open-handed blow, "which is the way an equal struck another equal." An indebted peasant might choose to surrender both his inner and his outer garment to a creditor, thus shaming him by standing naked before him. A soldier faced penalties for compelling a peasant to carry his equipment for more than a fixed distance. "In this setting, what are you to do when an imperial soldier requires you to carry his gear for a mile? Do it—and then keep going." Marcus J. Borg, *Jesus* (London: SPCK, 2011), 248–50.

144. *Discipleship*, DBWE 4: 133.

145. *Discipleship*, DBWE 4: 135. This distinction allows me to "differentiate between harm done to me personally, and harm done to me as bearer of my office, that is, in the responsibility given me by God. In the former case I am to act as Jesus commands, but in the latter case I am released from doing so." *Discipleship*, DBWE 4: 134.

146. *Discipleship*, DBWE 4: 135.

147. *Discipleship*, DBWE 4: 135.

148. *Ethics*, DBWE 6: 283–84.

149. "Basic Questions of a Christian Ethic," DBWE 10: 367.

150. "Basic Questions of a Christian Ethic," DBWE 10: 367. Bonhoeffer here again recalls Nietzsche by contradicting him. Nietzsche, he says, did not discover "the world beyond good and evil." It is implicit in the Christian message, which understands community between human beings and God to depend entirely on God's grace. "Basic Questions of a Christian Ethic," DBWE 10: 363. Christians "provide the justification for their acts, just as they alone bear responsibility for them. Christians create new tables, new decalogues, as Nietzsche said of the Overman." Nietzsche, says Bonhoeffer, quite unwittingly endowed the Overman with many of the qualities of Paul's and Luther's "free" Christian. "Traditional morals—even if propagated for Christians—or public opinion can never provide the standards for the action of Christians." "Basic Questions of a Christian Ethic," DBWE 10: 366–67.

151. *Ethics*, DBWE 6: 220.

152. *Discipleship*, DBWE 4: 135.

153. "Do not be overcome by evil, but overcome evil with good" (Rom. 12:21).

154. *Discipleship*, DBWE 4: 136.

155. *Discipleship*, DBWE 4: 136.

156. *Discipleship*, DBWE 4: 136.

157. *Discipleship*, DBWE 4: 144.

158. *Discipleship*, DBWE 4: 145.

159. *Discipleship*, DBWE 4: 136.

160. *Discipleship*, DBWE 4: 144.

161. *Letters and Papers*, DBWE 8: 49.

162. *Discipleship*, DBWE 8: 137.

163. *Letters and Papers*, DBWE 8: 41. Here again we encounter the same profound sense of personal responsibility before God that we find in *Discipleship* and the *Ethics*, now combined with an explicit assurance of God's forgiveness and consolation. God will not abandon the responsible actor, who risks everything freely in faith.

164. Green, Introduction, *Ethics*, DBWE 6: 19.

165. This represents a modest expansion of Luther's three estates, in which the preindustrial notion of the household (*oeconomicus*) is subdivided into family and work.

166. *Ethics*, DBWE 6: 389.

167. *Ethics*, DBWE 6: 68–69.

168. *Ethics*, DBWE 6: 393.

169. *Ethics*, DBWE 6: 69–70.

170. *Letters and Papers*, DBWE 8: 42. As Schroeder observes, it is the "incarnational character" of Bonhoeffer's ethics—the fact that the human encounter with God is always particular, concrete, historical—that "makes it so important to *read* history rather than simply to be swept along by it." Steven Schroeder, "The End of History and the New World Order," in Floyd and Marsh, 22.

171. *Letters and Papers*, DBWE 8: 43.

172. *Letters and Papers*, DBWE 8: 40.

173. "Basic Questions of a Christian Ethic," DBWE 10: 367.

174. Responsible action, Bonhoeffer allows, is limited by the requirement to surrender every action "to God's grace and judgment," and by the fact that other people have also to be granted the freedom to act responsibly. God and the neighbor, as we encounter them in Jesus Christ, set the parameters for responsible action. Responsible action is never "its own lord and master, nor is it unbounded or frivolous. Instead, it is creaturely and humble." *Ethics*, DBWE 6: 269.

175. John de Gruchy, "The Reception of Bonhoeffer's Theology," in de Gruchy, *Cambridge Companion*, 93–96, 103–4.

176. de Gruchy, "Reception of Bonhoeffer's Theology," in de Gruchy, *Cambridge Companion*, 97.

177. de Gruchy, "Reception of Bonhoeffer's Theology," in de Gruchy, *Cambridge Companion*, 104.

178. Wayne Whitson Floyd, "Dietrich Bonhoeffer," in *The Modern Theologians*, ed. David F. Ford (Malden, MA: Blackwell Publishing, 2005), 57.

179. Taylor, *Secular Age*, 592.

180. Taylor, *Secular Age*, 549.

181. *Letters and Papers*, DBWE 8: 479.

182. *Letters and Papers*, DBWE 8: 478–79.

183. *Discipleship*, DBWE 4: 217.

184. *Sanctorum Communio*, DBWE 1: 48.

185. *Sanctorum Communio*, DBWE 1: 33.

186. *Letters and Papers*, DBWE 8: 362.

187. *Letters and Papers*, DBWE 8: 501.

188. Barker, *Cross of Reality*, 436.

189. *Letters and Papers*, DBWE 8: 453.

190. Marsh, *Reclaiming Bonhoeffer*, 103.

191. *Ethics*, DBWE 6: 96.

192. "Sermon on Matthew 28:20," DBWE 10: 494.

193. Barth, *Romans*, 233.

194. *Creation and Fall*, DBWE 3: 142.

Bibliography

Baillie, John. *And the Life Everlasting.* Oxford: OUP, 1956.
Bainton, Roland H. *Here I Stand: A Life of Martin Luther.* Nashville: Abingdon Press, 1978.
Barker, H. Gaylon. *The Cross of Reality: Luther's Theologia Crucis and Bonhoeffer's Christology.* Augsburg Fortress, Publishers, 2015.
———. "Without God, We Live with God. Listening to Bonhoeffer's Witness in Today's Public Square." In de Gruchy, Plant, and Tietz, 156–67.
Barth, Karl. *Church Dogmatics I.1.* Translated by G. W. Bromiley. London: T&T Clark, 1975.
———. *Church Dogmatics I.2.* Translated by G. W. Bromiley, G. T. Thomson, and Harold Knight. London: T&T Clark, 2009.
———. *The Epistle to the Romans.* Translated by Edwyn C. Hoskyns. London: Oxford University Press, 1968.
———. "From a Letter to Superintendent Herrenbrück." In Smith, 89–92.
———. "Rudolf Bultmann – An Attempt to Understand Him." In Bartsch, Vol. II, 83–132.
———. *The Word of God and the Word of Man.* Translated by Douglas Horton. New York: Harper Torchbooks, 1957.
Bartsch, Hans-Werner. *Kerygma and Myth: A Theological Debate.* Volumes I and II. Translated by Reginald H. Fuller. London: SPCK, 1972.
Berger, Peter, Grace Davie, and Effie Fokas. *Religious America, Secular Europe? A Theme and Variations.* Farnham, Surrey: Ashgate Publishing Limited, 2008.
Bethge, Eberhard. *Dietrich Bonhoeffer: A Biography.* Translated by Eric Mosbacher, Peter and Betty Ross, Frank Clark, and William Glen-Doepel under the editorship of Edwin Robertson. Revised and edited by Victoria J. Barnett. Minneapolis: Fortress Press, 2000.
Bonhoeffer, Dietrich. *Act and Being: Transcendental Philosophy and Ontology in Systematic Theology.* DBWE 2. Edited by Wayne Whitson Floyd Jr. Translated by H. Martin Rumscheidt. Minneapolis: Fortress Press, 2009.

———. *Barcelona, Berlin, New York: 1928–1931*. DBWE 10. Edited by Clifford J. Green. Translated by Douglas W. Stott. Minneapolis: Fortress Press, 2008.

———. *Berlin: 1932–1933*. DBWE 12. Edited by Larry L. Rasmussen. Translated by Isabel Best and David Higgins, with Douglas W. Stott. Minneapolis: Fortress Press, 2009.

———. *Conspiracy and Imprisonment: 1940–1945*. DBWE 16. Edited by Mark S. Brocker. Translated by Lisa E. Dahill, with Douglas W. Stott. Minneapolis: Fortress Press, 2006.

———. *Creation and Fall: A Theological Exposition of Genesis 1–3*. DBWE 3. Edited by John W. de Gruchy. Translated by Douglas Stephen Bax. Minneapolis: Fortress Press, 2004.

———. *Discipleship*. DBWE 4. Edited by Geffrey B. Kelly and John D. Godsey. Translated by Barbara Green and Reinhard Krauss. Minneapolis: Fortress Press, 2003.

———. *Ecumenical, Academic, and Pastoral Work: 1931–1932*. DBWE 11. Edited by Victoria J. Barnett, Mark S. Brocker, and Michael B. Lukens. Translated by Anne Schmidt-Lange, with Isabel Best, Nicolas Humphrey, Marion Pauck, and Douglas W. Stott. Minneapolis: Fortress Press, 2012.

———. *Ethics*. DBWE 6. Edited by Clifford J. Green. Translated by Reinhard Krauss, Charles West, and Douglas W. Stott. Minneapolis: Fortress Press, 2005.

———. *Fiction from Tegel Prison*. DBWE 7. Edited by Clifford J. Green. Translated by Nancy Lukens. Minneapolis: Fortress Press, 1999.

———. *Indexes and Supplementary Materials*. DBWE 17. Edited by Victoria J. Barnett and Barbara Wojhoski, with Mark S. Brocker. Minneapolis: Fortress Press, 2014.

———. *Letters and Papers from Prison*. DBWE 8. Edited by John W. de Gruchy. Translated by Isabel Best, Lisa E. Dahill, Reinhard Krauss, and Nancy Lukens, with Barbara and Martin Rumscheidt, and Douglas W. Stott. Minneapolis: Fortress Press, 2010.

———. *Life Together* and *Prayerbook of the Bible*. DBWE 5. Edited by Geffrey B. Kelly. Translated by Daniel W. Bloesch and James H. Burtness. Minneapolis: Fortress Press, 2005.

———. *London, 1933–1935*. DBWE 13. Edited by Keith Clements. Translated by Isabel Best, with Douglas W. Stott. Minneapolis: Fortress Press, 2007.

———. *Sanctorum Communio: A Theological Study of the Sociology of the Church*. DBWE 1. Edited by Clifford J. Green. Translated by Reinhard Krauss and Nancy Lukens. Minneapolis: Fortress Press, 2009.

———. *Theological Education at Finkenwalde: 1935–1937*. DBWE 14. Edited by H. Gaylon Barker and Mark S. Brocker. Translated by Douglas W. Stott. Minneapolis: Fortress Press, 2013.

———. *Theological Education Underground: 1937–1940*. DBWE 15. Edited by Victoria J. Barnett. Translated by Victoria J. Barnett, Claudia D. Bergmann, Peter Frick, and Scott A. Moore, with Douglas W. Stott. Minneapolis: Fortress Press, 2012.

———. *Widerstand und Ergebung*. Gütersloh: Gütersloher Verlagshaus, 1998, 2011.

———. *The Young Bonhoeffer: 1918–1927*. DBWE 9. Edited by Paul Duane Matheny, Clifford J. Green, and Marshall D. Johnson. Translated by Mary Nebelsick, with Douglas W. Stott. Minneapolis: Fortress Press, 2003.
Borg, Marcus J. *Jesus*. London: SPCK, 2011.
Bruce, Steve. *Secularisation: In Defence of an Unfashionable Theory*. Oxford: OUP, 2011.
Bultmann, Rudolf. *Jesus and the Word*. Translated by Louise Pettibone Smith and Erminie Huntress Lantero. New York: Scribner, 1962, 1989.
———. "New Testament and Mythology." In Bartsch, Vol. I, 1–44.
Busch, Eberhard. *The Great Passion: An Introduction to Karl Barth's Theology*. Translated by Geoffrey W. Bromiley. Grand Rapids: Eerdmans, 2004.
Butler Bass, Diana. *Christianity After Religion*. New York: HarperCollins, 2012.
Dabrock, Peter. "Responding to 'Wirklichkeit': Reclaiming Bonhoeffer's Approach to Theological Ethics between Mystery and the Formation of the World." In Nielsen, Nissen and Tietz, 49–80.
de Gruchy, John W., ed. *The Cambridge Companion to Dietrich Bonhoeffer*. New York: Cambridge University Press, 1999.
———. Introduction to Bonhoeffer's *Letters and Papers from Prison*, 1–34.
———. *Led into Mystery*. London: SCM Press, 2013.
———. "The Reception of Bonhoeffer's Theology." In de Gruchy, *Cambridge Companion*, 93–109.
de Gruchy, John W., Stephen Plant, and Christiane Tietz, eds. *Dietrich Bonhoeffer's Theology Today: A Way between Fundamentalism and Secularism?* Gütersloh: Gütersloher Verlagshaus, 2009.
DeJonge, Michael P. "Bonhoeffer's Concept of the West." In Tietz and Zimmermann, 37–52.
———. *Bonhoeffer's Reception of Luther*. Oxford: OUP, 2017.
Dilthey, Wilhelm. *Introduction to the Human Sciences*. Edited by R. A. Makkreel and Frithjof Rodi. *Wilhelm Dilthey: Selected Works*, vol. 1. Princeton: Princeton University Press, 1989.
Dostoevsky, Fyodor M. *The Brothers Karamazov*. Translated by Constance Garnett. London: Heron Books, 1967.
Ebeling, Gerhard. *Word and Faith*. Translated by James W. Leitch. London: SCM, 1963.
Feil, Ernst. *The Theology of Dietrich Bonhoeffer*. Translated by Martin Rumscheidt. Philadelphia: Fortress Press, 1985.
Floyd, Wayne Whitson. "Dietrich Bonhoeffer." In Ford, 43–61.
———. Introduction to Bonhoeffer's *Act and Being*, 1–24.
———. "Kant, Hegel and Bonhoeffer." In Frick, 83–119.
Floyd, Wayne Whitson, and Charles Marsh, eds. *Theology and the Practice of Responsibility: Essays on Dietrich Bonhoeffer*. Valley Forge, PA: Trinity Press International, 1994.
Ford, David F., ed. *The Modern Theologians*. 3rd ed. Malden, MA: Blackwell Publishing, 2005.
Frick, Peter, ed. *Bonhoeffer's Intellectual Formation*. Tübingen: Mohr Siebeck, 2008.

Frick, Peter. "Nietzsche and Bonhoeffer." In Frick, 175–99.
———. "Rudolf Bultmann, Paul Tillich and Dietrich Bonhoeffer." In Frick, 225–44.
Green, Clifford J. *Bonhoeffer: A Theology of Sociality* (Rev. Ed.) Grand Rapids: Eerdmans, 1999.
———. "Bonhoeffer's Quest for Authentic Christianity: Beyond Fundamentalism, Nationalism, Religion and Secularism." In de Gruchy, Plant, and Tietz, 335–53.
———. Introduction to Bonhoeffer's *Sanctorum Communio*, 1–20.
———. Introduction to Bonhoeffer's *Ethics*, 1–44.
Greggs, Tom. "Religionless Christianity in a Complexly Religious and Secular World: Thinking Through and Beyond Bonhoeffer." In Plant and Wüstenberg, 111–25.
Gregor, Brian, and Jens Zimmermann, eds. *Bonhoeffer and Continental Thought*. Bloomington: Indiana University Press, 2009.
Hall, Douglas John. "Dietrich Bonhoeffer and the Ethics of Participation," www.ucalgary.ca/christchair/files/christchair/Hall_D.Bonhoeffer.PDFfile.
Hart, Kevin. "Bonhoeffer's 'Religious Clothes': The Naked Man, the Secret, and What We Hear." In Gregor and Zimmermann, 177–97.
Harvey, Barry A. "A Post-Critical Approach to a 'Religionless Christianity.'" In Floyd and Marsh, 39–58.
Hauerwas, Stanley. *Performing the Faith*. Eugene, OR: Wipf and Stock, 2015.
Holmes, Christopher R. J. "Beyond Bonhoeffer in Loyalty to Bonhoeffer: Reconsidering Bonhoeffer's Christological Aversion to Theological Metaphysics." In Mawson and Ziegler, 29–43.
Huber, Wolfgang. "Bonhoeffer and Modernity." In Floyd and Marsh, 5–19.
James, William. *The Varieties of Religious Experience*. Mineola, NY: Dover Publications, 2002.
Kelley, J. P. "Christological Concretion and Everyday Events in Three of Bonhoeffer's Sermons." In Kelly and Weborg, 100–13.
Kelly, Geffrey B. "Kierkegaard and Bonhoeffer." In Frick, 145–65.
Kelly, Geffrey B., and C. John Weborg, eds. *Reflections on Bonhoeffer: Essays in Honour of F. Burton Nelson*. Chicago: Covenant Publications, 1999.
Kirkpatrick, Matthew D., ed. *Engaging Bonhoeffer*. Minneapolis: Fortress Press, 2016.
Lash, Nicholas. *Holiness, Speech and Silence: Reflections on the Question of God*. Aldershot, HR: Ashgate Publishing Limited, 2004.
Marsh, Charles. *Reclaiming Dietrich Bonhoeffer*. New York: Oxford University Press, 1994.
———. *Strange Glory: A Life of Dietrich Bonhoeffer*. New York: Vintage Books, 2015.
Mawson, Michael, and Philip G. Ziegler, eds. *Christ, Church and World: New Studies in Bonhoeffer's Theology and Ethics*. London: Bloomsbury T&T Clark, 2016.
McLeod, Hugh. *The Religious Crisis of the 1960s*. Oxford: Oxford University Press, 2007.

Migliore, Daniel L. *Faith Seeking Understanding*. 2nd ed. Grand Rapids, MI: William B. Eerdmans Publishing Company, 2004.
Müller, Gerhard L., and Albrecht Schönherr. Afterword to Bonhoeffer's *Life Together*, 119–40.
Muller, Richard A. *Dictionary of Latin and Greek Theological Terms*. Grand Rapids: Baker Books, 1985.
Nielsen, Kirsten B., Ulrik Nissen, and Christiane Tietz, eds. *Mysteries in the Theology of Dietrich Bonhoeffer*. Göttingen: Vandenhoeck and Ruprecht, 2007.
Pangritz, Andreas. *Karl Barth in the Theology of Dietrich Bonhoeffer*. Translated by Barbara and Martin Rumscheidt. Grand Rapids: Eerdmans, 2000.
———. "Understanding Mystery." In Nielsen, Nissen, and Tietz, 9–26.
Plant, Stephen. "'We Believe in One Lord, Jesus Christ': A Pro-Nicene Revision of Bonhoeffer's 1933 Christology Lectures." In Mawson and Ziegler, 45–60.
Plant, Stephen, and Ralf K. Wüstenberg, eds. *Religion, Religionlessness and Contemporary Western Culture*. Frankfurt: Peter Lang GmbH, 2008.
Powell, Mark Allan. *Jesus as a Figure in History*. 2nd ed. Louisville, KY: Westminster John Knox Press, 2013.
Pugh, Jeffrey C. *Religionless Christianity: Dietrich Bonhoeffer in Troubled Times*. London: T&T Clark, 2008.
Rasmussen, Larry L. "Bonhoeffer, Gandhi, and Resistance." In Kelly and Weborg, 50–55.
Robertson, Edwin. *Bonhoeffer's Heritage: The Christian Way in a World without Religion*. London: Hodder & Stoughton, 1989.
Roof, W.C. "God is in the Details: Reflections on Religion's Public Presence in the United States in the Mid-1990s." *Sociology of Religion*, 57 (1996).
Rumscheidt, Martin. "The Formation of Bonhoeffer's Theology." In de Gruchy, *Cambridge Companion*, 50–70.
Scharffenorth, Ernst-Albert. Afterword to DBWE 12: *Berlin*, 483–507.
Schleiermacher, Friedrich. *On Religion*. Translated by Richard Crouter. Cambridge: Cambridge University Press, 1996.
Schliesser, Christine. "'Love of Life' – The Impact and Influence of Dietrich Bonhoeffer's Life and Thought on Jürgen Moltmann." In Kirkpatrick, 187–200.
Schroeder, Steven. "The End of History and the New World Order." In Floyd and Marsh, 21–38.
Schweitzer, Albert. *The Quest of the Historical Jesus*. Translated by W. Montgomery. Mineola, NY: Dover Publications, 2005.
Schwöbel, Christoph. "'Religion' and 'Religionlessness' in *Letters and Papers from Prison*." In Nielsen, Nissen, and Tietz, 159–84.
Smith, Ronald Gregor, ed. *World Come of Age. A Symposium on Dietrich Bonhoeffer*. Collins: London, 1967.
Spence, Alan. *Christology: A Guide for the Perplexed*. London: T&T Clark, 2008.
Stassen, Glen Harold. *A Thicker Jesus. Incarnational Discipleship in a Secular Age*. Louisville: Westminster John Knox Press, 2012.
Stevenson, J., ed. *Creeds, Councils and Controversies: Documents Illustrating the History of the Church, AD 337–461* (New Edition). London: SPCK, 1989.

Taylor, Charles. *A Secular Age*. Cambridge, MA: Harvard University Press, 2007.
———. *Varieties of Religion Today: William James Revisited*. Cambridge, MA: Harvard University Press, 2002.
Tietz, Christiane. "The Role of Jesus Christ for Christian Theology." In Mawson and Ziegler, 9–27.
Tietz, Christiane, and Jens Zimmermann, eds. *Bonhoeffer, Religion and Politics*. Frankfurt: Peter Lang GmbH, 2012.
Tödt, Heinz Eduard. *Authentic Faith: Bonhoeffer's Theological Ethics in Context*. Translated by David Stassen and Ilse Tödt. Grand Rapids: Eerdmans, 2007.
Torrance, Thomas F. *God and Rationality*. Edinburgh: T&T Clark, 1997.
Voas, David. "The Rise and Fall of Fuzzy Fidelity in Europe." *European Sociological Review*, vol. 25, no. 2 (2009): 155–68.
Ward, Graham. *The Politics of Discipleship: Becoming Postmaterial Citizens*. Grand Rapids, MI: Baker Academic, 2009.
Warner, Michael, Jonathan VanAntwerpen, and Craig Calhoun, eds. *Varieties of Secularism in a Secular Age*. Cambridge, MA: Harvard University Press, 2010.
Webster, John, ed. *The Cambridge Companion to Karl Barth*. New York: Cambridge University Press, 2000.
Weizsäcker, Friedrich von. *The World View of Physics*. Translated by Marjorie Grene. Chicago: University of Chicago Press, 1957.
Werpehowski, William. "Karl Barth and Politics." In Webster, 228–42.
Willmer, Haddon. "Costly Discipleship." In de Gruchy, *Cambridge Companion*, 173–89.
Wüstenberg, Ralf K. *A Theology of Life: Dietrich Bonhoeffer's Religionless Christianity*. Translated by Douglas W. Stott. Grand Rapids: Eerdmans, 1998.
Zimmermann, Jens. "Dietrich Bonhoeffer and Martin Heidegger: Two Different Visions of Humanity." In Gregor and Zimmermann, 102–33.

Index

absence: of fullness, 15; of God, 72, 132, 188–89; of history, 40; of independent existence, 172; of Jesus Christ, 131; of loved ones, 118; of meaning, 129, 141; of religion, 9–12, 71, 100, 163, 171, 188
alone before God, 183–84
America, 26, 122; and religion, 12–14, 23–24, 28, 32, 175; and theology, 47, 49, 64, 93. *See also* Europe
Anabaptists, 182
anthropology, 40, 63, 126, 189
anthropomorphism, 44, 47, 143
anxiety, 46, 54, 59, 118, 166, 192
Apostles' Creed, 43–44, 62
arcane discipline. *See* church
atonement, 79, 126, 130–32
authenticity, 58, 174, 177
autonomy, 10–11, 14, 16, 23, 26, 29, 48, 66, 72, 92–95, 108, 163, 186; ethical, 169, 172, 189. *See also* world come of age

Baillie, John, 139
Bainton, Roland, 103
Barker, H. Gaylon, 73, 101–2, 190
Barth, Karl, 10, 35–48, 50, 53, 57–60, 63–64, 67, 80–81, 129, 131–32, 149, 165–66, 191

Bell, George, 193
Berger, Peter, 13–15, 19, 23–24
Best, Payne, 173–74, 193
Bethge, Eberhard, 9, 37, 40–42, 50–52, 54, 56, 58, 61, 65, 67, 69, 75–76, 96, 117–20, 148, 154, 176–77, 180
Bible, 51, 55, 62, 72, 75, 99, 116–18, 121, 127–28, 135, 143–44, 155, 164, 171, 179
blessing, 118–20
Borg, Marcus, 196–97
boundaries, 79, 84, 86, 107, 144, 167–68, 172
Bruce, Steve, 15, 19–20, 22–24, 31
Bruno, Giordano, 11
Bultmann, Rudolf, 44–45, 61, 110, 126, 132–33
Busch, Eberhard, 179

cantus firmus, 71, 75, 101, 155, 171
Chalcedon, 86, 145–46, 155, 167, 178
Christianity. *See* Christology; church; religionless Christianity; worldliness
Christology, 41, 70, 85–86, 96–98, 116, 145, 155, 177
church, 44, 56, 89, 97–98, 104–5, 117, 137, 155, 173–78; arcane discipline, 43, 148–50, 160, 176;

church struggle (*Kirchenkampf*), 12, 75, 104; for others, 56, 75, 164, 176; and religion, 37, 53; self-preservation, 75–76, 164, 176. *See also* Jesus Christ, existing as church-community; theology, two kingdoms doctrine
conscience, 10, 59, 93, 108, 187, 192
conspiracy. *See* resistance
cross. *See* death on the

Dabrock, Peter, 92
death, 36, 40, 54–55, 57, 66, 107, 118, 135, 177; on the cross, 66, 131–32, 139, 173; from death to life, 37, 90, 166; sin and, 55, 71, 89
de Gruchy, John, 67, 98–99, 102, 148, 158–60, 187
DeJonge, Michael, 25–26, 41, 61–62, 87, 93–95, 106, 181–82
demythologization, 44–45, 126, 132–33
deus ex machina, 11, 54–55, 99, 178
Dilthey, Wihelm, 11, 27, 48–50, 166
discernment, 96, 187
discipleship, 90–91, 110–11, 149, 168, 185, 196
Dohnanyi, Hans von, 182
Dostoevsky, Fyodor, 59–60
duty, 26, 94, 96, 156, 187

Ebeling, Gerhard, 24, 38, 65, 116–18, 127, 134, 165
ecclesiology, 53, 77, 97, 177. *See also* church
ecumenical, 26, 193; ecumenical movement, 12, 75–76, 180–81
eternal life, 36, 133, 139, 157
eternity, 74, 118, 143; God in, 71, 87, 168, 184; and time, 36–37, 48
etsi deus non daretur, 10–11, 126–27
Europe, 11, 25–26; and religion, 12–14, 20–23, 27. *See also* America
evil. *See* violence and non-resistance
existentialism. *See* philosophy
extra calvinisticum. See theology

faith, 147–48
the fall, 85, 111, 126; fallen world, 84–85, 88, 170, 181–82, 190–91
Feil, Ernst, 40, 69–70, 97, 115, 117, 126–27, 143, 147, 158
Feuerbach, Ludwig, 63
fides directa, 160
fides reflexa, 160
finitum (in)capax infiniti. See theology
Floyd, Wayne Whitson, 80–82, 188
forgetfulness, 98, 103, 151
freedom, 37, 42, 77–78, 83–84, 90, 108, 124–25, 139, 156, 167, 169, 171–73, 187. *See also* vicarious representative action
Frick, Peter, 73

Gandhi, M. K. (Mahatma), 180, 195
genus majestaticum (majestic genus). *See* theology
Gerhardt, Paul, 150–51
Gethsemane, 73, 119
God: encounter with Jesus Christ, 75, 99, 130, 137, 164, 190–91; and history, 160, 183; knowledge of, 47, 64, 109, 156; name of, 73, 121, 136; new life, 49, 75, 126, 132, 164, 190; omnipotence, 72, 132, 165, 178–79; perfection, 71, 131–32, 162, 178, 185; powerlessness, 55, 58, 72, 98, 102, 179, 190; reconciliation with God, 74, 98, 157, 176; as stopgap, 54, 121, 178; the suffering God, 55, 72–73, 99, 124, 132, 164–65, 172–73, 179, 189–90, 195. *See also deus ex machina*; Jesus Christ
grace, 39, 46, 73, 92, 122, 124–25, 131, 143, 145, 148–49, 166, 175, 178, 190, 197; *apocastastasis*, 78, 98; cheap, 149–50, 161; costly, 149–50; justification by, 47, 59, 198
Green, Clifford, 26, 44, 50–54, 78, 93–95, 102, 104–6, 156
Greggs, Tom, 13
Grisebach, Eberhard, 105

Index

guardianship, 11, 50, 57, 72

Hall, Douglas John, 102–3
Hart, Kevin, 52
Harvey, Barry, 53, 65–66
Hauerwas, Stanley, 182
Hegel, Georg Wilhelm Friedrich, 107
Heidegger, Martin, 107–8
history, 10–12, 18–19, 28, 40, 49, 88, 143, 159, 170, 186–87, 198. *See also* God; Jesus Christ
Holmes, Christopher, 70–71
Huber, Wolfgang, 72
the human being: conformed to Christ, 77, 90, 126, 147, 159, 168; image of God (*imago dei*), 83–84, 90, 97, 169, 190–91; like God (*sicut deus*), 84–85, 108; for others, 189. *See also* God, new life; wholeness
humanism, 17–19, 24, 143, 157, 188

idealism. *See* philosophy
illusion of immediacy, 109, 168
immanence. *See* transcendence; world
incarnation, 131
individualism, 18, 24–25, 51–52, 65, 78, 83, 99, 106, 184, 189

James, William, 29, 32, 48–50; "Jamesian open space," 18, 30, 188
Jesus Christ: encounter with God, 124–25, 129–30, 143, 149, 156, 189, 191, 198; existing as church-community, 77, 91; fully human, wholly God, 77, 85–87, 189; hiddenness, 88–89, 127, 159, 191; historical Jesus, 87–89, 102, 110, 131, 168; the human being for others, 51, 75, 99, 119, 137, 172; the mediator, 87–88, 91–92, 109, 131, 147, 168–69; one reality in, 53, 77, 92–93, 98, 156–57, 167, 170–71, 173. *See also* death, on the cross; God, new life; God, powerlessness, God, suffering; resurrection

justice, 76, 103, 150–51, 157, 181–82, 187. *See also* law
justification, 57, 65, 88, 115, 159. *See also* grace

Kant, Immanuel, 80–81, 82, 96, 107
Kelley, J. P., 121–25, 145
Kelly, Geffrey, 161

Lash, Nicholas, 104
Lasserre, Jean, 180
law, 10, 17–18, 26, 36–38, 75, 92, 95, 120, 133, 139, 149, 156, 166, 184, 186. *See also* justice
legacy, 187–88
Luther, Martin, 41, 87, 103, 137, 150, 197. *See also* theology, *theologia crucis*; theology, two kingdoms doctrine

mandates, 186
Marsh, Charles, 70, 93, 113
martyrdom, 185
McLeod, Hugh, 30
meaning and promise, 128–29
meditation, 144–45, 157–58
metaphysics, 10, 26, 48, 51–52, 178, 191; and inwardness, 10, 51, 65
Migliore, Daniel, 79–80
Military Intelligence Office (*Abwehr*), 182
military service, 182, 196
miracle, 43, 89, 132, 142
Müller, Gerhard, 149
mystery, 43, 64, 141–43, 146–47, 155–56, 158–59
mysticism, 143–45, 157

naïveté, 159
nature, 16, 29, 88, 92
Naumann, Friedrich, 52–53, 65
Nazism (National Socialism), 12, 43, 58, 76, 103–4, 112, 124, 128, 149, 151, 176, 185–86
Nicholas of Cusa, 11

Niebuhr, Reinhold, 93, 180
Nietzsche, Friedrich, 73, 123, 138, 197
nonreligious language, 115–18, 125–27, 129–30, 133–34, 137. *See also* atonement; God; incarnation; meaning and promise; repentance; resurrection; revelation
nonresistance. *See* violence and nonresistance
nothingness, 103, 120, 128, 136

obedience, 53, 56, 85, 90, 96, 106, 111, 168, 178, 185
Old Testament, 42, 73–74, 115, 118–19, 135
ontology, 82, 107–8, 168, 170, 172. *See also* theology, of consciousness
O/otherness, 78–79, 86, 105–6, 131, 167–9, 190. *See also* God; personhood
orders of creation, preservation, 186

pacifism. *See* violence and nonresistance
pain, 49, 55, 75, 118–19, 142, 173
Pangritz, Andreas, 39–40, 44, 60–62, 71, 149–50
paradox, 85–86, 143, 145–47, 155, 158, 167
partiality, 52–54, 65–66, 165
peace, 12, 75–76, 180–82; in God, 38, 116, 143, 150, 195
perfection, 47, 74, 91, 123, 168, 175, 185. *See also* God
personhood, 79, 83, 144, 169
philosophy, 10; critical, 80–82; existential, 11, 55, 107–8, 128; idealism, 46, 82, 107, 144, 192; of life, 48–50, 123, 166; personalism, 105; pragmatism, 30, 48–50, 64; and theology, 52, 80–81; transcendental, 41, 82
piety, 37, 75, 143, 174
polyphony, 49, 155, 171

positivism of revelation, 35–40, 43, 60, 132, 149–50
Powell, Mark Allan, 110
prayer, 37, 43, 52, 76, 148, 157–58, 160, 176
preaching, 46, 64, 87, 94, 109, 149, 175
principle, 67, 89, 95–96, 170, 180, 183, 187
privilege, 3, 50, 55–57, 71, 120, 165, 177, 191
promise. *See* meaning and promise
providence, 152–53, 179
pseudo-Lutheranism, 92, 94–96, 111, 186
psychoanalysis, 55, 126
Pugh, Jeffrey, 137

Rasmussen, Larry, 195
reality. *See* one reality in Christ
reconciliation. *See* God
redemption, 74, 76, 88, 98, 150, 173
religion: Barth and. *See* Barth, Karl; definition of, 17, 19, 35; end of, 10–12, 24–25, 30–31, 58, 117, 164–65, 188; religious a priori, 9, 25, 45–46, 53, 63, 145, 172; true religion, 38–40. *See also* autonomy; *deus ex machina*; faith; guardianship; metaphysics and inwardness; nonreligious language; partiality; religionless Christianity; theology; privilege; world come of age
religionless Christianity, 35, 69, 71–76, 99–100, 137, 163–64, 171–73, 188–89
repentance, 115, 117, 126–27
resistance, 56, 163, 174, 182, 184
responsibility. *See* vicarious representative action
resurrection, 74, 83, 91, 111, 118, 133, 139, 159, 164, 172, 178, 189
revelation, 38–40, 42, 46–47, 58, 64, 73, 77, 81–83, 92, 99, 131, 142, 145, 148, 155–56, 167, 172, 179. *See also*

positivism of revelation; theology; transcendence
Robertson, Edwin, 126
Roof, Wade, 23
Rumscheidt, Martin, 37–38

sacraments, 43, 87, 104, 109, 148–49, 160, 176. *See also* theology (*finitum (in)capax infiniti*)
salvation: and the church, 54, 57, 78, 91; personal, 10, 26, 51, 73, 165; universal (*apocastastasis*). *See* grace
Scharffenorth, Ernst-Albert, 146
Schleiermacher, Friedrich, 63, 156
Schliesser, Christine, 195
Schönherr, Albrecht, 149
Schroeder, Steven, 198
Schweitzer, Albert, 88, 110
Schwöbel, Christoph, 35, 135
secular, secularism, 13–25, 28, 31, 58, 164–65. *See also* world; worldliness
Seeberg, Erich, 38
Seeberg, Reinhold, 9, 25, 45–46, 53
shame, 108
silence, 85, 141–44, 155
solitude, 184. *See also* alone before God
soul, 90, 142, 155
Spence, Alan, 39
spirit, 36–37, 53, 77–78, 91, 107, 133, 175; over-spiritualized, 119, 135; spirituality, 21–22, 30–31
Stassen, Glen, 106
state. *See* church; mandates; two kingdoms doctrine
Stellvertretung. *See* vicarious representative action
suffering. *See* God, the suffering God; theology, theodicy

Taylor, Charles, 15–19, 24–25, 28–30, 32, 188
theodicy. *See* theology
theologia crucis. *See* theology
theology: Christ-centered, 70; of consciousness, 81; of the cross (*theologia crucis*), 102–3; *extra calvinisticum*, 41; *finitum (in) capax infiniti*, 41–42, 61–62; *genus majestaticum*, 41, 61–62; liberal, 38, 40, 43–45, 49, 62, 88, 132, 156, 182; "new" or prison, 48, 71, 76–77, 96, 98–99, 119, 163, 166, 190; and philosophy, 52, 80–81; of revelation, 45, 63–64; the task of, 141–42, 147; theodicy, 126, 195; two kingdoms doctrine, 93–95. *See also* nonreligious interpretation; religionless Christianity
Tietz, Christiane, 79
Tödt, Heinz Eduard, 128–29
Torrance, Thomas, 59
transcendence, 15–16, 29–30, 40, 46–47, 51–52, 75, 79, 85–86, 115, 130–31, 142, 145, 156, 172, 188, 191; and immanence, 16–19, 29, 52. *See also* philosophy, transcendental; revelation
Troeltsch, Ernst, 25, 93
trust, 103, 177
two kingdoms doctrine. *See* theology
tyrannicide. *See* violence and non-resistance

vicarious representative action (*Stellvertretung*), 77, 79–80, 95–96, 106, 131–32, 170, 180, 186
violence and non-resistance, 180–87, 196–97. *See also* Gandhi
Voas, David, 15, 19–22, 24, 32

war. *See* violence and nonresistance
Ward, Graham, 21
Weizsäcker, Carl Friedrich von, 11, 26
wholeness, 17, 49, 53–54, 82, 85, 107, 141, 150–55, 171, 173, 189. *See also cantus firmus*, polyphony; providence
world come of age, 25, 35, 50, 57, 70, 99, 116, 130, 134, 149, 164, 188; modernity and plurality, 13–14, 19,

24, 32, 165. *See also* autonomy; secular, secularism
worldliness, 73–74, 91, 118, 120, 137, 148, 196
Wrede, William, 88, 110

Wüstenberg, Ralf, 35, 38–39, 45, 48–49, 51, 70, 116

Zimmermann, Jens, 79, 107–8

About the Author

Peter Hooton is responsible for the Research Secretariat which undertakes work in public theology at the Australian Centre for Christianity and Culture on Charles Sturt University (CSU)'s Canberra campus. He is a former career diplomat with experience in Africa, the Middle East, Asia, and the South Pacific. He has a PhD in theology from CSU and is a member of the University's Public and Contextual Theology Research Centre.

www.ingramcontent.com/pod-product-compliance
Lightning Source LLC
Chambersburg PA
CBHW050904300426
44111CB00010B/1377